1050 N

Illuminations

WALTER BENJAMIN

Illuminations

EDITED AND WITH AN INTRODUCTION BY HANNAH ARENDT

TRANSLATED BY HARRY ZOHN

SCHOCKEN BOOKS • NEW YORK

Published by arrangement with Harcourt Brace Jovanovich, Inc.
(A Helen and Kurt Wolff Book)

This reprint omits pages 141–144 of the original Harcourt, Brace
    & World edition.

The Introduction to this book, by Dr. Hannah Arendt, appeared originally
as an article in *The New Yorker.*

Acknowledgment is made for permission to quote from the following:
    From *The Trial*, by Franz Kafka, trans. by Edwin and Willa Muir.
Copyright 1937 and renewed 1965 by Alfred A. Knopf, Inc.
    From *The Castle*, by Franz Kafka. Copyright 1930, 1954 and renewed
1958 by Alfred A. Knopf, Inc. Reprinted by permission of the publisher.

Library of Congress Cataloging-in-Publication Data
Benjamin, Walter, 1892–1940.
    Illuminations.
    Translation of: Illuminationen.
    Reprint. Originally published: New York: Harcourt,
Brace & World, 1968.
"A Helen and Kurt Wolff book"—Verso t.p.
    Includes bibliographical references and index.
    I. Literature—Addresses, essays, lectures.
I. Arendt, Hannah.   II. Title.
PN37.B4413   1985   809   85-27865
ISBN 0-8052-0241-2

Manufactured in the United States of America

First SCHOCKEN paperback edition published in 1969

C9876543210

Contents

Introduction
Walter Benjamin: 1892-1940

I. THE HUNCHBACK

Fama, that much-coveted goddess, has many faces, and fame comes in many sorts and sizes—from the one-week notoriety of the cover story to the splendor of an everlasting name. Posthumous fame is one of Fama's rarer and least desired articles, although it is less arbitrary and often more solid than the other sorts, since it is only seldom bestowed upon mere merchandise. The one who stood most to profit is dead and hence it is not for sale. Such posthumous fame, uncommercial and unprofitable, has now come in Germany to the name and work of Walter Benjamin, a German-Jewish writer who was known, but not famous, as contributor to magazines and literary sections of newspapers for less than ten years prior to Hitler's seizure of power and his own emigration. There were few who still knew his name when he chose death in those early fall days of 1940 which for many of his origin and generation marked the darkest moment of the war—the fall of France, the threat to England, the still intact Hitler-Stalin pact whose most feared consequence at that moment was the close co-operation of the two most powerful secret police forces in Europe. Fifteen years later a two-volume edition of his writings was published in Germany and brought him almost immediately a *succès d'estime* that went far beyond the recognition among the few which he had known in his life. And since mere reputation, however high, as it rests on the judgment of the best, is never enough for writers and artists to make a living that only fame, the testimony of a multitude which need not be astronomical in size, can guarantee, one is doubly tempted to say (with Cicero), *Si vivi vicissent qui morte vicerunt*—how different everything would have been "if they had been victorious in life who have won victory in death."

Posthumous fame is too odd a thing to be blamed upon the blindness of the world or the corruption of a literary milieu. Nor can it be said that it is the bitter reward of those who were ahead of their time—as though history were a race track on which some contenders run so swiftly that they simply disappear from the spectator's range of vision. On the contrary, posthumous fame is usually preceded by the highest recognition among one's peers. When Kafka died in 1924, his few published books had not sold more than a couple of hundred copies, but his literary friends and the few readers who had almost accidentally stumbled on the short prose pieces (none of the novels was as yet published) knew beyond doubt that he was one of the masters of modern prose. Walter Benjamin had won such recognition early, and not only among those whose names at that time were still unknown, such as Gerhard Scholem, the friend of his youth, and Theodor Wiesengrund Adorno, his first and only disciple, who together are responsible for the posthumous edition of his works and letters.[1] Immediate, instinctive, one is tempted to say, recognition came from Hugo von Hofmannsthal, who published Benjamin's essay on Goethe's *Elective Affinities* in 1924, and from Bertolt Brecht, who upon receiving the news of Benjamin's death is reported to have said that this was the first real loss Hitler had caused to German literature. We cannot know if there is such a thing as altogether unappreciated genius, or whether it is the daydream of those who are not geniuses; but we can be reasonably sure that posthumous fame will not be their lot.

Fame is a social phenomenon; *ad gloriam non est satis unius opinio* (as Seneca remarked wisely and pedantically), "for fame the opinion of one is not enough," although it is enough for friendship and love. And no society can properly function without classification, without an arrangement of things and men in classes and prescribed types. This necessary classification is the basis for all social discrimination, and discrimination, present opinion to the contrary notwithstanding, is no less a constituent element of the social realm than equality is a constituent element of the political. The point is that in society everybody must answer the question of *what* he is—as distinct from the question of *who* he is—which his role is and his function, and the answer of course can never be: I am unique, not because of the implicit arrogance but because the answer would be meaningless. In the case of Benjamin the trouble (if such it was) can be diagnosed in retrospect with great precision; when Hofmannsthal had read the long essay on Goethe by the completely unknown author, he called it *"schlechthin unvergleichlich"* ("absolutely incomparable"), and the trouble was that he was literally right, it could not be compared with anything else in existing literature. The trouble with everything Benjamin wrote was that it always turned out to be *sui generis*.

Posthumous fame seems, then, to be the lot of the unclassifiable ones, that is, those whose work neither fits the existing order nor introduces a new genre that lends itself to future classification. Innumerable attempts to write à la Kafka, all of them dismal failures, have only served to emphasize Kafka's uniqueness, that absolute originality which can be traced to no predecessor and suffers no followers. This is what society can least come to terms with and upon which it will always be very reluctant to bestow its seal of approval. To put it bluntly, it would be as misleading today to recommend Walter Benjamin as a literary critic and essayist as it would have been misleading to recommend Kafka in 1924 as a short-story writer and novelist. To describe adequately his work and him as an author within our usual framework of reference, one would have to make a great many negative statements, such as: his erudition was great, but he was no scholar; his subject matter comprised texts and

their interpretation, but he was no philologist; he was greatly
attracted not by religion but by theology and the theological
type of interpretation for which the text itself is sacred, but he
was no theologian and he was not particularly interested in the
Bible; he was a born writer, but his greatest ambition was to produce a work consisting entirely of quotations; he was the first
German to translate Proust (together with Franz Hessel) and
St.-John Perse, and before that he had translated Baudelaire's
Tableaux parisiens, but he was no translator; he reviewed books
and wrote a number of essays on living and dead writers, but he
was no literary critic; he wrote a book about the German baroque and left behind a huge unfinished study of the French
nineteenth century, but he was no historian, literary or otherwise; I shall try to show that he thought poetically, but he was
neither a poet nor a philosopher.

Still, in the rare moments when he cared to define what he
was doing, Benjamin thought of himself as a literary critic, and
if he can be said at all to have aspired to a position in life it
would have been that of "the only true critic of German literature" (as Scholem put it in one of the few, very beautiful letters
to the friend that have been published), except that the very
notion of thus becoming a useful member of society would have
repelled him. No doubt he agreed with Baudelaire, "*Être un
homme utile m'a paru toujours quelque chose de bien hideux.*"
In the introductory paragraphs to the essay on *Elective Affinities*, Benjamin explained what he understood to be the task of the
literary critic. He begins by distinguishing between a commentary and a critique. (Without mentioning it, perhaps without
even being aware of it, he used the term *Kritik*, which in normal
usage means criticism, as Kant used it when he spoke of a *Critique
of Pure Reason*.)

Critique [he wrote] is concerned with the truth content of a work
of art, the commentary with its subject matter. The relationship between the two is determined by that basic law of literature according
to which the work's truth content is the more relevant the more in-
conspicuously and intimately it is bound up with its subject matter.
If therefore precisely those works turn out to endure whose truth is

most deeply embedded in their subject matter, the beholder who contemplates them long after their own time finds the *realia* all the more
striking in the work as they have faded away in the world. This
means that subject matter and truth content, united in the work's
early period, come apart during its afterlife; the subject matter becomes more striking while the truth content retains its original con-
cealment. To an ever-increasing extent, therefore, the interpretation
of the striking and the odd, that is, of the subject matter, becomes a
prerequisite for any later critic. One may liken him to a paleographer
in front of a parchment whose faded text is covered by the stronger
outlines of a script referring to that text. Just as the paleographer
would have to start with reading the script, the critic must start with
commenting on his text. And out of this activity there arises immediately an inestimable criterion of critical judgment: only now can
the critic ask the basic question of all criticism—namely, whether the
work's shining truth content is due to its subject matter or whether
the survival of the subject matter is due to the truth content. For as
they come apart in the work, they decide on its immortality. In this
sense the history of works of art prepares their critique, and this is
why historical distance increases their power. If, to use a simile, one
views the growing work as a funeral pyre, its commentator can be
likened to the chemist, its critic to an alchemist. While the former
is left with wood and ashes as the sole objects of his analysis, the latter is concerned only with the enigma of the flame itself: the enigma
of being alive. Thus the critic inquires about the truth whose living
flame goes on burning over the heavy logs of the past and the light
ashes of life gone by.

The critic as an alchemist practicing the obscure art of
transmuting the futile elements of the real into the shining, enduring gold of truth, or rather watching and interpreting the
historical process that brings about such magical transfiguration—
whatever we may think of this figure, it hardly corresponds to
anything we usually have in mind when we classify a writer as
a literary critic.

There is, however, another less objective element than the
mere fact of being unclassifiable which is involved in the life of
those who "have won victory in death." It is the element of bad
luck, and this factor, very prominent in Benjamin's life, cannot
be ignored here because he himself, who probably never thought
or dreamed about posthumous fame, was so extraordinarily aware

of it. In his writing and also in conversation he used to speak about the "little hunchback," the *"bucklicht Männlein,"* a German fairy-tale figure out of *Des Knaben Wunderhorn*, the famous collection of German folk poetry.

Will ich in mein' Keller gehn,	Will ich in mein Küchel gehn,
Will mein Weinlein zapfen;	Will mein Süpplein kochen;
Steht ein bucklicht Männlein da,	Steht ein bucklicht Männlein da,
Tät mir'n Krug wegschnappen.	Hat mein Töpflein brochen.*

The hunchback was an early acquaintance of Benjamin, who had first met him when, still a child, he found the poem in a children's book, and he never forgot. But only once (at the end of *A Berlin Childhood around 1900*), when anticipating death he attempted to get hold of "his 'entire life' . . . as it is said to pass before the eyes of the dying," did he clearly state who and what it was that had terrified him so early in life and was to accompany him until his death. His mother, like millions of other mothers in Germany, used to say, "Mr. Bungle sends his regards" (*Ungeschickt lässt grüssen*) whenever one of the countless little catastrophes of childhood had taken place. And the child knew of course what this strange bungling was all about. The mother referred to the "little hunchback," who caused the objects to play their mischievous tricks upon children; it was he who had tripped you up when you fell and knocked the thing out of your hand when it went to pieces. And after the child came the grown-up man who knew what the child was still ignorant of, namely, that it was not he who had provoked "the little one" by looking at him—as though he had been the boy who wished to learn what fear was—but that the hunchback had looked at him and that bungling was a misfortune. For "anyone whom the little man looks at pays no attention; not to himself and not to the

* When I go down to the cellar / There to draw some wine, / A little hunchback who's in there / Grabs that jug of mine. When I go into my kitchen, / There my soup to make, / A little hunchback who's in there / My little pot did break.

little man. In consternation he stands before a pile of debris"
(*Schriften* I, 650-52).

Thanks to the recent publication of his letters, the story of
Benjamin's life may now be sketched in broad outline; and it
would be tempting indeed to tell it as a sequence of such piles
of debris since there is hardly any question that he himself
viewed it in that way. But the point of the matter is that he
knew very well of the mysterious interplay, the place "at which
weakness and genius coincide," which he so masterfully diagnosed in Proust. For he was of course also speaking about himself when, in complete agreement, he quoted what Jacques
Rivière had said about Proust: he "died of the same inexperience
that permitted him to write his works. He died of ignorance . . .
because he did not know how to make a fire or open a window"
("The Image of Proust"). Like Proust, he was wholly incapable of changing "his life's conditions even when they were
about to crush him." (With a precision suggesting a sleepwalker
his clumsiness invariably guided him to the very center of a misfortune, or wherever something of the sort might lurk. Thus, in
the winter of 1939-40 the danger of bombing made him decide
to leave Paris for a safer place. Well, no bomb was ever dropped
on Paris, but Meaux, where Benjamin went, was a troop center
and probably one of the very few places in France that was
seriously endangered in those months of the phony war.) But
like Proust, he had every reason to bless the curse and to repeat
the strange prayer at the end of the folk poem with which he
closes his childhood memoir:

> Liebes Kindlein, ach, ich bitt,
> Bet fürs bucklicht Männlein mit.*

In retrospect, the inextricable net woven of merit, great gifts,
clumsiness, and misfortune into which his life was caught can
be detected even in the first pure piece of luck that opened Benjamin's career as a writer. Through the good offices of a friend,
he had been able to place "Goethe's *Elective Affinities*" in Hof-

* O dear child, I beg of you,
  Pray for the little hunchback too.

mannsthal's *Neue Deutsche Beiträge* (1924-25). This study, a masterpiece of German prose and still of unique stature in the general field of German literary criticism and the specialized field of Goethe scholarship, had already been rejected several times, and Hofmannsthal's enthusiastic approval came at a moment when Benjamin almost despaired of "finding a taker for it" (*Briefe* I, 300). But there was a decisive misfortune, apparently never fully understood, which under the given circumstances was necessarily connected with this chance. The only material security which this first public breakthrough could have led to was the *Habilitation*, the first step of the university career for which Benjamin was then preparing himself. This, to be sure, would not yet have enabled him to make a living—the so-called *Privatdozent* received no salary—but it would probably have induced his father to support him until he received a full professorship, since this was a common practice in those days. It is now hard to understand how he and his friends could ever have doubted that a *Habilitation* under a not unusual university professor was bound to end with a catastrophe. If the gentlemen involved declared later that they did not understand a single word of the study, *The Origin of German Tragedy*, which Benjamin had submitted, they can certainly be believed. How were they to understand a writer whose greatest pride it was that "the writing consists largely of quotations—the craziest mosaic technique imaginable"—and who placed the greatest emphasis on the six mottoes that preceded the study: "No one . . . could gather any rarer or more precious ones"? (*Briefe* I, 366). It was as if a real master had fashioned some unique object, only to offer it for sale at the nearest bargain center. Truly, neither anti-Semitism nor ill will toward an outsider—Benjamin had taken his degree in Switzerland during the war and was no one's disciple—nor the customary academic suspicion of anything that is not guaranteed to be mediocre need have been involved.

However—and this is where bungling and bad luck come in—in the Germany of that time there was another way, and it was precisely his Goethe essay that spoiled Benjamin's only chance for a university career. As often with Benjamin's writings, this study was inspired by polemics, and the attack concerned Friedrich Gundolf's book on Goethe. Benjamin's critique was definitive, and yet Benjamin could have expected more understanding from Gundolf and other members of the circle around Stefan George, a group with whose intellectual world he had been quite familiar in his youth, than from the "establishment"; and he probably need not have been a member of the circle to earn his academic accreditation under one of these men who at that time were just beginning to get a fairly comfortable foothold in the academic world. But the one thing he should not have done was to mount an attack on the most prominent and most capable academic member of the circle so vehement that everyone was bound to know, as he explained retrospectively later, that he had "just as little to do with academe . . . as with the monuments which men like Gundolf or Ernst Bertram have erected." (*Briefe* II, 523). Yes, that is how it was. And it was Benjamin's bungling or his misfortune to have announced this to the world before he was admitted to the university.

Yet one certainly cannot say that he consciously disregarded due caution. On the contrary, he was aware that "Mr. Bungle sends his regards" and took more precautions than anyone else I have known. But his system of provisions against possible dangers, including the "Chinese courtesy" mentioned by Scholem,[2] invariably, in a strange and mysterious way, disregarded the real danger. For just as he fled from the safe Paris to the dangerous Meaux at the beginning of the war—to the front, as it were—his essay on Goethe inspired in him the wholly unnecessary worry that Hofmannsthal might take amiss a very cautious critical remark about Rudolf Borchardt, one of the chief contributors to his periodical. Yet he expected only good things from having found for this "attack upon the ideology of George's school . . . this one place where they will find it hard to ignore the invective" (*Briefe* I, 341). They did not find it hard at all. For no one was more isolated than Benjamin, so utterly alone. Even the authority of Hofmannsthal—"the new patron," as Benjamin called him in the first burst of happiness (*Briefe* I, 327)—could not alter this situation. His voice hardly mattered compared with the very real power of the George school, an influential group in which, as with all such entities, only ideological allegiance counted, since only ideology, not rank and quality, can hold a group together. Despite their pose of being above politics, George's disciples were fully as conversant with the basic principles of literary maneuvers as the professors were with the fundamentals of academic politics or the hacks and journalists with the ABC of "one good turn deserves another."

Benjamin, however, did not know the score. He never knew how to handle such things, was never able to move among such people, not even when "the adversities of outer life which sometimes come from all sides, like wolves" (*Briefe* I, 298), had already afforded him some insight into the ways of the world. Whenever he tried to adjust and be co-operative so as to get some firm ground under his feet somehow, things were sure to go wrong.

A major study on Goethe from the viewpoint of Marxism—in the middle twenties he came very close to joining the Communist Party—never appeared in print, either in the Great Russian Encyclopedia, for which it was intended, or in present-day Germany. Klaus Mann, who had commissioned a review of Brecht's *Threepenny Novel* for his periodical *Die Sammlung*, returned the manuscript because Benjamin had asked 250 French francs—then about 10 dollars—for it and he wanted to pay only 150. His commentary on Brecht's poetry did not appear in his lifetime. And the most serious difficulties finally developed with the Institute for Social Research, which, originally (and now again) part of the University of Frankfurt, had emigrated to America and on which Benjamin depended financially. Its guiding spirits, Theodor W. Adorno and Max Horkheimer, were "dialectical materialists" and in their opinion Benjamin's thinking was "undialectic," moved in "materialistic categories, which by no means coincide with Marxist ones," was "lacking in mediation" insofar as, in an essay on Baudelaire, he had related "certain conspicuous elements within the superstructure . . . directly, perhaps even causally, to corresponding elements in the substructure." The result was that Benjamin's original essay, "The Paris of the Second Empire in the Works of Baudelaire," was not printed, either then in the magazine of the Institute or in the posthumous two-volume edition of his writings. (Parts of it have now been published—"Der Flâneur" in *Die Neue Rundschau,* December 1967, and "Die Moderne" in *Das Argument,* March 1968.)

Benjamin probably was the most peculiar Marxist ever produced by this movement, which God knows has had its full share of oddities. The theoretical aspect that was bound to fascinate him was the doctrine of the superstructure, which was only briefly sketched by Marx but then assumed a disproportionate role in the movement as it was joined by a disproportionately large number of intellectuals, hence by people who were interested only in the superstructure. Benjamin used this doctrine only as a heuristic-methodological stimulus and was hardly interested in its historical or philosophical background. What fascinated him about the matter was that the spirit and its material manifestation were so intimately connected that it seemed permissible to discover everywhere Baudelaire's *correspondances,* which clarified and illuminated one another if they were properly correlated, so that finally they would no longer require any interpretative or explanatory commentary. He was concerned with the correlation between a street scene, a speculation on the stock exchange, a poem, a thought, with the hidden line which holds them together and enables the historian or philologist to recognize that they must all be placed in the same period. When Adorno criticized Benjamin's "wide-eyed presentation of actualities" (*Briefe* II, 793), he hit the nail right on its head; this is precisely what Benjamin was doing and wanted to do. Strongly influenced by surrealism, it was the "attempt to capture the portrait of history in the most insignificant representations of reality, its scraps, as it were" (*Briefe* II, 685). Benjamin had a passion for small, even minute things; Scholem tells about his ambition to get one hundred lines onto the ordinary page of a notebook and about his admiration for two grains of wheat in the Jewish section of the Musée Cluny "on which a kindred soul had inscribed the complete *Shema Israel.*" [3] For him the size of an object was in an inverse ratio to its significance. And this passion, far from being a whim, derived directly from the only world view that ever had a decisive influence on him, from Goethe's conviction of the factual existence of an *Urphänomen*, an archetypal phenomenon, a concrete thing to be discovered in the world of appearances in which "significance" (*Bedeutung*, the most Goethean of words, keeps recurring in Benjamin's writings) and appearance, word and thing, idea and experience, would coincide. The smaller the object, the more likely it seemed that it could contain in the most concentrated form everything else; hence his delight that two grains of wheat should contain the entire *Shema Israel*, the very essence of Judaism, tiniest essence appearing on tiniest entity, from which in both cases everything else originates that, however, in significance cannot be compared with its origin. In other words, what profoundly fascinated Benjamin from the beginning was never an idea, it was always a phenomenon. "What seems paradoxical about everything that is justly called beautiful is the fact that it appears" (*Schriften* I, 349), and this paradox—or, more simply, the wonder of appearance—was always at the center of all his concerns.

How remote these studies were from Marxism and dialectical materialism is confirmed by their central figure, the *flâneur*.[4] It is to him, aimlessly strolling through the crowds in the big cities in studied contrast to their hurried, purposeful activity, that things reveal themselves in their secret meaning: "The true picture of the past *flits* by" ("Philosophy of History"), and only the *flâneur* who idly strolls by receives the message. With great acumen Adorno has pointed to the static element in Benjamin: "To understand Benjamin properly one must feel behind his every sentence the conversion of extreme agitation into something static, indeed, the static notion of movement itself" (*Schriften* I, xix). Naturally, nothing could be more "undialectic" than this attitude in which the "angel of history" (in the ninth of the "Theses on the Philosophy of History") does not dialectically move forward into the future, but has his face "turned toward the past." "Where a chain of events appears to *us*, *he* sees one single catastrophe which keeps piling wreckage upon wreckage and hurls it in front of his feet. The angel would like to stay, awaken the dead, and join

together what has been smashed to pieces." (Which would presumably mean the end of history.) "But a storm is blowing from
Paradise" and "irresistibly propels him into the future to which
his back is turned, while the pile of ruins before him grows skyward. What we call progress is *this* storm." In this angel, which
Benjamin saw in Klee's "Angelus Novus," the *flâneur* experiences
his final transfiguration. For just as the *flâneur*, through the *gestus*
of purposeless strolling, turns his back to the crowd even as he
is propelled and swept by it, so the "angel of history," who looks
at nothing but the expanse of ruins of the past, is blown backwards into the future by the storm of progress. That such thinking should ever have bothered with a consistent, dialectically
sensible, rationally explainable process seems absurd.

It should also be obvious that such thinking neither aimed nor
could arrive at binding, generally valid statements, but that these
were replaced, as Adorno critically remarks, "by metaphorical
ones" (*Briefe* II, 785). In his concern with directly, actually
demonstrable concrete facts, with single events and occurrences
whose "significance" is manifest, Benjamin was not much interested in theories or "ideas" which did not immediately assume the
most precise outward shape imaginable. To this very complex
but still highly realistic mode of thought the Marxian relationship between superstructure and substructure became, in a precise sense, a metaphorical one. If, for example—and this would
certainly be in the spirit of Benjamin's thought—the abstract
concept *Vernunft* (reason) is traced back to its origin in the
verb *vernehmen* (to perceive, to hear), it may be thought that
a word from the sphere of the superstructure has been given
back its sensual substructure, or, conversely, that a concept has
been transformed into a metaphor—provided that "metaphor" is
understood in its original, nonallegorical sense of *metapherein*
(to transfer). For a metaphor establishes a connection which is
sensually perceived in its immediacy and requires no interpretation, while an allegory always proceeds from an abstract notion and then invents something palpable to represent it almost
at will. The allegory must be explained before it can become
meaningful, a solution must be found to the riddle it presents, so

that the often laborious interpretation of allegorical figures always unhappily reminds one of the solving of puzzles even when no more ingenuity is demanded than in the allegorical representation of death by a skeleton. Since Homer the metaphor has borne that element of the poetic which conveys cognition; its use establishes the *correspondances* between physically most remote things—as when in the *Iliad* the tearing onslaught of fear and grief on the hearts of the Achaians corresponds to the combined onslaught of the winds from north and west on the dark waters (*Iliad* IX, 1-8); or when the approaching of the army moving to battle in line after line corresponds to the sea's long billows which, driven by the wind, gather head far out on the sea, roll to shore line after line, and then burst on the land in thunder (*Iliad* IV, 422-23). Metaphors are the means by which the oneness of the world is poetically brought about. What is so hard to understand about Benjamin is that without being a poet he *thought poetically* and therefore was bound to regard the metaphor as the greatest gift of language. Linguistic "transference" enables us to give material form to the invisible—"A mighty fortress is our God"—and thus to render it capable of being experienced. He had no trouble understanding the theory of the superstructure as the final doctrine of metaphorical thinking—precisely because without much ado and eschewing all "mediations" he directly related the superstructure to the so-called "material" substructure, which to him meant the totality of sensually experienced data. He evidently was fascinated by the very thing that the others branded as "vulgar-Marxist" or "undialectical" thinking.

It seems plausible that Benjamin, whose spiritual existence had been formed and informed by Goethe, a poet and not a philosopher, and whose interest was almost exclusively aroused by poets and novelists, although he had studied philosophy, should have found it easier to communicate with poets than with theoreticians, whether of the dialectical or the metaphysical variety. And there is indeed no question but that his friendship with Brecht—unique in that here the greatest living German poet met the most important critic of the time, a fact both were fully aware of—was the second and incomparably more important stroke of good fortune in Benjamin's life. It promptly had the most adverse consequences; it antagonized the few friends he had, it endangered his relation to the Institute of Social Research, toward whose "suggestions" he had every reason "to be docile" (*Briefe* II, 683), and the only reason it did not cost him his friendship with Scholem was Scholem's abiding loyalty and admirable generosity in all matters concerning his friend. Both Adorno and Scholem blamed Brecht's "disastrous influence" [5] (Scholem) for Benjamin's clearly undialectic usage of Marxian categories and his determined break with all metaphysics; and the trouble was that Benjamin, usually quite inclined to compromises albeit mostly unnecessary ones, knew and maintained that his friendship with Brecht constituted an absolute limit not only to docility but even to diplomacy, for "my agreeing with Brecht's production is one of the most important and most strategic points in my entire position" (*Briefe* II, 594). In Brecht he found a poet of rare intellectual powers and, almost as important for him at the time, someone on the Left who, despite all talk about dialectics, was no more of a dialectical thinker than he was, but whose intelligence was uncommonly close to reality. With Brecht he could practice what Brecht himself called "crude thinking" (*das plumpe Denken*): "The main thing is to learn how to think crudely. Crude thinking, that is the thinking of the great," said Brecht, and Benjamin added by way of elucidation: "There are many people whose idea of a dialectician is a lover of subtleties. . . . Crude thoughts, on the contrary, should be part and parcel of dialectical thinking, because they are nothing but the referral of theory to practice . . . a thought must be crude to come into its own in action." [6] Well, what attracted Benjamin to crude thinking was probably not so much a referral to practice as to reality, and to him this reality manifested itself most directly in the proverbs and idioms of everyday language. "Proverbs are a school of crude thinking," he writes in the same context; and the art of taking proverbial and idiomatic speech literally enabled Benjamin—as it did Kafka, in whom figures of speech are often clearly discernible as a source of inspiration and furnish the key to many a "riddle"—to write a prose of such singularly enchanting and enchanted closeness to reality.

Wherever one looks in Benjamin's life, one will find the little hunchback. Long before the outbreak of the Third Reich he was playing his evil tricks, causing publishers who had promised Benjamin an annual stipend for reading manuscripts or editing a periodical for them to go bankrupt before the first number appeared. Later the hunchback did allow a collection of magnificent German letters, made with infinite care and provided with the most marvelous commentaries, to be printed—under the title *Deutsche Menschen* and with the motto *"Von Ehre ohne Ruhm/ Von Grösse ohne Glanz/Von Würde ohne Sold"* (Of Honor without Fame/Of Greatness without Splendor/Of Dignity without Pay); but then he saw to it that it ended in the cellar of the bankrupt Swiss publisher, instead of being distributed, as intended by Benjamin, who signed the selection with a pseudonym, in Nazi Germany. And in this cellar the edition was discovered in 1962, at the very moment when a new edition had come off the press in Germany. (One would also charge it to the little hunchback that often the few things that were to take a good turn first presented themselves in an unpleasant guise. A case in point is the translation of *Anabase* by Alexis Saint-Léger Léger [St.-John Perse] which Benjamin, who thought the work "of little importance" [*Briefe* I, 381], undertook because, like the Proust translation, the assignment had been procured for him by Hofmannsthal. The translation did not appear in Germany until after the war, yet Benjamin owed to it his contact with Léger, who, being a diplomat, was able to intervene and persuade the French government to spare Benjamin a second internment in France during the war—a privilege that very few other refugees enjoyed.) And then after mischief came "the piles of debris," the last of which, prior to the catastrophe at the Spanish border, was the threat he had felt, since 1938, that the Institute for Social Research in New York, the only "material and moral support" of his Paris existence (*Briefe* II, 839), would desert him. "The very circumstances that greatly endanger my European situation will probably make emigration to the U.S.A. impossible for me," so he wrote in April of 1939 (*Briefe* II, 810), still under the impact of the "blow" which Adorno's letter rejecting the first version of the Baudelaire study had dealt him in November of 1938 (*Briefe* II, 790).

Scholem is surely right when he says that next to Proust, Benjamin felt the closest personal affinity with Kafka among contemporary authors, and undoubtedly Benjamin had the "field of ruins and the disaster area" of his own work in mind when he wrote that "an understa⟩ ⟨ing of [Kafka's] production involves, among other things, the s..⟩ple recognition that he was a failure" (*Briefe* II, 614). What Benjamin said of Kafka with such unique aptness applies to himself as well: "The circumstances of this failure are multifarious. One is tempted to say: once he was certain of eventual failure, everything worked out for him *en route* as in a dream" (*Briefe* II, 764). He did not need to read Kafka to think like Kafka. When "The Stoker" was all he had read of Kafka, he had already quoted Goethe's statement about hope in his essay on *Elective Affinities:* "Hope passed over their heads like a star that falls from the sky"; and the sentence with which he concludes this study reads as though Kafka had written it: "Only for the sake of the hopeless ones have we been given hope" (*Schriften* I, 140).

On September 26, 1940, Walter Benjamin, who was about to emigrate to America, took his life at the Franco-Spanish border. There were various reasons for this. The Gestapo had confiscated his Paris apartment, which contained his library (he had been able to get "the more important half" out of Germany) and many of his manuscripts, and he had reason to be concerned also about the others which, through the good offices of George Bataille, had been placed in the Bibliothèque Nationale prior to his flight from Paris to Lourdes, in unoccupied France.[7] How was he to live without a library, how could he earn a living without the extensive collection of quotations and excerpts among his manuscripts? Besides, nothing drew him to America, where, as he used to say, people would probably find no other use for him than to cart him up and down the country to exhibit him as the "last European." But the immediate occasion for Benjamin's suicide was an uncommon stroke of bad luck. Through the armistice agreement between Vichy France and the Third Reich, refugees from Hitler Germany—*les refugiés provenant d'Allemagne*, as they were officially referred to in France—were in danger of being shipped back to Germany, presumably only if they were political opponents. To save this category of refugees—which, it should be noted, never included the unpolitical mass of Jews who later turned out to be the most endangered of all—the United States had distributed a number of emergency visas through its consulates in unoccupied France. Thanks to the efforts of the Institute in New York, Benjamin was among the first to receive such a visa in Marseilles. Also, he quickly obtained a Spanish transit visa to enable him to get to Lisbon and board a ship there. However, he did not have a French exit visa, which at that time was still required and which the French government, eager to please the Gestapo, invariably denied to German refugees. In general this presented no great difficulty, since a relatively short and none too arduous road to be covered by foot over the mountains to Port Bou was well known and was not guarded by the French border police. Still, for Benjamin, apparently suffering from a cardiac condition (*Briefe* II, 841), even the shortest walk was a great exertion, and he must have arrived in a state of serious exhaustion. The small group of refugees that he had joined reached the Spanish border town only to learn that Spain had closed the border that same day and that the border officials did not honor visas made out in Marseilles. The refugees were supposed to return to France by the same route the next day. During the night Benjamin took his life, whereupon the border officials, upon whom this suicide had made an impression, allowed his companions to proceed to Portugal. A few weeks later the embargo on visas was lifted again. One day earlier Benjamin would have got through without any trouble; one day later the people in Marseilles would have known that for the time being it was impossible to pass through Spain. Only on that particular day was the catastrophe possible.

II. THE DARK TIMES

> *"Anyone who cannot cope with life while he is alive needs one hand to ward off a little his despair over his fate . . . but with his other hand he can jot down what he sees among the ruins, for he sees different and more things than the others; after all, he is dead in his own lifetime and the real survivor."*
>
> —Franz Kafka, DIARIES, entry of October 19, 1921

> *"Like one who keeps afloat on a shipwreck by climbing to the top of a mast that is already crumbling. But from there he has a chance to give a signal leading to his rescue."*
>
> —Walter Benjamin in a letter to
> Gerhard Scholem dated April 17, 1931

Often an era most clearly brands with its seal those who have been least influenced by it, who have been most remote from it, and who therefore have suffered most. So it was with Proust, with Kafka, with Karl Kraus, and with Benjamin. His gestures and the way he held his head when listening and talking; the way he moved; his manners, but especially his style of speaking, down to his choice of words and the shape of his syntax; finally, his downright idiosyncratic tastes—all this seemed so old-fashioned, as though he had drifted out of the nineteenth century into the twentieth the way one is driven onto the coast of a strange land. Did he ever feel at home in twentieth-century Germany? One has reason to doubt it. In 1913, when he first visited France as a very young man, the streets of Paris were "almost more homelike" (*Briefe* I, 56) to him after a few days than the familiar streets of Berlin. He may have felt even then, and he certainly felt twenty years later, how much the trip from Berlin to Paris was tantamount to a trip in time—not from one country to another, but from the twentieth century back to the nineteenth. There was the *nation par excellence* whose culture had determined the Europe of the nineteenth century and for which Haussmann had rebuilt Paris, "the capital of the nineteenth century," as Benjamin was to call it. This Paris was not yet cosmopolitan, to be sure, but it was profoundly European, and thus it has, with unparalleled naturalness, offered itself to all homeless people as a second home ever since the middle of the last century. Neither the pronounced xenophobia of its inhabitants nor the sophisticated harassment by the local police has ever been able to change this. Long before his emigration Benjamin knew how "very exceptional [it was] to make the kind of contact with a Frenchman that would enable one to prolong a conversation with him beyond the first quarter of an hour" (*Briefe* I, 445). Later, when he was domiciled in Paris as a refugee, his innate nobility prevented him from developing his slight acquaintances —chief among them was Gide—into connections and from making new contacts. (Werner Kraft—so we learned recently—took him to see Charles du Bos, who was, by virtue of his "enthusiasm for German literature," a kind of key figure for German emigrants. Werner Kraft had the better connections—what irony! [8]) In his strikingly judicious review of Benjamin's works and letters as well as of the secondary literature, Pierre Missac has pointed out how greatly Benjamin must have suffered because he did not get the "reception" in France that was due him.[9] This is correct, of course, but it surely did not come as a surprise.

No matter how irritating and offensive all this may have been, the city itself compensated for everything. Its boulevards, Benjamin discovered as early as 1913, are formed by houses which "do not seem made to be lived in, but are like stone sets for people to walk between" (*Briefe* I, 56). This city, around which one still can travel in a circle past the old gates, has remained what the cities of the Middle Ages, severely walled off and protected against the outside, once were: an interior, but without the narrowness of medieval streets, a generously built and planned open-air *intérieur* with the arch of the sky like a majestic ceiling above it. "The finest thing here about all art and all activity is the fact that they leave the few remainders of the original and the natural their splendor" (*Briefe* I, 421). Indeed, they help them to acquire new luster. It is the uniform façades, lining the streets like inside walls, that make one feel more physically sheltered in this city than in any other. The arcades which connect the great boulevards and offer protection from inclement weather exerted such an enormous fascination over Benjamin that he referred to his projected major work on the nineteenth century and its capital simply as "The Arcades" (*Passagenarbeit*); and these passageways are indeed like a symbol of Paris, because they clearly are inside and outside at the same time and thus represent its true nature in quintessential form. In Paris a stranger feels at home because he can inhabit the city the way he lives in his own four walls. And just as one inhabits an apartment, and makes it comfortable, by living in it instead of just using it for sleeping, eating, and working, so one inhabits a city by strolling through it without aim or purpose, with one's stay secured by the countless cafés which line the streets and past which the life of the city, the flow of pedestrians, moves along. To this day Paris is the only one among the large cities which can be comfortably covered on foot, and more than any other city it is dependent for its liveliness on people who pass by in the streets, so that the modern automobile traffic endangers its very existence not only for technical reasons. The wasteland of an American suburb, or the residential districts of many towns, where all of street life takes place on the roadway and where one can walk on the sidewalks, by now reduced to footpaths, for miles on end without encountering a human being, is the very opposite of Paris. What all other cities seem to permit only reluctantly to the dregs of society—strolling, idling, *flânerie*—Paris streets actually invite everyone to do. Thus, ever since the Second Empire the city has been the paradise of all those who need to chase after no livelihood, pursue no career, reach no goal—the paradise, then, of bohemians, and not only of artists and writers but of all those who have gathered about them because they could not be integrated either politically—being homeless or stateless—or socially.

Without considering this background of the city which became a decisive experience for the young Benjamin one can hardly understand why the *flâneur* became the key figure in his writings. The extent to which this strolling determined the pace of his thinking was perhaps most clearly revealed in the peculiarities of his gait, which Max Rychner described as "at once advancing and tarrying, a strange mixture of both." [10] It was the walk of a *flâneur*, and it was so striking because, like the dandy and the snob, the *flâneur* had his home in the nineteenth century, an age of security in which children of upper-middle-class families were assured of an income without having to work, so that they had no reason to hurry. And just as the city taught Benjamin *flânerie*, the nineteenth century's secret style of walking and thinking, it naturally aroused in him a feeling for French literature as well, and this almost irrevocably estranged him from normal German intellectual life. "In Germany I feel quite isolated in my efforts and interests among those of my generation, while in France there are certain forces—the writers Giraudoux and, especially, Aragon; the surrealist movement—in which I see at work what occupies me too"—so he wrote to Hofmannsthal in 1927 (*Briefe* I, 446), when, having returned from a trip to Moscow and convinced that literary projects sailing under the Communist flag were unfeasible, he was setting out to consolidate his "Paris position" (*Briefe* I, 444-45). (Eight years earlier he had mentioned the "incredible feeling of kinship" which Péguy had inspired in him: "No written work has ever touched me so closely and given me such a sense of communion" [*Briefe* I, 217].) Well, he did not succeed in consolidating anything, and success would hardly have been possible. Only in postwar Paris have foreigners—and presumably that is what everyone not born in France is called in Paris to this day—been able to occupy "positions." On the other hand, Benjamin was forced into a position which actually did not exist anywhere, which, in fact, could not be identified and diagnosed as such until afterwards. It was the position on the "top of the mast" from which the tempestuous times could be surveyed better than from a safe harbor, even though the distress signals of the "shipwreck," of this one man who had not learned to swim either with or against the tide, were hardly noticed—either by those who had never exposed themselves to these seas or by those who were capable of moving even in this element.

Viewed from the outside, it was the position of the free-lance writer who lives by his pen; however, as only Max Rychner seems to have observed, he did so in a "peculiar way," for "his publications were anything but frequent" and "it was never quite clear . . . to what extent he was able to draw upon other resources." [11] Rychner's suspicions were justified in every respect. Not only were "other resources" at his disposal prior to his emigration, but behind the façade of free-lance writing he led the considerably freer, albeit constantly endangered, life of an *homme de lettres* whose home was a library that had been gathered with extreme care but was by no means intended as a working tool; it consisted of treasures whose value, as Benjamin often repeated, was proved by the fact that he had not read them—a library, then, which was guaranteed not to be useful or at the service of any profession. Such an existence was something unknown in Germany, and almost equally unknown was the occupation which Benjamin, only because he had to make a living, derived from it: not the occupation of a literary historian and scholar with the requisite number of fat tomes to his credit, but that of a critic and essayist who regarded even the essay form as too vulgarly extensive and would have preferred the aphorism if he had not been paid by the line. He was certainly not unaware of the fact that his professional ambitions were directed at something that simply did not exist in Germany, where, despite Lichtenberg, Lessing, Schlegel, Heine, and Nietzsche, aphorisms have never been appreciated and people have usually thought of criticism as something disreputably subversive which might be enjoyed—if at all—only in the cultural section of a newspaper. It was no accident that Benjamin chose the French language for expressing this ambition: *"Le but que je m'avais proposé . . . c'est d'être considéré comme le premier critique de la littérature allemande. La difficulté c'est que, depuis plus de cinquante ans, la critique littéraire en Allemagne n'est plus considérée comme un genre sérieux. Se faire une situation dans la critique, cela . . . veut dire: la recréer comme genre"* ("The goal I set for myself . . . is to be regarded as the foremost critic of German literature. The trouble is that for more than fifty years literary criticism in Germany has not been considered a serious genre. To create a place in criticism for oneself means to re-create it as a genre") (*Briefe* II, 505).

There is no doubt that Benjamin owed this choice of a profession to early French influences, to the proximity of the great neighbor on the other side of the Rhine which inspired in him so intimate a sense of affinity. But it is much more symptomatic that even this selection of a profession was actually motivated by hard times and financial woes. If one wants to express the "profession" he had prepared himself for spontaneously, although perhaps not deliberately, in social categories, one has to go back to Wilhelminian Germany in which he grew up and where his first plans for the future took shape. Then one could say that Benjamin did not prepare for anything but the "profession" of a private collector and totally independent scholar, what was then called *Privatgelehrter*. Under the circumstances of the time his studies, which he had begun before the First World War, could have ended only with a university career, but unbaptized Jews were still barred from such a career, as they were from any career in the civil service. Such Jews were permitted a *Habilitation* and at most could attain the rank of an unpaid *Extraordinarius;* it was a career which presupposed rather than provided an assured income. The doctorate which Benjamin decided to take only "out of consideration for my family" (*Briefe* I, 216) and his subsequent attempt at *Habilitation* were intended as the basis for his family's readiness to place such an income at his disposal.

This situation changed abruptly after the war: the inflation had impoverished, even dispossessed, large numbers of the bourgeoisie, and in the Weimar Republic a university career was open even to unbaptized Jews. The unhappy story of the *Habilitation* shows clearly how little Benjamin took these altered circumstances into account and how greatly he continued to be dominated by prewar ideas in all financial matters. For from the outset the *Habilitation* had only been intended to call his father "to order" by supplying "evidence of public recognition" (*Briefe* I, 293) and to make him grant his son, who was in his thirties at that time, an income that was adequate and, one should add, commensurate with his social standing. At no time, not even when he had already come close to the Communists, did he doubt that despite his chronic conflicts with his parents he was entitled to such a subvention and that their demand that he "work for a living" was "unspeakable" (*Briefe* I, 292). When his father said later that he could not or would not increase the monthly stipend he was paying anyway, even if his son achieved the *Habilitation*, this naturally removed the basis of Benjamin's entire undertaking. Until his parents' death in 1930, Benjamin was able to solve the problem of his livelihood by moving back into the parental home, living there first with his family (he had a wife and a son), and after his separation—which came soon enough—by himself. (He was not divorced until 1930.) It is evident that this arrangement caused him a great deal of suffering, but it is just as evident that in all probability he never seriously considered another solution. It is also striking that despite his permanent financial trouble he managed throughout these years constantly to enlarge his library. His one attempt to deny himself this expensive passion—he visited the great auction houses the way others frequent gambling casinos—and his resolution even to sell something "in an emergency" ended with his feeling obliged to "deaden the pain of this readiness" (*Briefe* I, 340) by making fresh purchases; and his one demonstrable attempt to free himself from financial dependence on his family ended with the proposal that his father immediately give him "funds enabling me to buy an interest in a secondhand bookstore" (*Briefe* I, 292). This is the only gainful employment that Benjamin ever considered. Nothing came of it, of course.

In view of the realities of the Germany of the twenties and of Benjamin's awareness that he would never be able to make a living with his pen—"there are places in which I can earn a minimum and places in which I can live on a minimum, but there is no place where I can do both" (*Briefe* II, 563)—his whole attitude may strike one as unpardonably irresponsible. Yet it was anything but a case of irresponsibility. It is reasonable to assume that it is just as hard for rich people grown poor to believe in their poverty as it is for poor people turned rich to believe in their wealth; the former seem carried away by a recklessness of which they are totally unaware, the latter seem possessed by a stinginess which actually is nothing but the old ingrained fear of what the next day may bring.

Moreover, in his attitude to financial problems Benjamin was by no means an isolated case. If anything, his outlook was typical of an entire generation of German-Jewish intellectuals, although probably no one else fared so badly with it. Its basis was the mentality of the fathers, successful businessmen who did not think too highly of their own achievements and whose dream it was that their sons were destined for higher things. It was the secularized version of the ancient Jewish belief that those who "learn" —the Torah or the Talmud, that is, God's Law—were the true elite of the people and should not be bothered with so vulgar an occupation as making money or working for it. This is not to say that in this generation there were no father-son conflicts; on the contrary, the literature of the time is full of them, and if Freud had lived and carried on his inquiries in a country and language other than the German-Jewish milieu which supplied his patients, we might never have heard of an Oedipus complex.[12] But as a rule these conflicts were resolved by the sons' laying claim to being geniuses, or, in the case of the numerous Communists from well-to-do homes, to being devoted to the welfare of mankind—in any case, to aspiring to things higher than making money—and the fathers were more than willing to grant that this was a valid excuse for not making a living. Where such claims were not made or recognized, catastrophe was just around the corner. Benjamin was a case in point: his father never recognized his claims, and their relations were extraordinarily bad. Another such case was Kafka, who—possibly because he really was something like a genius—was quite free of the genius mania of his environment, never claimed to be a genius, and ensured his financial independence by taking an ordinary job at the Prague workmen's compensation office. (His relations with his father were of course equally bad, but for different reasons.) And still, no sooner had Kafka taken this position than he saw in it a "running start for suicides," as though he were obeying an order that says "You have to earn your grave." [13]

For Benjamin, at any rate, a monthly stipend remained the only possible form of income, and in order to receive one after his parents' death he was ready, or thought he was, to do many things: to study Hebrew for three hundred marks a month if the Zionists thought it would do them some good, or to think dialectically, with all the mediating trimmings, for one thousand French francs if there was no other way of doing business with the Marxists. The fact that despite being down and out he later did neither is worthy of admiration, and so is the infinite patience with which Scholem, who had worked very hard to get Benjamin a stipend for the study of Hebrew from the university in Jerusalem, allowed himself to be put off for years. No one, of course, was prepared to subsidize him in the only "position" for which he was born, that of an *homme de lettres*, a position of whose unique prospects neither the Zionists nor the Marxists were, or could have been, aware.

Today the *homme de lettres* strikes us as a rather harmless, marginal figure, as though he were actually to be equated with the figure of the *Privatgelehrter* that has always had a touch of the comic. Benjamin, who felt so close to French that the language became for him a "sort of alibi" (*Briefe* II, 505) for his existence, probably knew about the *homme de lettres*'s origins in prerevolutionary France as well as about his extraordinary career in the French Revolution. In contrast to the later writers and literati, the "*écrivains et littérateurs*" as even Larousse defines the *hommes de lettres*, these men, though they did live in the world of the written and printed word and were, above all, surrounded by books, were neither obliged nor willing to write and read professionally, in order to earn a living. Unlike the class of the intellectuals, who offer their services either to the state as experts, specialists, and officials, or to society for diversion and instruction, the *hommes de lettres* always strove to keep aloof from both the state and society. Their material existence was based on income without work, and their intellectual attitude rested upon their resolute refusal to be integrated politically or socially. On the basis of this dual independence they could afford that attitude of superior disdain which gave rise to La Rochefoucauld's contemptuous insights into human behavior, the worldly wisdom of Montaigne, the aphoristic trenchancy of Pascal's thought, the boldness and open-mindedness of Montesquieu's political reflections. It cannot be my task here to discuss the circumstances which eventually turned the *hommes de lettres* into revolutionaries in the eighteenth century nor the way in which their successors in the nineteenth and twentieth centuries split into the class of the "cultured" on the one hand and of the professional revolutionaries on the other. I mention this historical background only because in Benjamin the element of culture combined in such a unique way with the element of the revolutionary and rebellious. It was as though shortly before its disappearance the figure of the *homme de lettres* was destined to show itself once more in the fullness of its possibilities, although—or, possibly, because—it had lost its material basis in such a catastrophic way, so that the purely intellectual passion which makes this figure so lovable might unfold in all its most telling and impressive possibilities.

There certainly was no dearth of reasons to rebel against his origins, the milieu of German-Jewish society in Imperial Germany, in which Benjamin grew up, nor was there any lack of justification for taking a stand against the Weimar Republic, in which he refused to take up a profession. In *A Berlin Childhood around 1900* Benjamin describes the house from which he came as a "mausoleum long intended for me" (*Schriften* I, 643). Characteristically enough, his father was an art dealer and antiquarian; the family was a wealthy and run-of-the-mill assimilated one; one of his grandparents was Orthodox, the other belonged to a Reform congregation. "In my childhood I was a prisoner of the old and the new West. In those days my clan inhabited these two districts with an attitude mingled of stubbornness and self-confidence, turning them into a ghetto which it regarded as its fief" (*Schriften* I, 643). The stubbornness was toward their Jewishness; it was only stubbornness that made them cling to it. The self-confidence was inspired by their position in the non-Jewish environment in which they had, after all, achieved quite a bit. Just how much was shown on days when guests were expected. On such occasions the inside of the sideboard, which seemed to be the center of the house and thus "with good reason resembled the temple mountains," was opened, and now it was possible "to show off treasures such as idols like to be surrounded with." Then "the house's hoard of silver" appeared, and what was displayed "was there not tenfold, but twentyfold or thirtyfold. And when I looked at these long, long rows of mocha spoons or knife rests, fruit knives or oyster forks, the enjoyment of this profusion struggled with the fear that those who were being expected might all look alike, just as our cutlery did" (*Schriften* I, 632). Even the child knew that something was radically wrong, and not only because there were poor people ("The poor—for the rich children of my age they existed only as beggars. And it was a great advance in my understanding when for the first time poverty dawned on me in the ignominy of poorly paid work" [*Schriften* I, 632]) but because "stubbornness" within and "self-confidence" without were producing an atmosphere of insecurity and self-consciousness which truly was anything but suitable for the raising of children. This was true not only of Benjamin or Berlin West * or Germany. With what passion did Kafka try to persuade his sister to put her ten-year-old son in a boarding school, so as to save him from "the special mentality which is particularly virulent among wealthy Prague Jews and which cannot be kept away from children . . . this petty, dirty, sly mentality." [14]

What was involved, then, was what had since the 1870s or 1880s been called the Jewish question and existed in that form only in the German-speaking Central Europe of those decades. Today this question has been washed away, as it were, by the catastrophe of European Jewry and is justly forgotten, although one still encounters it occasionally in the language of the older generation of German Zionists whose thinking habits derive from the first decades of this century. Besides, it never was anything

---

* A fashionable residential area of Berlin.

but the concern of the Jewish intelligentsia and had no significance for the majority of Central European Jewry. For the intellectuals, however, it was of great importance, for their own Jewishness, which played hardly any role in their spiritual household, determined their social life to an extraordinary degree and therefore presented itself to them as a moral question of the first order. In this moral form the Jewish question marked, in Kafka's words, "the terrible inner condition of these generations." [15] No matter how insignificant this problem may appear to us in the face of what actually happened later, we cannot disregard it here, for neither Benjamin nor Kafka nor Karl Kraus can be understood without it. For simplicity's sake I shall state the problem exactly as it was stated and endlessly discussed then—namely, in an article entitled "German-Jewish Mt. Parnassus" ("Deutsch-jüdischer Parnass") which created a great stir when Moritz Goldstein published it in 1912 in the distinguished journal *Der Kunstwart*.

According to Goldstein, the problem as it appeared to the Jewish intelligentsia had a dual aspect, the non-Jewish environment and assimilated Jewish society, and in his view the problem was insoluble. With respect to the non-Jewish environment, "We Jews administer the intellectual property of a people which denies us the right and the ability to do so." And further: "It is easy to show the absurdity of our adversaries' arguments and prove that their enmity is unfounded. What would be gained by this? That their hatred is *genuine*. When all calumnies have been refuted, all distortions rectified, all false judgments about us rejected, antipathy will remain as something irrefutable. Anyone who does not realize this is beyond help." It was the failure to realize this that was felt to be unbearable about Jewish society, whose representatives, on the one hand, wished to remain Jews and, on the other, did not want to acknowledge their Jewishness: "We shall openly drum the problem that they are shirking into them. We shall force them to own up to their Jewishness or to have themselves baptized." But even if this was successful, even if the mendacity of this milieu could be exposed and escaped— what would be gained by it? A "leap into modern Hebrew literature" was impossible for the current generation. Hence: "Our relationship to Germany is one of unrequited love. Let us be manly enough at last to tear the beloved out of our hearts. . . . I have stated what we *must* want to do; I have also stated why we *cannot* want it. My intention was to point up the problem. It is not my fault that I know of no solution." (For himself, Herr Goldstein solved the problem six years later when he became cultural editor of the *Vossische Zeitung*. And what else could he have done?)

One could dispose of Moritz Goldstein by saying that he simply reproduced what Benjamin in another context called "a major part of the *vulgar* anti-Semitic as well as the Zionist ideology" (*Briefe* I, 152-53), if one did not encounter in Kafka, on a far more serious level, a similar formulation of the problem and the same confession of its insolubility. In a letter to Max Brod about German-Jewish writers he said that the Jewish question or "the despair over it was their inspiration—an inspiration as respectable as any other but fraught, upon closer examination, with distressing peculiarities. For one thing, what their despair discharged itself in could not be German literature which on the surface it appeared to be," because the problem was not really a German one. Thus they lived "among three impossibilities . . . : the impossibility of not writing" as they could get rid of their inspiration only by writing; "the impossibility of writing in German"—Kafka considered their use of the German language as the "overt or covert, or possibly self-tormenting usurpation of an alien property, which has not been acquired but stolen, (relatively) quickly picked up, and which remains someone else's possession even if not a single linguistic mistake can be pointed out"; and finally, "the impossibility of writing differently," since no other language was available. "One could almost add a fourth impossibility," says Kafka in conclusion, "the impossibility of writing, for this despair was not something that could be mitigated through writing"—as is normal for poets, to whom a god has given to say what men suffer and endure. Rather, despair has become here "an enemy of life *and* of writing; writing was here only a moratorium, as it is for someone who writes his last will and testament just before he hangs himself." [16]

Nothing could be easier than to demonstrate that Kafka was wrong and that his own work, which speaks the purest German prose of the century, is the best refutation of his views. But such a demonstration, apart from being in bad taste, is all the more superfluous as Kafka himself was so very much aware of it—"If I indiscriminately write down a sentence," he once noted in his Diaries, "it already is perfect" [17]—just as he was the only one to know that *"Mauscheln"* (speaking a Yiddishized German), though despised by all German-speaking people, Jews or non-Jews, did have a legitimate place in the German language, being nothing else but óne of the numerous German dialects. And since he rightly thought that "within the German language, only the dialects and, besides them, the most personal High German are really alive," it naturally was no less legitimate to change from *Mauscheln*, or from Yiddish, to High German than it was to change from Low German or the Alemannic dialect. If one reads Kafka's remarks about the Jewish troupe of actors which so fascinated him, it becomes clear that what attracted him were less the specifically Jewish elements than the liveliness of language and gesture.

To be sure, we have some difficulty today in understanding these problems or taking them seriously, especially since it is so tempting to misinterpret and dismiss them as mere reaction to an anti-Semitic milieu and thus as an expression of self-hatred. But nothing could be more misleading when dealing with men of the human stature and intellectual rank of Kafka, Kraus, and Benjamin. What gave their criticism its bitter sharpness was never anti-Semitism as such, but the reaction to it of the Jewish middle class, with which the intellectuals by no means identified. There, too, it was not a matter of the frequently undignified apologetic attitude of official Jewry, with which the intellectuals had hardly any contact, but of the lying denial of the very existence of widespread anti-Semitism, of the isolation from reality staged with all the devices of self-deception by the Jewish bourgeoisie, an isolation which for Kafka, and not only for him, included the often hostile and always haughty separation from the Jewish people, the so-called *Ostjuden* (Jews from Eastern Europe) who were, though one knew better, blamed by them for anti-Semitism. The decisive factor in all this was the loss of reality, aided and abetted by the wealth of these classes. "Among poor people," wrote Kafka, "the world, the bustle of work, so to speak, irresistibly enters the huts . . . and does not allow the musty, polluted, child-consuming air of a nicely furnished family room to be generated." [18] They fought against Jewish society because it would not permit them to live in the world as it happened to be, without illusions—thus, for example, to be prepared for the murder of Walther Rathenau (in 1922): to Kafka it was "incomprehensible that they should have let him live as long as that." [19] What finally determined the acuteness of the problem was the fact that it did not merely, or even primarily, manifest itself as a break between the generations from which one could have escaped by leaving home and family. To only very few German-Jewish writers did the problem present itself in this way, and these few were surrounded by all those others who are already forgotten but from whom they are clearly distinguishable only today when posterity has settled the question of who is who. ("Their political function," wrote Benjamin, "is to establish not parties but cliques, their literary function to produce not schools but fashions, and their economic function to set into the world not producers but agents. Agents or smarties who know how to spend their poverty as if it were riches and who make whoopee out of their yawning vacuity. One could not establish oneself more comfortably in an uncomfortable situation." [20]) Kafka, who exemplified this situation in the above-mentioned letter by "linguistic impossibilities," adding that they could "also be called something quite different," points to a "linguistic middle class" between, as it were, proletarian dialect and high-class prose; it is "nothing but ashes which can be given a semblance of life only by overeager Jewish hands rummaging through them." One need hardly add that the overwhelming majority of Jewish intellectuals belonged to this "middle class"; according to Kafka, they constituted "the hell of German-Jewish letters," in which Karl

Kraus held sway as "the great overseer and taskmaster" without noticing how much "he himself belongs in this hell among those to be chastised." [21] That these things may be seen quite differently from a non-Jewish perspective becomes apparent when one reads in one of Benjamin's essays what Brecht said about Karl Kraus: "When the age died by its own hand, he was that hand" (*Schriften* II, 174).

For the Jews of that generation (Kafka and Moritz Goldstein were but ten years older than Benjamin) the available forms of rebellion were Zionism and Communism, and it is noteworthy that their fathers often condemned the Zionist rebellion more bitterly than the Communist. Both were escape routes from illusion into reality, from mendacity and self-deception to an honest existence. But this is only how it appears in retrospect. At the time when Benjamin tried, first, a half-hearted Zionism and then a basically no less half-hearted Communism, the two ideologies faced each other with the greatest hostility: the Communists were defaming Zionists as Jewish Fascists [22] and the Zionists were calling the young Jewish Communists "red assimilationists." In a remarkable and probably unique manner Benjamin kept both routes open for himself for years; he persisted in considering the road to Palestine long after he had become a Marxist, without allowing himself to be swayed in the least by the opinions of his Marxist-oriented friends, particularly the Jews among them. This shows clearly how little the "positive" aspect of either ideology interested him, and that what mattered to him in both instances was the "negative" factor of criticism of existing conditions, a way out of bourgeois illusions and untruthfulness, a position outside the literary as well as the academic establishment. He was quite young when he adopted this radically critical attitude, probably without suspecting to what isolation and loneliness it would eventually lead him. Thus we read, for example, in a letter written in 1918, that Walther Rathenau, claiming to represent Germany in foreign affairs, and Rudolf Borchardt, making a similar claim with respect to German spiritual affairs, had in common the "*will* to lie," "the objective mendacity" (*Briefe* I, 189 ff). Neither wanted to "serve" a cause through his works—in

Borchardt's case, the "spiritual and linguistic resources" of the people; in Rathenau's, the nation—but both used their works and talents as "sovereign means in the service of an absolute will to power." In addition, there were the littérateurs who placed their gifts in the service of a career and social status: "To be a littérateur is to live under the sign of mere intellect, just as prostitution is to live under the sign of mere sex" (*Schriften* II, 179). Just as a prostitute betrays sexual love, a littérateur betrays the mind, and it was this betrayal of the mind which the best among the Jews could not forgive their colleagues in literary life. In the same vein Benjamin wrote five years later—one year after the assassination of Rathenau—to a close German friend: ". . . Jews today ruin even the best German cause which they publicly champion, because their public statement is necessarily venal (in a deeper sense) and cannot adduce proof of its authenticity" (*Briefe* I, 310). He went on to say that only the private, almost "secret relationships between Germans and Jews" were legitimate, while "everything about German-Jewish relations that works in public today causes harm." There was much truth in these words. Written from the perspective of the Jewish question at that time, they supply evidence of the darkness of a period in which one could rightly say, "The light of the public darkens everything" (Heidegger).

As early as 1913 Benjamin weighed the position of Zionism "as a possibility and thus perhaps a necessary commitment" (*Briefe* I, 44) in the sense of this dual rebellion against the parental home and German-Jewish literary life. Two years later he met Gerhard Scholem, encountering in him for the first and only time "Judaism in living form"; soon afterwards came the beginning of that curious, endless consideration, extending over a period of almost twenty years, of emigration to Palestine. "Under certain, by no means impossible conditions I am ready if not determined [to go to Palestine]. Here in Austria the Jews (the decent ones, those who are not making money) talk of nothing else." So he wrote in 1919 (*Briefe* I, 222), but at the same time he regarded such a plan as an "act of violence" (*Briefe* I, 208), unfeasible unless it turned out to be necessary. Whenever such financial or political necessity arose, he reconsidered the project and did not go. It is hard to say whether he was still serious about it after the separation from his wife, who had come from a Zionist milieu. But it is certain that even during his Paris exile he announced that he might go "to Jerusalem in October or November, after a more or less definitive conclusion of my studies" (*Briefe* II, 655). What strikes one as indecison in the letters, as though he were vacillating between Zionism and Marxism, in truth was probably due to the bitter insight that all solutions were not only objectively false and inappropriate to reality, but would lead him personally to a false salvation, no matter whether that salvation was labeled Moscow or Jerusalem. He felt that he would deprive himself of the positive cognitive chances of his own position—"on the top of a mast that is already crumbling" or "dead in his own lifetime and the real survivor" among the ruins. He had settled down in the desperate conditions which corresponded to reality; there he wanted to remain in order to "denature" his own writings "like methylated spirits . . . at the risk of making them unfit for consumption" by anyone then alive but with the chance of being preserved all the more reliably for an unknown future.

For the insolubility of the Jewish question for that generation by no means consisted only in their speaking and writing German or in the fact that their "production plant" was located in Europe—in Benjamin's case, in Berlin West or in Paris, something about which he did "not have the slightest illusions" (*Briefe* II, 531). What was decisive was that these men did not wish to "return" either to the ranks of the Jewish people or to Judaism, and could not desire to do so—not because they believed in "progress" and an automatic disappearance of anti-Semitism or because they were too "assimilated" and too alienated from their Jewish heritage, but because all traditions and cultures as well as all "belonging" had become equally questionable to them. This is what they felt was wrong with the "return" to the Jewish fold as proposed by the Zionists; they could all have said what Kafka once said about being a member of the Jewish people: ". . . My people, provided that I have one." [23]

No doubt, the Jewish question was of great importance for this generation of Jewish writers and explains much of the personal despair so prominent in nearly everything they wrote. But the most clear-sighted among them were led by their personal conflicts to a much more general and more radical problem, namely, to questioning the relevance of the Western tradition as a whole. Not just Marxism as a doctrine but the Communist revolutionary movement exerted a powerful attraction on them because it implied more than a criticism of existing social and political conditions and took into account the totality of political and spiritual traditions. For Benjamin, at any rate, this question of the past and of tradition as such was decisive, and precisely in the sense in which Scholem, warning his friend against the dangers to his thinking inherent in Marxism, posed it, albeit without being aware of the problem. Benjamin, he wrote, was running the risk of forfeiting the chance of becoming "the legitimate continuer of the most fruitful and most genuine traditions of a Hamann and a Humboldt" (*Briefe* II, 526). What he did not understand was that such a return to and continuation of the past was the very thing which "the morality of [his] insights," to which Scholem appealed, was bound to rule out for Benjamin.[24]

It seems tempting to believe, and would indeed be a comforting thought, that those few who ventured out onto the most exposed positions of the time and paid the full price of isolation at least thought of themselves as the precursors of a new age. That certainly was not the case. In his essay on Karl Kraus, Benjamin brought up this question: Does Kraus stand "at the threshold of a new age?" "Alas, by no means. He stands at the threshold of the Last Judgment" (*Schriften* II, 174). And at this threshold there really stood all those who later became the masters of the "new age"; they looked upon the dawn of a new age basically as a decline and viewed history along with the traditions which led up to this decline as a field of ruins.[25] No one has expressed this more clearly than Benjamin in his "Theses on the Philosophy of History," and nowhere has he said it more unequivocally than in a letter from Paris dated 1935: "Actually, I hardly feel constrained to try to make head or tail of this condition of the world.

On this planet a great number of civilizations have perished in blood and horror. Naturally, one must wish for the planet that one day it will experience a civilization that has abandoned blood and horror; in fact, I am . . . inclined to assume that our planet is waiting for this. But it is terribly doubtful whether *we* can bring such a present to its hundred- or four-hundred-millionth birthday party. And if we don't, the planet will finally punish us, its unthoughtful well-wishers, by presenting us with the Last Judgment" * (*Briefe* II, 698).

Well, in this respect the last thirty years have hardly brought much that could be called new.

III. THE PEARL DIVER

Full fathom five thy father lies,
  Of his bones are coral made,
Those are pearls that were his eyes.
  Nothing of him that doth fade
But doth suffer a sea-change
Into something rich and strange.
        —THE TEMPEST, I, 2

Insofar as the past has been transmitted as tradition, it possesses authority; insofar as authority presents itself historically, it becomes tradition. Walter Benjamin knew that the break in tradition and the loss of authority which occurred in his lifetime were irreparable, and he concluded that he had to discover new ways of dealing with the past. In this he became a master when he discovered that the transmissibility of the past had been replaced by its citability and that in place of its authority there had arisen a strange power to settle down, piecemeal, in the present and to deprive it of "peace of mind," the mindless peace of complacency. "Quotations in my works are like robbers by the roadside who make an armed attack and relieve an idler of his convictions" (*Schriften* I, 571). This discovery of the modern function of quotations, according to Benjamin, who exemplified

* *Weltgericht* (Last Judgment) plays on the dual meaning of *Gericht* (judgment; dish). (Translator's note.)

it by Karl Kraus, was born out of despair—not the despair of a past that refuses "to throw its light on the future" and lets the human mind "wander in darkness" as in Tocqueville, but out of the despair of the present and the desire to destroy it; hence their power is "not the strength to preserve but to cleanse, to tear out of context, to destroy" (*Schriften* II, 192). Still, the discoverers and lovers of this destructive power originally were inspired by an entirely different intention, the intention to preserve; and only because they did not let themselves be fooled by the professional "preservers" all around them did they finally discover that the destructive power of quotations was "the only one which still contains the hope that something from this period will survive—for no other reason than that it was torn out of it." In this form of "thought fragments," quotations have the double task of interrupting the flow of the presentation with "transcendent force" (*Schriften* I, 142-43) and at the same time of concentrating within themselves that which is presented. As to their weight in Benjamin's writings, quotations are comparable only to the very dissimilar Biblical citations which so often replace the immanent consistency of argumentation in medieval treatises.

I have already mentioned that collecting was Benjamin's central passion. It started early with what he himself called his "bibliomania" but soon extended into something far more characteristic, not so much of the person as of his work: the collecting of quotations. (Not that he ever stopped collecting books. Shortly before the fall of France he seriously considered exchanging his edition of the Collected Works of Kafka, which had recently appeared in five volumes, for a few first editions of Kafka's early writings—an undertaking which naturally was bound to remain incomprehensible to any nonbibliophile.) The "inner need to own a library" (*Briefe* I, 193) asserted itself around 1916, at the time when Benjamin turned in his studies to Romanticism as the "last movement that once more saved tradition" (*Briefe* I, 138). That a certain destructive force was active even in this passion for the past, so characteristic of heirs and late-comers, Benjamin did not discover until much later, when he had already lost his faith in tradition and in the indestructibility of the world. (This will be discussed presently.) In those days, encouraged by Scholem, he still believed that his own estrangement from tradition was probably due to his Jewishness and that there might be a way back for him as there was for his friend, who was preparing to emigrate to Jerusalem. (As early as 1920, when he was not yet seriously beset by financial worries, he thought of learning Hebrew.) He never went as far on this road as did Kafka, who after all his efforts stated bluntly that he had no use for anything Jewish except the Hasidic tales which Buber had just prepared for modern usage—"into everything else I just drift, and another current of air carries me away again." [26] Was he, then, despite all doubts, to go back to the German or European past and help with the tradition of its literature?

Presumably this is the form in which the problem presented itself to him in the early twenties, before he turned to Marxism. That is when he chose the German Baroque Age as a subject for his *Habilitation* thesis, a choice that is very characteristic of the ambiguity of this entire, still unresolved cluster of problems. For in the German literary and poetic tradition the Baroque has, with the exception of the great church chorales of the time, never really been alive. Goethe rightly said that when he was eighteen years old, German literature was no older. And Benjamin's choice, baroque in a double sense, has an exact counterpart in Scholem's strange decision to approach Judaism via the Cabala, that is, that part of Hebrew literature which is untransmitted and untransmissible in terms of Jewish tradition, in which it has always had the odor of something downright disreputable. Nothing showed more clearly—so one is inclined to say today—that there was no such thing as a "return" either to the German or the European or the Jewish tradition than the choice of these fields of study. It was an implicit admission that the past spoke directly only through things that had not been handed down, whose seeming closeness to the present was thus due precisely to their exotic character, which ruled out all claims to a binding authority. Obligative truths were replaced by what was in some sense significant or interesting, and this of course meant—as no

one knew better than Benjamin—that the "consistence of truth
. . . has been lost" (*Briefe* II, 763). Outstanding among the
properties that formed this "consistence of truth" was, at least
for Benjamin, whose early philosophical interest was theologically inspired, that truth concerned a secret and that the revelation of this secret had authority. Truth, so Benjamin said shortly
before he became fully aware of the irreparable break in tradition
and the loss of authority, is not "an unveiling which destroys the
secret, but the revelation which does it justice" (*Schriften* I, 146).
Once this truth had come into the human world at the appropriate moment in history—be it as the Greek *a-letheia*, visually
perceptible to the eyes of the mind and comprehended by us as
"un-concealment" ("*Unverborgenheit*"—Heidegger), or as the
acoustically perceptible word of God as we know it from the
European religions of revelation—it was this "consistence" peculiar to it which made it tangible, as it were, so that it could be
handed down by tradition. Tradition transforms truth into wisdom, and wisdom is the consistence of transmissible truth. In
other words, even if truth should appear in our world, it could
not lead to wisdom, because it would no longer have the characteristics which it could acquire only through universal recognition of its validity. Benjamin discusses these matters in connection
with Kafka and says that of course "Kafka was far from being
the first to face this situation. Many had accommodated themselves to it, adhering to truth or whatever they regarded as truth
at any given time and, with a more or less heavy heart, forgoing
its transmissibility. Kafka's real genius was that he tried something
entirely new: he sacrificed truth for the sake of clinging to the
transmissibility" (*Briefe* II, 763). He did so by making decisive
changes in traditional parables or inventing new ones in traditional style; [27] however, these "do not modestly lie at the feet of
the doctrine," as do the haggadic tales in the Talmud, but "unexpectedly raise a heavy claw" against it. Even Kafka's reaching
down to the sea bottom of the past had this peculiar duality of
wanting to preserve and wanting to destroy. He wanted to preserve it even though it was not truth, if only for the sake of this
"new beauty in what is vanishing" (see Benjamin's essay on

Leskov); and he knew, on the other hand, that there is no more effective way to break the spell of tradition than to cut out the "rich and strange," coral and pearls, from what had been handed down in one solid piece.

Benjamin exemplified this ambiguity of gesture in regard to the past by analyzing the collector's passion which was his own. Collecting springs from a variety of motives which are not easily understood. As Benjamin was probably the first to emphasize, collecting is the passion of children, for whom things are not yet commodities and are not valued according to their usefulness, and it is also the hobby of the rich, who own enough not to need anything useful and hence can afford to make "the transfiguration of objects" (*Schriften* I, 416) their business. In this they must of necessity discover the beautiful, which needs "disinterested delight" (Kant) to be recognized. At any rate, a collected object possesses only an amateur value and no use value whatsoever. (Benjamin was not yet aware of the fact that collecting can also be an eminently sound and often highly profitable form of investment.) And inasmuch as collecting can fasten on any category of objects (not just art objects, which are in any case removed from the everyday world of use objects because they are "good" for nothing) and thus, as it were, redeem the object as a thing since it now is no longer a means to an end but has its intrinsic worth, Benjamin could understand the collector's passion as an attitude akin to that of the revolutionary. Like the revolutionary, the collector "dreams his way not only into a remote or bygone world, but at the same time into a better one in which, to be sure, people are not provided with what they need any more than they are in the everyday world, but in which things are liberated from the drudgery of usefulness" (*Schriften* I, 416). Collecting is the redemption of things which is to complement the redemption of man. Even the reading of his books is something questionable to a true bibliophile: " 'And you have read all these?' Anatole France is said to have been asked by an admirer of his library. 'Not one-tenth of them. I don't suppose you use your Sèvres china every day?' " ("Unpacking My Library"). (In Benjamin's library there were collections of rare children's books and of books by mentally deranged authors; since he was interested neither in child psychology nor in psychiatry, these books, like many others among his treasures, literally were not good for anything, serving neither to divert nor to instruct.) Closely connected with this is the fetish character which Benjamin explicitly claimed for collected objects. The value of genuineness which is decisive for the collector as well as for the market determined by him has replaced the "cult value" and is its secularization.

These reflections, like so much else in Benjamin, have something of the ingeniously brilliant which is not characteristic of his essential insights, which are, for the most part, quite down-to-earth. Still, they are striking examples of the *flânerie* in his thinking, of the way his mind worked, when he, like the *flâneur* in the city, entrusted himself to chance as a guide on his intellectual journeys of exploration. Just as strolling through the treasures of the past is the inheritor's luxurious privilege, so is the "collector's attitude, in the highest sense, the attitude of the heir" ("Unpacking My Library") who, by taking possession of things—and "ownership is the most profound relationship that one can have to objects" (*ibid.*)—establishes himself in the past, so as to achieve, undisturbed by the present, "a renewal of the old world." And since this "deepest urge" in the collector has no public significance whatsoever but results in a strictly private hobby, everything "that is said from the angle of the true collector" is bound to appear as "whimsical" as the typically Jean Paulian vision of one of those writers "who write books not because they are poor, but because they are dissatisfied with the books which they could buy but do not like" (*ibid.*). Upon closer examination, however, this whimsicality has some noteworthy and not so harmless peculiarities. There is, for one thing, the gesture, so significant of an era of public darkness, with which the collector not only withdraws from the public into the privacy of his four walls but takes along with him all kinds of treasures that once were public property to decorate them. (This, of course, is not today's collector, who gets hold of whatever has or, in his estimate, will have a market value or can enhance his social status, but the collector who, like Benjamin, seeks strange things that are considered valueless.) Also, in his passion for the past for its own sake, born of his contempt for the present as such and therefore rather heedless of objective quality, there already appears a disturbing factor to announce that tradition may be the last thing to guide him and traditional values by no means be as safe in his hands as one might have assumed at first glance.

For tradition puts the past in order, not just chronologically but first of all systematically in that it separates the positive from the negative, the orthodox from the heretical, and which is obligatory and relevant from the mass of irrelevant or merely interesting opinions and data. The collector's passion, on the other hand, is not only unsystematic but borders on the chaotic, not so much because it is a passion as because it is not primarily kindled by the quality of the object—something that is classifiable—but is inflamed by its "genuineness," its uniqueness, something that defies any systematic classification. Therefore, while tradition discriminates, the collector levels all differences; and this leveling— so that "the positive and the negative . . . predilection and rejection are here closely contiguous" (*Schriften* II, 313)—takes place even if the collector has made tradition itself his special field and carefully eliminated everything not recognized by it. Against tradition the collector pits the criterion of genuineness; to the authoritative he opposes the sign of origin. To express this way of thinking in theoretical terms: he replaces content with pure originality or authenticity, something that only French Existentialism established as a quality *per se* detached from all specific characteristics. If one carries this way of thinking to its logical conclusion, the result is a strange inversion of the original collector's drive: "The genuine picture may be old, but the genuine thought is new. It is of the present. This present may be meager, granted. But no matter what it is like, one must firmly take it by the horns to be able to consult the past. It is the bull whose blood must fill the pit if the shades of the departed are to appear at its edge" (*Schriften* II, 314). Out of this present when it has been sacrificed for the invocation of the past arises then "the deadly impact of thought" which is directed against tradition and the authority of the past.

Thus the heir and preserver unexpectedly turns into a destroyer. "The true, greatly misunderstood passion of the collector is always anarchistic, destructive. For this is its dialectics: to combine with loyalty to an object, to individual items, to things sheltered in his care, a stubborn subversive protest against the typical, the classifiable." [28] The collector destroys the context in which his object once was only part of a greater, living entity, and since only the uniquely genuine will do for him he must cleanse the chosen object of everything that is typical about it. The figure of the collector, as old-fashioned as that of the *flâneur*, could assume such eminently modern features in Benjamin because history itself—that is, the break in tradition which took place at the beginning of this century—had already relieved him of this task of destruction and he only needed to bend down, as it were, to select his precious fragments from the pile of debris. In other words, the things themselves offered, particularly to a man who firmly faced the present, an aspect which had previously been discoverable only from the collector's whimsical perspective.

I do not know when Benjamin discovered the remarkable co-incidence of his old-fashioned inclinations with the realities of the times; it must have been in the mid-twenties, when he began the serious study of Kafka, only to discover shortly thereafter in Brecht the poet who was most at home in this century. I do not mean to assert that Benjamin shifted his emphasis from the collecting of books to the collecting of quotations (exclusive with him) overnight or even within one year, although there is some evidence in the letters of a conscious shifting of emphasis. At any rate, nothing was more characteristic of him in the thirties than the little notebooks with black covers which he always carried with him and in which he tirelessly entered in the form of quotations what daily living and reading netted him in the way of "pearls" and "coral." On occasion he read from them aloud, showed them around like items from a choice and precious collection. And in this collection, which by then was anything but whimsical, it was easy to find next to an obscure love poem from the eighteenth century the latest newspaper item, next to Goecking's "Der erste Schnee" a report from Vienna dated summer 1939, saying that the local gas company had "stopped supplying gas to Jews. The gas consumption of the Jewish population involved a loss for the gas company, since the biggest consumers were the ones who did not pay their bills. The Jews used the gas especially for committing suicide" (*Briefe* II, 820). Here indeed the shades of the departed were invoked only from the sacrificial pit of the present.

The close affinity between the break in tradition and the seemingly whimsical figure of the collector who gathers his fragments and scraps from the debris of the past is perhaps best illustrated by the fact, astonishing only at first glance, that there probably was no period before ours in which old and ancient things, many of them long forgotten by tradition, have become general educational material which is handed to schoolboys everywhere in hundreds of thousands of copies. This amazing revival, particularly of classical culture, which since the forties has been especially noticeable in relatively traditionless America, began in Europe in the twenties. There it was initiated by those who were most aware of the irreparability of the break in tradition—thus in Germany, and not only there, first and foremost by Martin Heidegger, whose extraordinary, and extraordinarily early, success in the twenties was essentially due to a "listening to the tradition that does not give itself up to the past but thinks of the present." [29] Without realizing it, Benjamin actually had more in common with Heidegger's remarkable sense for living eyes and living bones that had sea-changed into pearls and coral, and as such could be saved and lifted into the present only by doing violence to their context in interpreting them with "the deadly impact" of new thoughts, than he did with the dialectical subtleties of his Marxist friends. For just as the above-cited closing sentence from the Goethe essay sounds as though Kafka had written it, the following words from a letter to Hofmannsthal dated 1924 make one think of some of Heidegger's essays written in the forties and fifties: "The conviction which guides me in my literary attempts . . . [is] that each truth has its home, its ancestral palace, in language, that this palace was built with the oldest *logoi,* and that to a truth thus founded the insights of the sciences will remain inferior for as long as they make do here and there in the area of language like nomads, as it were, in the conviction of the sign character of language which produces the irresponsible arbitrariness of their terminology" (*Briefe* I, 329). In the spirit of Benjamin's early work on the philosophy of language, words are "the opposite of all communication directed toward the outside," just as truth is "the death of intention." Anyone who seeks truth fares like the man in the fable about the veiled picture at Saïs; "this is caused not by some mysterious monstrousness of the content to be unveiled but by the nature of truth before which even the purest fire of searching is extinguished as though under water" (*Schriften* I, 151, 152).

From the Goethe essay on, quotations are at the center of every work of Benjamin's. This very fact distinguishes his writings from scholarly works of all kinds in which it is the function of quotations to verify and document opinions, wherefore they can safely be relegated to the Notes. This is out of the question in Benjamin. When he was working on his study of German tragedy, he boasted of a collection of "over 600 quotations very systematically and clearly arranged" (*Briefe* I, 339); like the later notebooks, this collection was not an accumulation of excerpts intended to facilitate the writing of the study but constituted the main work, with the writing as something secondary. The main work consisted in tearing fragments out of their context and arranging them afresh in such a way that they illustrated one another and were able to prove their *raison d'être* in a free-floating state, as it were. It definitely was a sort of surrealistic montage. Benjamin's ideal of producing a work consisting entirely of quotations, one that was mounted so masterfully that it could dispense with any accompanying text, may strike one as whimsical in the extreme and self-destructive to boot, but it was not, any more than were the contemporaneous surrealistic experiments which arose from similar impulses. To the extent that an accompanying text by the author proved unavoidable, it was a matter of fashioning it in such a way as to preserve "the intention of such investigations," namely, "to plumb the depths of language and thought . . . by drilling rather than excavating" (*Briefe* I, 329), so as not to ruin everything with explanations that seek to provide a causal or systematic connection. In so doing Benjamin was quite aware that this new method of "drilling" resulted in a certain "forcing of insights . . . whose inelegant pedantry, however, is preferable to today's almost universal habit of falsifying them"; it was equally clear to him that this method was bound to be "the cause of certain obscurities" (*Briefe* I, 330). What mattered to him above all was to avoid anything that might be reminiscent of empathy, as though a given subject of investigation had a message in readiness which easily communicated itself, or could be communicated, to the reader or spectator: "*No poem is intended for the reader, no picture for the beholder, no symphony for the listener*" ("The Task of the Translator"; italics added).

This sentence, written quite early, could serve as motto for all of Benjamin's literary criticism. It should not be misunderstood as another dadaist affront of an audience that even then had already become quite used to all sorts of merely capricious shock effects and "put-ons." Benjamin deals here with thought things, particularly those of a linguistic nature, which, according to him, "retain their meaning, possibly their best significance, if they are not *a priori* applied exclusively to man. For example, one could speak of an unforgettable life or moment even if all men had forgotten them. If the nature of such a life or moment required that it not be forgotten, that predicate would not contain a falsehood but merely a claim that is not being fulfilled by men, and perhaps also a reference to a realm in which it *is* fulfilled: God's remembrance" (*ibid.*). Benjamin later gave up this theological background but not the theory and not his method of drilling to obtain the essential in the form of quotations—as one obtains water by drilling for it from a source concealed in the depths of the earth. This method is like the modern equivalent of ritual invocations, and the spirits that now arise invariably are those spiritual essences from a past that have suffered the Shakespearean "sea-change" from living eyes to pearls, from living bones to coral. For Benjamin to quote is to name, and naming rather than speaking, the word rather than the sentence, brings truth to light. As one may read in the preface to the *Origin of German Tragedy*, Benjamin regarded truth as an exclusively acoustical phenomenon: "Not Plato but Adam," who gave things their names, was to him the "father of philosophy." Hence tradition was the form in which these name-giving words were transmitted; it too was an essentially acoustical phenomenon. He felt himself so akin to Kafka precisely because the latter, current misinterpretations notwithstanding, had "no far-sightedness or 'prophetic vision,'" but listened to tradition, and "he who listens hard does not see" ("Max Brod's Book on Kafka").

There are good reasons why Benjamin's philosophical interest from the outset concentrated on the philosophy of language, and why finally naming through quoting became for him the only possible and appropriate way of dealing with the past without the aid of tradition. Any period to which its own past has become as questionable as it has to us must eventually come up against the phenomenon of language, for in it the past is contained ineradicably, thwarting all attemts to get rid of it once and for all. The Greek *polis* will continue to exist at the bottom of our political existence—that is, at the bottom of the sea—for as long as we use the word "politics." This is what the semanticists, who with good reason attack language as the one bulwark behind which the past hides—its confusion, as they say—fail to understand. They are absolutely right: in the final analysis all problems are linguistic problems; they simply do not know the implications of what they are saying.

But Benjamin, who could not yet have read Wittgenstein, let alone his successors, knew a great deal about these very things, because from the beginning the problem of truth had presented itself to him as a "revelation . . . which must be heard, that is, which lies in the metaphysically acoustical sphere." To him, therefore, language was by no means primarily the gift of speech which distinguishes man from other living beings, but, on the contrary, "the world essence . . . from which speech arises"

(*Briefe* I, 197), which incidentally comes quite close to Heidegger's position that "man can speak only insofar as he is the sayer." Thus there is "a language of truth, the tensionless and even silent depository of the ultimate secrets which all thought is concerned with" ("The Task of the Translator"), and this is "the true language" whose existence we assume unthinkingly as soon as we translate from one language into another. That is why Benjamin places at the center of his essay "The Task of the Translator" the astonishing quotation from Mallarmé in which the spoken languages in their multiplicity and diversity suffocate, as it were, by virtue of their Babel-like tumult, the "*immortelle parole*," which cannot even be thought, since "thinking is writing without implement or whispers, silently," and thus prevent the voice of truth from being heard on earth with the force of material, tangible evidence. Whatever theoretical revisions Benjamin may subsequently have made in these theological-metaphysical convictions, his basic approach, decisive for all his literary studies, remained unchanged: not to investigate the utilitarian or communicative functions of linguistic creations, but to understand them in their crystallized and thus ultimately fragmentary form as intentionless and noncommunicative utterances of a "world essence." What else does this mean than that he understood language as an essentially poetic phenomenon? And this is precisely what the last sentence of the Mallarmé aphorism, which he does not quote, says in unequivocal clarity: "*Seulement, sachons n'existerait pas le vers: lui, philosophiquement remunère le défaut des langues, complément supérieur*"—all this were true if poetry did not exist, the poem that philosophically makes good the defect of languages, is their superior complement.[30] All of which says no more, though in a slightly more complex way, than what I mentioned before—namely, that we are dealing here with something which may not be unique but is certainly extremely rare: the gift of *thinking poetically*.

And this thinking, fed by the present, works with the "thought fragments" it can wrest from the past and gather about itself. Like a pearl diver who descends to the bottom of the sea, not to excavate the bottom and bring it to light but to pry loose the rich and the strange, the pearls and the coral in the depths, and to carry them to the surface, this thinking delves into the depths of the past—but not in order to resuscitate it the way it was and to contribute to the renewal of extinct ages. What guides this thinking is the conviction that although the living is subject to the ruin of the time, the process of decay is at the same time a process of crystallization, that in the depth of the sea, into which sinks and is dissolved what once was alive, some things "suffer a sea-change" and survive in new crystallized forms and shapes that remain immune to the elements, as though they waited only for the pearl diver who one day will come down to them and bring them up into the world of the living— as "thought fragments," as something "rich and strange," and perhaps even as everlasting *Urphänomene*.

HANNAH ARENDT

Notes

1. Walter Benjamin, *Schriften*, Frankfurt a.M., Suhrkamp Verlag, 1955, 2 vols., and *Briefe*, Frankfurt a.M., 1966, 2 vols. The following references are to these editions.

2. Yearbook of the Leo Baeck Institute, 1965, p. 117.

3. *Op. cit.*

4. The classical description of the *flâneur* occurs in Baudelaire's famous essay on Constantin Guys "Le Peintre de la vie moderne"—see Pléiade edition, pp. 877-83. Benjamin frequently refers to it indirectly and quotes from it in the Baudelaire essay.

5. Both have recently reiterated this—Scholem in his Leo Baeck Memorial Lecture of 1965, in which he said, "I am inclined to consider Brecht's influence on Benjamin's output in the thirties baleful, and in some respects disastrous," and Adorno in a statement to his disciple Rolf Tiedemann according to which Benjamin admitted to Adorno that he had written "his essay on the Work of Art in order to outdo Brecht, whom he was afraid of, in radicalism" (quoted in Rolf Tiedemann, *Studien zur Philosophie Walter Benjamins*, Frankfurt, 1965, p. 89). It is improbable that Benjamin should have expressed fear of Brecht, and Adorno seems not to claim that he did. As for the rest of the statement, it is, unfortunately, all too likely that Benjamin made it because he was afraid of Adorno. It is true that Benjamin was very shy in his dealings with people he had not known since his youth, but he was afraid only of people he was dependent upon. Such a dependence on Brecht would have come about only if he had followed Brecht's suggestion that he move from Paris to Brecht's vicinity in considerably less expensive Denmark. As it turned out, Benjamin had serious doubts about such an exclusive "dependence on one person" in a strange country with a "quite unfamiliar language" (*Briefe* II, 596, 599).

6. In the review of the *Dreigroschenroman*. Cf. *Versuche über Brecht*, Frankfurt, 1966, p. 90.

7. It now seems that nearly everything has been saved. The manuscripts hidden in Paris were, in accordance with Benjamin's instructions, sent to Theodor W. Adorno; according to Tiedemann (*op. cit.*, p. 212), they are now in Adorno's "private collection" in Frank-

furt. Reprints and copies of most texts are also in Gershom Scholem's personal collection in Jerusalem. The material confiscated by the Gestapo has turned up in the German Democratic Republic. See "Der Benjamin-Nachlass in Potsdam" by Rosemarie Heise in *alternative*, October-December, 1967.

8. Cf. "Walter Benjamin hinter seinen Briefen," *Merkur*, March 1967.

9. Cf. Pierre Missac, "L'Eclat et le secret: Walter Benjamin," *Critique*, Nos. 231-32, 1966.

10. Max Rychner, the recently deceased editor of the *Neue Schweizer Rundschau*, was one of the most cultivated and most refined figures in the intellectual life of the time. Like Adorno, Ernst Bloch, and Scholem, he published his "Erinnerungen an Walter Benjamin" in *Der Monat*, September, 1960.

11. *Ibid.*

12. Kafka, whose outlook on these matters was more realistic than that of any of his contemporaries, said that "the father complex which is the intellectual nourishment of many . . . concerns the Judaism of the fathers . . . the vague consent of the fathers (this vagueness was the outrage)" to their sons' leaving of the Jewish fold: "with their hind legs they were still stuck to the Judaism of their fathers, and with the forelegs they found no new ground" (Franz Kafka, *Briefe*, p. 337).

13. *Ibid.*, p. 55.

14. *Ibid.*, p. 339.

15. *Ibid.*, p. 337.

16. *Ibid.*, pp. 336-38.

17. Franz Kafka, *Tagebücher*, p. 42.

18. Franz Kafka, *Briefe*, p. 347.

19. *Ibid.*, p. 378.

20. In "Der Autor als Produzent," a lecture given in Paris in 1934, in which Benjamin quotes an earlier essay on the intellectual Left. See *Versuche über Brecht*, p. 109.

21. Quoted in Max Brod, *Franz Kafkas Glauben und Lehre*, Winterthur, 1948.

22. Brecht, for instance, told Benjamin that his essay on Kafka gave aid and comfort to Jewish Fascism. See *Versuche*, p. 123.

23. Franz Kafka, *Briefe*, p. 183.

24. In the above-mentioned article Pierre Missac deals with the same passage and writes: "*Sans sous-estimer la valeur d'une telle réussite [d'être le successeur de Hamann et de Humboldt], on peut penser que Benjamin recherchait aussi dans le Marxisme un moyen d'y échapper.*" (Without underestimating the value of such a success [being the successor of Hamann and Humboldt], it is possible to think that Benjamin also sought in Marxism a means of escaping it.)

25. One is immediately reminded of Brecht's poem "On the Poor B.B."—

Fröhlich machet das Haus den Esser: er leert es.
Von diesen Städten wird bleiben: der durch sie hindurchging,
    der Wind!
Fröhlich machet das Haus den Esser: er leert es.
Wir wissen, dass wir Vorläufige sind
Und nach uns wird kommen: nichts Nennenswertes.

("Of these cities will remain that which blew through them, the wind./The house makes the feaster merry. He cleans it out./We know we're only temporary and after us will follow/Nothing worth talking about." *The Manual of Piety*, New York, 1966.)

Worth noting, too, is a remarkable aphorism of Kafka in the "Notes from the Year 1920" under the title "He": "Everything he does appears to him extraordinarily new but also, because of the impossible abundance of the new, extraordinarily amateurish, indeed hardly tolerable, incapable of becoming historical, tearing asunder the chain of generations, breaking off for the first time the music of the world which until now could at least be divined in all its depth. Sometimes in his conceit he is more worried about the world than about himself."

The predecessor of this mood is, again, Baudelaire. "*Le monde va finir. La seule raison pour laquelle il pouvait durer, c'est qu'elle existe. Que cette raison est faible, comparée à toutes celles qui annoncent le contraire, particulièrement à celle-ci: qu'est-ce que le monde a désormais à faire sous le ciel? ... Quant à moi qui sens quelquefois en moi le ridicule d'un prophète, je sais que je n'y trouverai jamais la charité d'un médecin. Perdu dans ce vilain monde, coudoyé par les foules, je suis comme un homme lassé dont l'oeil ne voit en arrière, dans les années profondes, que désabusement et amertume, et devant lui qu'un orage où rien de neuf n'est contenu, ni enseignement ni douleur.*" From *Journaux intimes*, Pléiade edition, pp. 1195-97.

26. Cf. Kafka, *Briefe*, p. 173.

27. A selection appeared under the title *Parables and Paradoxes* in a bilingual edition (Schocken Books, New York, 1961).

28. Benjamin, "Lob der Puppe," *Literarische Welt*, January 10, 1930.

29. See Martin Heidegger, *Kants These über das Sein*, Frankfurt, 1962, p. 8.

30. For the aphorism by Mallarmé, see "Variations sur un sujet" under the subtitle "Crise des vers," Pléiade edition, pp. 363-64.

Illuminations

Unpacking My Library

A Talk about Book Collecting

I am unpacking my library. Yes, I am. The books are not yet on the shelves, not yet touched by the mild boredom of order. I cannot march up and down their ranks to pass them in review before a friendly audience. You need not fear any of that. Instead, I must ask you to join me in the disorder of crates that have been wrenched open, the air saturated with the dust of wood, the floor covered with torn paper, to join me among piles of volumes that are seeing daylight again after two years of darkness, so that you may be ready to share with me a bit of the mood—it is certainly not an elegiac mood but, rather, one of anticipation—which these books arouse in a genuine collector. For such a man is speaking to you, and on closer scrutiny he proves to be speaking only about himself. Would it not be presumptuous of me if, in order to appear convincingly objective and down-to-earth, I enumerated for you the main sections or prize pieces of a library, if I presented you with their history or even their usefulness to a writer? I, for one, have in mind something less obscure, something more palpable than that; what I am really concerned with is giving you some insight into the relationship of a book collector to his possessions, into collecting rather than a collection. If I do this by elaborating on the various ways of acquiring books, this is something entirely arbitrary. This or any other procedure is merely a dam against the spring tide of memories which surges toward any collector as he contemplates his possessions. Every passion borders on the chaotic, but the collector's passion borders on the chaos of memories. More than that: the chance, the fate, that suffuse the past before my eyes are conspicuously present in the accustomed confusion of these books. For what else is this collection but a disorder to which habit has accommodated itself to such an extent that it can appear as order? You have all heard of people whom the loss of their books has turned into invalids, or of those who in order to acquire them became criminals. These are the very areas in which any order is a balancing act of extreme precariousness. "The only exact knowledge there is," said Anatole France, "is the knowledge of the date of publication and the format of books." And indeed, if there is a counterpart to the confusion of a library, it is the order of its catalogue.

Thus there is in the life of a collector a dialectical tension between the poles of disorder and order. Naturally, his existence is tied to many other things as well: to a very mysterious relationship to ownership, something about which we shall have more to say later; also, to a relationship to objects which does not emphasize their functional, utilitarian value—that is, their usefulness—but studies and loves them as the scene, the stage, of their fate. The most profound enchantment for the collector is the locking of individual items within a magic circle in which they are fixed as the final thrill, the thrill of acquisition, passes over them. Everything remembered and thought, everything conscious, becomes the pedestal, the frame, the base, the lock of his property. The period, the region, the craftsmanship, the former ownership—for a true collector the whole background of an item adds up to a magic encyclopedia whose quintessence is the fate of his object. In this circumscribed area, then, it may be surmised how the great physiognomists—and collectors are the physiognomists of the world of objects—turn into interpreters of fate. One has only to watch a collector handle the objects in his glass case. As he holds them in his hands, he seems to be seeing through them into their distant past as though inspired. So much for the magical side of the collector—his old-age image, I might call it.

Habent sua fata libelli: these words may have been intended as a general statement about books. So books like *The Divine Comedy*, Spinoza's *Ethics*, and *The Origin of Species* have their fates. A collector, however, interprets this Latin saying differently. For him, not only books but also copies of books have their fates. And in this sense, the most important fate of a copy is its encounter with him, with his own collection. I am not exaggerating when I say that to a true collector the acquisition of an old book is its rebirth. This is the childlike element which in a collector mingles with the element of old age. For children can accomplish the renewal of existence in a hundred unfailing ways. Among children, collecting is only one process of renewal; other processes are the painting of objects, the cutting out of figures, the application of decals—the whole range of childlike modes of acquisition, from touching things to giving them names. To renew the old world—that is the collector's deepest desire when he is driven to acquire new things, and that is why a collector of older books is closer to the wellsprings of collecting than the acquirer of luxury editions. How do books cross the threshold of a collection and become the property of a collector? The history of their acquisition is the subject of the following remarks.

Of all the ways of acquiring books, writing them oneself is regarded as the most praiseworthy method. At this point many of you will remember with pleasure the large library which Jean Paul's poor little schoolmaster Wutz gradually acquired by writing, himself, all the works whose titles interested him in book-fair catalogues; after all, he could not afford to buy them. Writers are really people who write books not because they are poor, but because they are dissatisfied with the books which they could buy but do not like. You, ladies and gentlemen, may regard this as a whimsical definition of a writer. But everything said from the angle of a real collector is whimsical. Of the customary modes of acquisition, the one most appropriate to a collector would be the borrowing of a book with its attendant non-returning. The book borrower of real stature whom we envisage here proves himself to be an inveterate collector of books not so much by the fervor with which he guards his borrowed treasures and by the deaf ear which he turns to all reminders from the everyday world of legality as by his failure to read these books. If my experience may serve as evidence, a man is more likely to return a borrowed book upon occasion than to read it. And the non-reading of books, you will object, should be characteristic of collectors? This is news to me, you may say. It is not news at all. Experts will bear me out when I say that it is the oldest thing in the world. Suffice it to quote the answer which Anatole France gave to a philistine who admired his library and then finished with the standard question, "And you have read all these books, Monsieur France?" "Not one-tenth of them. I don't suppose you use your Sèvres china every day?"

Incidentally, I have put the right to such an attitude to the test. For years, for at least the first third of its existence, my library consisted of no more than two or three shelves which increased only by inches each year. This was its militant age, when no book was allowed to enter it without the certification that I had not read it. Thus I might never have acquired a library extensive enough to be worthy of the name if there had not been an inflation. Suddenly the emphasis shifted; books acquired real value, or, at any rate, were difficult to obtain. At least this is how it seemed in Switzerland. At the eleventh hour I sent my first major book orders from there and in this way was able to secure such irreplaceable items as *Der blaue Reiter* and Bachofen's *Sage von Tanaquil*, which could still be obtained from the publishers at that time.

Well—so you may say—after exploring all these byways we should finally reach the wide highway of book acquisition, namely, the purchasing of books. This is indeed a wide highway, but not a comfortable one. The purchasing done by a book collector has very little in common with that done in a bookshop by a student getting a textbook, a man of the world buying a present for his lady, or a businessman intending to while away his next train journey. I have made my most memorable purchases on trips, as a transient. Property and possession belong to the tactical sphere. Collectors are people with a tactical instinct; their experience teaches them that when they capture a strange city, the smallest antique shop can be a fortress, the most remote stationery store a key position. How many cities have revealed themselves to me in the marches I undertook in the pursuit of books!

By no means all of the most important purchases are made on the premises of a dealer. Catalogues play a far greater part. And even though the purchaser may be thoroughly acquainted with the book ordered from a catalogue, the individual copy always remains a surprise and the order always a bit of a gamble. There are grievous disappointments, but also happy finds. I remember, for instance, that I once ordered a book with colored illustrations for my old collection of children's books only because it contained fairy tales by Albert Ludwig Grimm and was published at Grimma, Thuringia. Grimma was also the place of publication of a book of fables edited by the same Albert Ludwig Grimm. With its sixteen illustrations my copy of this book of fables was the only extant example of the early work of the great German book illustrator Lyser, who lived in Hamburg around the middle of the last century. Well, my reaction to the consonance of the names had been correct. In this case too I discovered the work of Lyser, namely *Linas Märchenbuch*, a work which has remained unknown to his bibliographers and which deserves a more detailed reference than this first one I am introducing here.

The acquisition of books is by no means a matter of money or expert knowledge alone. Not even both factors together suffice for the establishment of a real library, which is always somewhat impenetrable and at the same time uniquely itself. Anyone who buys from catalogues must have flair in addition to the qualities I have mentioned. Dates, place names, formats, previous owners, bindings, and the like: all these details must tell him something—not as dry, isolated facts, but as a harmonious whole; from the quality and intensity of this harmony he must be able to recognize whether a book is for him or not. An auction requires yet another set of qualities in a collector. To the reader of a catalogue the book itself must speak, or possibly its previous ownership if the provenance of the copy has been established. A man who wishes to participate at an auction must pay equal attention to the book and to his competitors, in addition to keeping a cool enough head to avoid being carried away in the competition. It is a frequent occurrence that someone gets stuck with a high purchase price because he kept raising his bid—more to assert himself than to acquire the book. On the other hand, one of the finest memories of a collector is the moment when he rescued a book to which he might never have given a thought, much less a wishful look, because he found it lonely and abandoned on the market place and bought it to give it its freedom—the way the prince bought a beautiful slave girl in *The Arabian Nights*. To a book collector, you see, the true freedom of all books is somewhere on his shelves.

To this day, Balzac's *Peau de chagrin* stands out from long rows of French volumes in my library as a memento of my most exciting experience at an auction. This happened in 1915 at the Rümann auction put up by Emil Hirsch, one of the greatest of book experts and most distinguished of dealers. The edition in question appeared in 1838 in Paris, Place de la Bourse. As I pick up my copy, I see not only its number in the Rümann collection, but even the label of the shop in which the first owner bought the book over ninety years ago for one-eightieth of today's price. "Papeterie I. Flanneau," it says. A fine age in which it was still possible to buy such a de luxe edition at a stationery dealer's! The steel engravings of this book were designed by the foremost French graphic artist and executed by the foremost engravers. But I was going to tell you how I acquired this book. I had gone to Emil Hirsch's for an advance inspection and had handled forty or fifty volumes; that particular volume had inspired in me the ardent desire to hold on to it forever. The day of the auction came. As chance would have it, in the sequence of the auction this copy of *La Peau de chagrin* was preceded by a complete set of its illustrations printed separately on India paper. The bidders sat at a long table; diagonally across from me sat the man who was the focus of all eyes at the first bid, the famous Munich collector Baron von Simolin. He was greatly interested in this set, but he had rival bidders; in short, there was a spirited contest which resulted in the highest bid of the entire auction—far in excess of three thousand marks. No one seemed to have expected such a high figure, and all those present were quite excited. Emil Hirsch remained unconcerned, and whether he wanted to save time or was guided by some other consideration, he proceeded to the next item, with no one really paying attention. He called out the price, and with my heart pounding and with the full realization that I was unable to compete with any of those big collectors I bid a somewhat higher amount. Without arousing the bidders' attention, the auctioneer went through the usual routine—"Do I hear more?" and three bangs of his gavel, with an eternity seeming to separate each from the next—and proceeded to add the auctioneer's charge. For a student like me the sum was still considerable. The following morning at the pawnshop is no longer part of this story, and I prefer to speak about another incident which I should like to call the negative of an auction. It happened last year at a Berlin auction. The collection of books that was offered was a miscellany in quality and subject matter, and only a number of rare works on occultism and natural philosophy were worthy of note. I bid for a number of them, but each time I noticed a gentleman in the front row who seemed only to have waited for my bid to counter with his own, evidently prepared to top any offer. After this had been repeated several times, I gave up all hope of acquiring the book which I was most interested in that day. It was the rare *Fragmente aus dem Nachlass eines jungen Physikers* [Posthumous Fragments of a Young Physicist] which Johann Wilhelm Ritter published in two volumes at Heidelberg in 1810. This work has never been reprinted, but I have always considered its preface, in which the author-editor tells the story of his life in the guise of an obituary for his supposedly deceased unnamed friend—with whom he is really identical—as the most important sample of personal prose of German Romanticism. Just as the item came up I had a brain wave. It was simple enough: since my bid was bound to give the item to the other man, I must not bid at all. I controlled myself and remained silent. What I had hoped for came about: no interest, no bid, and the book was put aside. I deemed it wise to let several days go by, and when I appeared on the premises after a week, I found the book in the secondhand department and benefited by the lack of interest when I acquired it.

Once you have approached the mountains of cases in order to mine the books from them and bring them to the light of day —or, rather, of night—what memories crowd in upon you! Nothing highlights the fascination of unpacking more clearly than the difficulty of stopping this activity. I had started at noon, and it was midnight before I had worked my way to the last cases. Now I put my hands on two volumes bound in faded boards which, strictly speaking, do not belong in a book case at all: two albums with stick-in pictures which my mother pasted in as a child and which I inherited. They are the seeds of a collection of children's books which is growing steadily even today, though no longer in my garden. There is no living library that does not harbor a number of booklike creations from fringe areas. They need not be stick-in albums or family albums, autograph books or portfolios containing pamphlets or religious tracts; some people become attached to leaflets and prospectuses, others to handwriting facsimiles or typewritten copies of unobtainable books; and certainly periodicals can form the prismatic fringes of a library. But to get back to those albums: Actually, inheritance is the soundest way of acquiring a collection. For a collector's attitude toward his possessions stems from an owner's feeling of responsibility toward his property. Thus it is, in the highest sense, the attitude of an heir, and the most distinguished trait of a collection will always be its transmissibility. You should know that in saying this I fully realize that my discussion of the mental climate of collecting will confirm many of you in your conviction that this passion is behind the times, in your distrust of the collector type. Nothing is further from my mind than to shake either your conviction or your distrust. But one thing should be noted: the phenomenon of collecting loses its meaning as it loses its personal owner. Even though public collections may be less objectionable socially and more useful academically than private collections, the objects get their due only in the latter. I do know that time is running out for the type that I am discussing here and have been representing before you a bit *ex officio*. But, as Hegel put it, only when it is dark does the owl of Minerva begin its flight. Only in extinction is the collector comprehended.

Now I am on the last half-emptied case and it is way past midnight. Other thoughts fill me than the ones I am talking about —not thoughts but images, memories. Memories of the cities in which I found so many things: Riga, Naples, Munich, Danzig, Moscow, Florence, Basel, Paris; memories of Rosenthal's sumptuous rooms in Munich, of the Danzig Stockturm where the late Hans Rhaue was domiciled, of Süssengut's musty book cellar in North Berlin; memories of the rooms where these books had been housed, of my student's den in Munich, of my room in Bern, of the solitude of Iseltwald on the Lake of Brienz, and finally of my boyhood room, the former location of only four or five of the several thousand volumes that are piled up around me. O bliss of the collector, bliss of the man of leisure! Of no one has less been expected, and no one has had a greater sense of well-being than the man who has been able to carry on his disreputable existence in the mask of Spitzweg's "Bookworm." For inside him there are spirits, or at least little genii, which have seen to it that for a collector—and I mean a real collector, a collector as he ought to be—ownership is the most intimate relationship that one can have to objects. Not that they come alive in him; it is he who lives in them. So I have erected one of his dwellings, with books as the building stones, before you, and now he is going to disappear inside, as is only fitting.

The Task of the Translator

An Introduction to the Translation
of Baudelaire's TABLEAUX PARISIENS

In the appreciation of a work of art or an art form, consideration of the receiver never proves fruitful. Not only is any reference to a certain public or its representatives misleading, but even the concept of an "ideal" receiver is detrimental in the theoretical consideration of art, since all it posits is the existence and nature of man as such. Art, in the same way, posits man's physical and spiritual existence, but in none of its works is it concerned with his response. No poem is intended for the reader, no picture for the beholder, no symphony for the listener.

Is a translation meant for readers who do not understand the original? This would seem to explain adequately the divergence of their standing in the realm of art. Moreover, it seems to be the only conceivable reason for saying "the same thing" repeatedly. For what does a literary work "say"? What does it communicate? It "tells" very little to those who understand it. Its essential quality is not statement or the imparting of information. Yet any translation which intends to perform a transmitting function cannot transmit anything but information—hence, something inessential. This is the hallmark of bad translations. But do we not generally regard as the essential substance of a literary work what it contains in addition to information—as even a poor translator will admit—the unfathomable, the mysterious, the "poetic," something that a translator can reproduce only if he is also a poet? This, actually, is the cause of another characteristic of inferior translation, which consequently we may define as the inaccurate transmission of an inessential content. This will be true whenever a translation undertakes to serve the reader. However, if it were intended for the reader, the same would have to apply to the original. If the original does not exist for the reader's sake, how could the translation be understood on the basis of this premise?

Translation is a mode. To comprehend it as mode one must go back to the original, for that contains the law governing the translation: its translatability. The question of whether a work is translatable has a dual meaning. Either: Will an adequate translator ever be found among the totality of its readers? Or, more pertinently: Does its nature lend itself to translation and, therefore, in view of the significance of the mode, call for it? In principle, the first question can be decided only contingently; the second, however, apodictically. Only superficial thinking will deny the independent meaning of the latter and declare both questions to be of equal significance. . . . It should be pointed out that certain correlative concepts retain their meaning, and possibly their foremost significance, if they are referred exclusively to man. One might, for example, speak of an unforgettable life or moment even if all men had forgotten it. If the nature of such a life or moment required that it be unforgotten, that predicate would not imply a falsehood but merely a claim not fulfilled by men, and probably also a reference to a realm in which it *is* fulfilled: God's remembrance. Analogously, the translatability of linguistic creations ought to be considered even if men should prove unable to translate them. Given a strict concept of translation, would they not really be translatable to some degree? The question as to whether the translation of certain linguistic creations is called for ought to be posed in this sense. For this thought is valid here: If translation is a mode, translatability must be an essential feature of certain works.

Translatability is an essential quality of certain works, which is not to say that it is essential that they be translated; it means rather that a specific significance inherent in the original manifests itself in its translatability. It is plausible that no translation, however good it may be, can have any significance as regards the original. Yet, by virtue of its translatability the original is closely connected with the translation; in fact, this connection is all the closer since it is no longer of importance to the original. We may call this connection a natural one, or, more specifically, a vital connection. Just as the manifestations of life are intimately connected with the phenomenon of life without being of importance to it, a translation issues from the original—not so much from its life as from its afterlife. For a translation comes later than the original, and since the important works of world literature never find their chosen translators at the time of their origin, their translation marks their stage of continued life. The idea of life and afterlife in works of art should be regarded with an entirely unmetaphorical objectivity. Even in times of narrowly prejudiced thought there was an inkling that life was not limited to organic corporeality. But it cannot be a matter of extending its dominion under the feeble scepter of the soul, as Fechner tried to do, or, conversely, of basing its definition on the even less conclusive factors of animality, such as sensation, which characterize life only occasionally. The concept of life is given its due only if everything that has a history of its own, and is not merely the setting for history, is credited with life. In the final analysis, the range of life must be determined by history rather than by nature, least of all by such tenuous factors as sensation and soul. The philosopher's task consists in comprehending all of natural life through the more encompassing life of history. And indeed, is not the continued life of works of art far easier to recognize than the continual life of animal species? The history of the great works of art tells us about their antecedents, their realization in the age of the artist, their potentially eternal afterlife in succeeding generations. Where this last manifests itself, it is called fame.

Translations that are more than transmissions of subject matter come into being when in the course of its survival a work has reached the age of its fame. Contrary, therefore, to the claims of bad translators, such translations do not so much serve the work as owe their existence to it. The life of the originals attains in them to its ever-renewed latest and most abundant flowering.

Being a special and high form of life, this flowering is governed by a special, high purposiveness. The relationship between life and purposefulness, seemingly obvious yet almost beyond the grasp of the intellect, reveals itself only if the ultimate purpose toward which all single functions tend is sought not in its own sphere but in a higher one. All purposeful manifestations of life, including their very purposiveness, in the final analysis have their end not in life, but in the expression of its nature, in the representation of its significance. Translation thus ultimately serves the purpose of expressing the central reciprocal relationship between languages. It cannot possibly reveal or establish this hidden relationship itself; but it can represent it by realizing it in embryonic or intensive form. This representation of hidden significance through an embryonic attempt at making it visible is of so singular a nature that it is rarely met with in the sphere of nonlinguistic life. This, in its analogies and symbols, can draw on other ways of suggesting meaning than intensive—that is, anticipative, intimating—realization. As for the posited central kinship of languages, it is marked by a distinctive convergence. Languages are not strangers to one another, but are, a priori and apart from all historical relationships, interrelated in what they want to express.

With this attempt at an explication our study appears to rejoin, after futile detours, the traditional theory of translation. If the kinship of languages is to be demonstrated by translations, how else can this be done but by conveying the form and meaning of the original as accurately as possible? To be sure, that theory would be hard put to define the nature of this accuracy and therefore could shed no light on what is important in a translation. Actually, however, the kinship of languages is brought out by a translation far more profoundly and clearly than in the superficial and indefinable similarity of two works of literature. To grasp the genuine relationship between an original and a translation requires an investigation analogous to the argumentation by which a critique of cognition would have to prove the impossibility of an image theory. There it is a matter of showing that in cognition there could be no objectivity, not even a claim to it, if it dealt with images of reality; here it can be demonstrated that no translation would be possible if in its ultimate essence it strove for likeness to the original. For in its afterlife—which could not be called that if it were not a transformation and a renewal of something living—the original undergoes a change. Even words with fixed meaning can undergo a maturing process. The obvious tendency of a writer's literary style may in time wither away, only to give rise to immanent tendencies in the literary creation. What sounded fresh once may sound hackneyed later; what was once current may someday sound quaint. To seek the essence of such changes, as well as the equally constant changes in meaning, in the subjectivity of posterity rather than in the very life of language and its works, would mean—even allowing for the crudest psychologism—to confuse the root cause of a thing with its essence. More pertinently, it would mean denying, by an impotence of thought, one of the most powerful and fruitful historical processes. And even if one tried to turn an author's last stroke of the pen into the *coup de grâce* of his work, this still would not save that dead theory of translation. For just as the tenor and the significance of the great works of literature undergo a complete transformation over the centuries, the mother tongue of the translator is transformed as well. While a poet's words endure in his own language, even the greatest translation is destined to become part of the growth of its own language and eventually to be absorbed by its renewal. Translation is so far removed from being the sterile equation of two dead languages that of all literary forms it is the one charged with the special mission of watching over the maturing process of the original language and the birth pangs of its own.

If the kinship of languages manifests itself in translations, this is not accomplished through a vague alikeness between adaptation and original. It stands to reason that kinship does not necessarily involve likeness. The concept of kinship as used here is in accord with its more restricted common usage: in both cases, it cannot be defined adequately by identity of origin, although in defining the more restricted usage the concept of origin remains indispensable. Wherein resides the relatedness of two languages, apart from historical considerations? Certainly not in the similarity between works of literature or words. Rather, all suprahistorical kinship of languages rests in the intention underlying each language as a whole—an intention, however, which no single language can attain by itself but which is realized only by the totality of their intentions supplementing each other: pure language. While all individual elements of foreign languages—words, sentences, structure—are mutually exclusive, these languages supplement one another in their intentions. Without distinguishing the intended object from the mode of intention, no firm grasp of this basic law of a philosophy of language can be achieved. The words *Brot* and *pain* "intend" the same object, but the modes of this intention are not the same. It is owing to these modes that the word *Brot* means something different to a German than the word *pain* to a Frenchman, that these words are not interchangeable for them, that, in fact, they strive to exclude each other. As to the intended object, however, the two words mean the very same thing. While the modes of intention in these two words are in conflict, intention and object of intention complement each of the two languages from which they are derived; there the object is complementary to the intention. In the individual, unsupplemented languages, meaning is never found in relative independence, as in individual words or sentences; rather, it is in a constant state of flux—until it is able to emerge as pure language from the harmony of all the various modes of intention. Until then, it remains hidden in the languages. If, however, these languages continue to grow in this manner until the end of their time, it is translation which catches fire on the eternal life of the works and the perpetual renewal of language. Translation keeps putting the hallowed growth of languages to the test: How far removed is their hidden meaning from revelation, how close can it be brought by the knowledge of this remoteness?

This, to be sure, is to admit that all translation is only a somewhat provisional way of coming to terms with the foreignness of languages. An instant and final rather than a temporary and provisional solution of this foreignness remains out of the reach of mankind; at any rate, it eludes any direct attempt. Indirectly, however, the growth of religions ripens the hidden seed into a higher development of language. Although translation, unlike art, cannot claim permanence for its products, its goal is undeniably a final, conclusive, decisive stage of all linguistic creation. In translation the original rises into a higher and purer linguistic air, as it were. It cannot live there permanently, to be sure, and it certainly does not reach it in its entirety. Yet, in a singularly impressive manner, at least it points the way to this region: the predestined, hitherto inaccessible realm of reconciliation and fulfillment of languages. The transfer can never be total, but what reaches this region is that element in a translation which goes beyond transmittal of subject matter. This nucleus is best defined as the element that does not lend itself to translation. Even when all the surface content has been extracted and transmitted, the primary concern of the genuine translator remains elusive. Unlike the words of the original, it is not translatable, because the relationship between content and language is quite different in the original and the translation. While content and language form a certain unity in the original, like a fruit and its skin, the language of the translation envelops its content like a royal robe with ample folds. For it signifies a more exalted language than its own and thus remains unsuited to its content, overpowering and alien. This disjunction prevents translation and at the same time makes it superfluous. For any translation of a work originating in a specific stage of linguistic history represents, in regard to a specific aspect of its content, translation into all other languages. Thus translation, ironically, transplants the original into a more definitive linguistic realm since it can no longer be displaced by a secondary rendering. The original can only be raised there anew and at other points of time. It is no mere coincidence that the word "ironic" here brings the Romanticists to mind. They, more than any others, were gifted with an insight into the life of literary works which has its highest testimony in translation. To be sure, they hardly recognized translation in this sense, but devoted their entire attention to criticism, another, if a lesser, factor in the continued life of literary works. But even though the Romanticists virtually ignored translation in their theoretical writings, their own great translations testify to their sense of the essential nature and the dignity of this literary mode. There is abundant evidence that this sense is not necessarily most pronounced in a poet; in fact, he may be least open to it. Not even literary history suggests the traditional notion that great poets have been eminent translators and lesser poets have been indifferent translators. A number of the most eminent ones, such as Luther, Voss, and Schlegel, are incomparably more important as translators than as creative writers; some of the great among them, such as Hölderlin and Stefan George, cannot be simply subsumed as poets, and quite particularly not if we consider them as translators. As translation is a mode of its own, the task of the translator, too, may be regarded as distinct and clearly differentiated from the task of the poet.

The task of the translator consists in finding that intended effect [*Intention*] upon the language into which he is translating which produces in it the echo of the original. This is a feature of translation which basically differentiates it from the poet's work, because the effort of the latter is never directed at the language as such, at its totality, but solely and immediately at specific linguistic contextual aspects. Unlike a work of literature, translation does not find itself in the center of the language forest but on the outside facing the wooded ridge; it calls into it without entering, aiming at that single spot where the echo is able to give, in its own language, the reverberation of the work in the alien one. Not only does the aim of translation differ from that of a literary work—it intends language as a whole, taking an individual work in an alien language as a point of departure—but it is a different effort altogether. The intention of the poet is spontaneous, primary, graphic; that of the translator is derivative, ultimate, ideational. For the great motif of integrating many tongues into one true language is at work. This language is one in which the independent sentences, works of literature, critical judgments, will never communicate—for they remain dependent on translation; but in it the languages themselves, supplemented and reconciled in their mode of signification, harmonize. If there is such a thing as a language of truth, the tensionless and even silent depository of the ultimate truth which all thought strives for, then this language of truth is—the true language. And this very language, whose divination and description is the only perfection a philosopher can hope for, is concealed in concentrated fashion in translations. There is no muse of philosophy, nor is there one of translation. But despite the claims of sentimental artists, these two are not banausic. For there is a philosophical genius that is characterized by a yearning for that language which manifests itself in translations. *"Les langues imparfaites en cela que plusieurs, manque la suprême: penser étant écrire sans accessoires, ni chuchotement mais tacite encore l'immortelle parole, la diversité, sur terre, des idiomes empêche personne de proférer les mots qui, sinon se trouveraient, par une frappe unique, elle-même matériellement la vérité."* * If what Mallarmé evokes here is fully fathomable to a philosopher, translation, with its rudiments of such a language, is midway between poetry and doctrine. Its products are less sharply defined, but it leaves no less of a mark on history.

If the task of the translator is viewed in this light, the roads toward a solution seem to be all the more obscure and impenetrable. Indeed, the problem of ripening the seed of pure language in a translation seems to be insoluble, determinable in no solution. For is not the ground cut from under such a solution if the reproduction of the sense ceases to be decisive? Viewed negatively, this is actually the meaning of all the foregoing. The traditional

* "The imperfection of languages consists in their plurality, the supreme one is lacking: thinking is writing without accessories or even whispering, the immortal word still remains silent; the diversity of idioms on earth prevents everybody from uttering the words which otherwise, at one single stroke, would materialize as truth."

concepts in any discussion of translations are fidelity and license—
the freedom of faithful reproduction and, in its service, fidelity
to the word. These ideas seem to be no longer serviceable to a
theory that looks for other things in a translation than reproduction of meaning. To be sure, traditional usage makes these
terms appear as if in constant conflict with each other. What can
fidelity really do for the rendering of meaning? Fidelity in the
translation of individual words can almost never fully reproduce
the meaning they have in the original. For sense in its poetic significance is not limited to meaning, but derives from the connotations conveyed by the word chosen to express it. We say of
words that they have emotional connotations. A literal rendering
of the syntax completely demolishes the theory of reproduction
of meaning and is a direct threat to comprehensibility. The nineteenth century considered Hölderlin's translations of Sophocles
as monstrous examples of such literalness. Finally, it is self-evident
how greatly fidelity in reproducing the form impedes the rendering of the sense. Thus no case for literalness can be based on
a desire to retain the meaning. Meaning is served far better—and
literature and language far worse—by the unrestrained license of
bad translators. Of necessity, therefore, the demand for literalness, whose justification is obvious, whose legitimate ground is
quite obscure, must be understood in a more meaningful context.
Fragments of a vessel which are to be glued together must match
one another in the smallest details, although they need not be
like one another. In the same way a translation, instead of re-
sembling the meaning of the original, must lovingly and in detail
incorporate the original's mode of signification, thus making both
the original and the translation recognizable as fragments of a
greater language, just as fragments are part of a vessel. For this
very reason translation must in large measure refrain from wanting to communicate something, from rendering the sense, and in
this the original is important to it only insofar as it has already
relieved the translator and his translation of the effort of assem-
bling and expressing what is to be conveyed. In the realm of
translation, too, the words ἐν ἀρχῇ ἦν ὁ λόγος [in the beginning
was the word] apply. On the other hand, as regards the mean-

ing, the language of a translation can—in fact, must—let itself go, so that it gives voice to the *intentio* of the original not as reproduction but as harmony, as a supplement to the language in which it expresses itself, as its own kind of *intentio*. Therefore it is not the highest praise of a translation, particularly in the age of its origin, to say that it reads as if it had originally been written in that language. Rather, the significance of fidelity as ensured by literalness is that the work reflects the great longing for linguistic complementation. A real translation is transparent; it does not cover the original, does not block its light, but allows the pure language, as though reinforced by its own medium, to shine upon the original all the more fully. This may be achieved, above all, by a literal rendering of the syntax which proves words rather than sentences to be the primary element of the translator. For if the sentence is the wall before the language of the original, literalness is the arcade.

Fidelity and freedom in translation have traditionally been regarded as conflicting tendencies. This deeper interpretation of the one apparently does not serve to reconcile the two; in fact, it seems to deny the other all justification. For what is meant by freedom but that the rendering of the sense is no longer to be regarded as all-important? Only if the sense of a linguistic creation may be equated with the information it conveys does some ultimate, decisive element remain beyond all communication—quite close and yet infinitely remote, concealed or distinguishable, fragmented or powerful. In all language and linguistic creations there remains in addition to what can be conveyed something that cannot be communicated; depending on the context in which it appears, it is something that symbolizes or something symbolized. It is the former only in the finite products of language, the latter in the evolving of the languages themselves. And that which seeks to represent, to produce itself in the evolving of languages, is that very nucleus of pure language. Though concealed and fragmentary, it is an active force in life as the symbolized thing itself, whereas it inhabits linguistic creations only in symbolized form. While that ultimate essence, pure language, in the various tongues is tied only to linguistic elements and their changes, in linguistic creations it is weighted with a heavy, alien meaning. To relieve it of this, to turn the symbolizing into the symbolized, to regain pure language fully formed in the linguistic flux, is the tremendous and only capacity of translation. In this pure language—which no longer means or expresses anything but is, as expressionless and creative Word, that which is meant in all languages—all information, all sense, and all intention finally encounter a stratum in which they are destined to be extinguished. This very stratum furnishes a new and higher justification for free translation; this justification does not derive from the sense of what is to be conveyed, for the emancipation from this sense is the task of fidelity. Rather, for the sake of pure language, a free translation bases the test on its own language. It is the task of the translator to release in his own language that pure language which is under the spell of another, to liberate the language imprisoned in a work in his re-creation of that work. For the sake of pure language he breaks through decayed barriers of his own language. Luther, Voss, Hölderlin, and George have extended the boundaries of the German language.— And what of the sense in its importance for the relationship between translation and original? A simile may help here. Just as a tangent touches a circle lightly and at but one point, with this touch rather than with the point setting the law according to which it is to continue on its straight path to infinity, a translation touches the original lightly and only at the infinitely small point of the sense, thereupon pursuing its own course according to the laws of fidelity in the freedom of linguistic flux. Without explicitly naming or substantiating it, Rudolf Pannwitz has characterized the true significance of this freedom. His observations are contained in *Die Krisis der europäischen Kultur* and rank with Goethe's Notes to the *Westöstlicher Divan* as the best comment on the theory of translation that has been published in Germany. Pannwitz writes: "Our translations, even the best ones, proceed from a wrong premise. They want to turn Hindi, Greek, English into German instead of turning German into Hindi, Greek, English. Our translators have a far greater reverence for the usage of their own language than for the spirit of the foreign works.

... The basic error of the translator is that he preserves the state in which his own language happens to be instead of allowing his language to be powerfully affected by the foreign tongue. Particularly when translating from a language very remote from his own he must go back to the primal elements of language itself and penetrate to the point where work, image, and tone converge. He must expand and deepen his language by means of the foreign language. It is not generally realized to what extent this is possible, to what extent any language can be transformed, how language differs from language almost the way dialect differs from dialect; however, this last is true only if one takes language seriously enough, not if one takes it lightly."

The extent to which a translation manages to be in keeping with the nature of this mode is determined objectively by the translatability of the original. The lower the quality and distinction of its language, the larger the extent to which it is information, the less fertile a field is it for translation, until the utter preponderance of content, far from being the lever for a translation of distinctive mode, renders it impossible. The higher the level of a work, the more does it remain translatable even if its meaning is touched upon only fleetingly. This, of course, applies to originals only. Translations, on the other hand, prove to be untranslatable not because of any inherent difficulty, but because of the looseness with which meaning attaches to them. Confirmation of this as well as of every other important aspect is supplied by Hölderlin's translations, particularly those of the two tragedies by Sophocles. In them the harmony of the languages is so profound that sense is touched by language only the way an aeolian harp is touched by the wind. Hölderlin's translations are prototypes of their kind; they are to even the most perfect renderings of their texts as a prototype is to a model. This can be demonstrated by comparing Hölderlin's and Rudolf Borchardt's translations of Pindar's Third Pythian Ode. For this very reason Hölderlin's translations in particular are subject to the enormous danger inherent in all translations: the gates of a language thus expanded and modified may slam shut and enclose the translator with silence. Hölderlin's translations from Sophocles were his last work; in them meaning plunges from abyss to abyss until it threatens to become lost in the bottomless depths of language. There is, however, a stop. It is vouchsafed to Holy Writ alone, in which meaning has ceased to be the watershed for the flow of language and the flow of revelation. Where a text is identical with truth or dogma, where it is supposed to be "the true language" in all its literalness and without the mediation of meaning, this text is unconditionally translatable. In such case translations are called for only because of the plurality of languages. Just as, in the original, language and revelation are one without any tension, so the translation must be one with the original in the form of the interlinear version, in which literalness and freedom are united. For to some degree all great texts contain their potential translation between the lines; this is true to the highest degree of sacred writings. The interlinear version of the Scriptures is the prototype or ideal of all translation.

The Storyteller

Reflections on the Works of Nikolai Leskov

I

Familiar though his name may be to us, the storyteller in his living immediacy is by no means a present force. He has already become something remote from us and something that is getting even more distant. To present someone like Leskov as a storyteller does not mean bringing him closer to us but, rather, increasing our distance from him. Viewed from a certain distance, the great, simple outlines which define the storyteller stand out in him, or rather, they become visible in him, just as in a rock a human head or an animal's body may appear to an observer at the proper distance and angle of vision. This distance and this angle of vision are prescribed for us by an experience which we may have almost every day. It teaches us that the art of storytelling is coming to an end. Less and less frequently do we encounter people with the ability to tell a tale properly. More and more often there is embarrassment all around when the wish to hear a story is expressed. It is as if something that seemed inalienable to us, the securest among our possessions, were taken from us: the ability to exchange experiences. — social / perform. functions

One reason for this phenomenon is obvious: experience has

fallen in value. And it looks as if it is continuing to fall into bot-tomlessness. Every glance at a newspaper demonstrates that it has reached a new low, that our picture, not only of the external world but of the moral world as well, overnight has undergone changes which were never thought possible. With the [First] World War a process began to become apparent which has not halted since then. Was it not noticeable at the end of the war that men returned from the battlefield grown silent—not richer, but poorer in communicable experience? What ten years later was poured out in the flood of war books was anything but ex-perience that goes from mouth to mouth. And there was nothing remarkable about that. For never has experience been contra-dicted more thoroughly than strategic experience by tactical warfare, economic experience by inflation, bodily experience by mechanical warfare, moral experience by those in power. A gen-eration that had gone to school on a horse-drawn streetcar now stood under the open sky in a countryside in which nothing re-mained unchanged but the clouds, and beneath these clouds, in a field of force of destructive torrents and explosions, was the tiny, fragile human body.

(I I)   MODERN STORY, FORM OVER
                                    CONTENT

Experience which is passed on from mouth to mouth is the source from which all storytellers have drawn. And among those who have written down the tales, it is the great ones whose writ-ten version differs least from the speech of the many nameless storytellers. Incidentally, among the last named there are two groups which, to be sure, overlap in many ways. And the figure of the storyteller gets its full corporeality only for the one who can picture them both. "When someone goes on a trip, he has something to tell about," goes the German saying, and people imagine the storyteller as someone who has come from afar. But they enjoy no less listening to the man who has stayed at home, making an honest living, and who knows the local tales and tra-ditions. If one wants to picture these two groups through their archaic representatives, one is embodied in the resident tiller of the soil, and the other in the trading seaman. Indeed, each sphere of life has, as it were, produced its own tribe of storytellers. Each of these tribes preserves some of its characteristics centuries later. Thus, among nineteenth-century German storytellers, writers like Hebel and Gotthelf stem from the first tribe, writers like Sealsfield and Gerstäcker from the second. With these tribes, however, as stated above, it is only a matter of basic types. The actual extension of the realm of storytelling in its full historical breadth is inconceivable without the most intimate interpenetration of these two archaic types. Such an interpenetration was achieved particularly by the Middle Ages in their trade structure. The resident master craftsman and the traveling journeymen worked together in the same rooms; and every master had been a traveling journeyman before he settled down in his home town or somewhere else. If peasants and seamen were past masters of storytelling, the artisan class was its university. In it was combined the lore of faraway places, such as a much-traveled man brings home, with the lore of the past, as it best reveals itself to natives of a place.

III   ⌐TELLS A STORy⌐

Leskov was at home in distant places as well as distant times. He was a member of the Greek Orthodox Church, a man with genuine religious interests. But he was a no less sincere opponent of ecclesiastic bureaucracy. Since he was not able to get along any better with secular officialdom, the official positions he held were not of long duration. Of all his posts, the one he held for a long time as Russian representative of a big English firm was presumably the most useful one for his writing. For this firm he traveled through Russia, and these trips advanced his worldly wisdom as much as they did his knowledge of conditions in Russia. In this way he had an opportunity of becoming acquainted with the organization of the sects in the country. This left its mark on his works of fiction. In the Russian legends Leskov saw allies in his fight against Orthodox bureaucracy. There are a number of his legendary tales whose focus is a righteous man, seldom an ascetic, usually a simple, active man who becomes a saint apparently in the most natural way in the world. Mystical exaltation is not Leskov's forte. Even though he occasionally liked to indulge in the miraculous, even in piousness he prefers to stick with a sturdy nature. He sees the prototype in the man who finds his way about the world without getting too deeply involved with it.

He displayed a corresponding attitude in worldly matters. It is in keeping with this that be began to write late, at the age of twenty-nine. That was after his commercial travels. His first printed work was entitled "Why Are Books Expensive in Kiev?" A number of other writings about the working class, alcoholism, police doctors, and unemployed salesmen are precursors of his works of fiction.

IV

An orientation toward practical interests is characteristic of many born storytellers. More pronouncedly than in Leskov this trait can be recognized, for example, in Gotthelf, who gave his peasants agricultural advice; it is found in Nodier, who concerned himself with the perils of gas light; and Hebel, who slipped bits of scientific instruction for his readers into his *Schatz-kästlein*, is in this line as well. All this points to the nature of every real story. It contains, openly or covertly, something useful. The usefulness may, in one case, consist in a moral; in another, in some practical advice; in a third, in a proverb or maxim. In every case the storyteller is a man who has counsel for his readers. But if today "having counsel" is beginning to have an old-fashioned ring, this is because the communicability of experience is decreasing. In consequence we have no counsel either for ourselves or for others. After all, counsel is less an answer to a question than a proposal concerning the continuation of a story which is just unfolding. To seek this counsel one would first have to be able to tell the story. (Quite apart from the fact that a man is receptive to counsel only to the extent that he allows his situation to speak.) Counsel woven into the fabric of

real life is wisdom. The art of storytelling is reaching its end because the epic side of truth, wisdom, is dying out. This, however,
is a process that has been going on for a long time. And nothing
would be more fatuous than to want to see in it merely a "symptom of decay," let alone a "modern" symptom. It is, rather, only
a concomitant symptom of the secular productive forces of history, a concomitant that has quite gradually removed narrative
from the realm of living speech and at the same time is making
it possible to see a new beauty in what is vanishing.

v

The earliest symptom of a process whose end is the decline
of storytelling is the rise of the novel at the beginning of modern times. What distinguishes the novel from the story (and
from the epic in the narrower sense) is its essential dependence
on the book. The dissemination of the novel became possible
only with the invention of printing. What can be handed on
orally, the wealth of the epic, is of a different kind from what
constitutes the stock in trade of the novel. What differentiates
the novel from all other forms of prose literature—the fairy tale,
the legend, even the novella—is that it neither comes from oral
tradition nor goes into it. This distinguishes it from storytelling
in particular. The storyteller takes what he tells from experience
—his own or that reported by others. And he in turn makes it
the experience of those who are listening to his tale. The novelist
has isolated himself. The birthplace of the novel is the solitary
individual, who is no longer able to express himself by giving
examples of his most important concerns, is himself uncounseled,
and cannot counsel others. To write a novel means to carry the
incommensurable to extremes in the representation of human
life. In the midst of life's fullness, and through the representation
of this fullness, the novel gives evidence of the profound perplexity of the living. Even the first great book of the genre, *Don
Quixote*, teaches how the spiritual greatness, the boldness, the
helpfulness of one of the noblest of men, Don Quixote, are completely devoid of counsel and do not contain the slightest scin-

tilla of wisdom. If now and then, in the course of the centuries, efforts have been made—most effectively, perhaps, in *Wilhelm Meisters Wanderjahre*—to implant instruction in the novel, these attempts have always amounted to a modification of the novel form. The *Bildungsroman*, on the other hand, does not deviate in any way from the basic structure of the novel. By integrating the social process with the development of a person, it bestows the most frangible justification on the order determining it. The legitimacy it provides stands in direct opposition to reality. Particularly in the *Bildungsroman*, it is this inadequacy that is actualized.

VI

One must imagine the transformation of epic forms occurring in rhythms comparable to those of the change that has come over the earth's surface in the course of thousands of centuries. Hardly any other forms of human communication have taken shape more slowly, been lost more slowly. It took the novel, whose beginnings go back to antiquity, hundreds of years before it encountered in the evolving middle class those elements which were favorable to its flowering. With the appearance of these elements, storytelling began quite slowly to recede into the archaic; in many ways, it is true, it took hold of the new material, but it was not really determined by it. On the other hand, we recognize that with the full control of the middle class, which has the press as one of its most important instruments in fully developed capitalism, there emerges a form of communication which, no matter how far back its origin may lie, never before influenced the epic form in a decisive way. But now it does exert such an influence. And it turns out that it confronts storytelling as no less of a stranger than did the novel, but in a more menacing way, and that it also brings about a crisis in the novel. This new form of communication is information.

Villemessant, the founder of *Le Figaro*, characterized the nature of information in a famous formulation. "To my readers," he used to say, "an attic fire in the Latin Quarter is more important than a revolution in Madrid." This makes strikingly clear that it is no longer intelligence coming from afar, but the information which supplies a handle for what is nearest that gets the readiest hearing. The intelligence that came from afar—whether the spatial kind from foreign countries or the temporal kind of tradition—possessed an authority which gave it validity, even when it was not subject to verification. Information, however, lays claim to prompt verifiability. The prime requirement is that it appear "understandable in itself." Often it is no more exact than the intelligence of earlier centuries was. But while the latter was inclined to borrow from the miraculous, it is indispensable for information to sound plausible. Because of this it proves incompatible with the spirit of storytelling. If the art of storytelling has become rare, the dissemination of information has had a decisive share in this state of affairs.

Every morning brings us the news of the globe, and yet we are poor in noteworthy stories. This is because no event any longer comes to us without already being shot through with explanation. In other words, by now almost nothing that happens benefits storytelling; almost everything benefits information. Actually, it is half the art of storytelling to keep a story free from explanation as one reproduces it. Leskov is a master at this (compare pieces like "The Deception" and "The White Eagle"). The most extraordinary things, marvelous things, are related with the greatest accuracy, but the psychological connection of the events is not forced on the reader. It is left up to him to interpret things the way he understands them, and thus the narrative achieves an amplitude that information lacks.

VII

Leskov was grounded in the classics. The first storyteller of the Greeks was Herodotus. In the fourteenth chapter of the third book of his *Histories* there is a story from which much can be learned. It deals with Psammenitus.

When the Egyptian king Psammenitus had been beaten and captured by the Persian king Cambyses, Cambyses was bent on humbling his prisoner. He gave orders to place Psammenitus on the road along which the Persian triumphal procession was to pass. And he further arranged that the prisoner should see his daughter pass by as a maid going to the well with her pitcher. While all the Egyptians were lamenting and bewailing this spectacle, Psammenitus stood alone, mute and motionless, his eyes fixed on the ground; and when presently he saw his son, who was being taken along in the procession to be executed, he likewise remained unmoved. But when afterwards he recognized one of his servants, an old, impoverished man, in the ranks of the prisoners, he beat his fists against his head and gave all the signs of deepest mourning.

From this story it may be seen what the nature of true storytelling is. The value of information does not survive the moment in which it was new. It lives only at that moment; it has to surrender to it completely and explain itself to it without losing any time. A story is different. It does not expend itself. It preserves and concentrates its strength and is capable of releasing it even after a long time. Thus Montaigne referred to this Egyptian king and asked himself why he mourned only when he caught sight of his servant. Montaigne answers: "Since he was already overfull of grief, it took only the smallest increase for it to burst through its dams." Thus Montaigne. But one could also say: The king is not moved by the fate of those of royal blood, for it is his own fate. Or: We are moved by much on the stage that does not move us in real life; to the king, this servant is only an actor. Or: Great grief is pent up and breaks forth only with relaxation. Seeing this servant was the relaxation. Herodotus offers no explanations. His report is the driest. That is why this story from ancient Egypt is still capable after thousands of years of arousing astonishment and thoughtfulness. It resembles the seeds of grain which have lain for centuries in the chambers of the pyramids shut up air-tight and have retained their germinative power to this day.

as opposed to sentimental promiscuity

VIII

There is nothing that commends a story to memory more effectively than that chaste compactness which precludes psychological analysis. And the more natural the process by which the storyteller forgoes psychological shading, the greater becomes the story's claim to a place in the memory of the listener, the more completely is it integrated into his own experience, the greater will be his inclination to repeat it to someone else someday, sooner or later. This process of assimilation, which takes place in depth, requires a state of relaxation which is becoming rarer and rarer. If sleep is the apogee of physical relaxation, boredom is the apogee of mental relaxation. Boredom is the dream bird that hatches the egg of experience. A rustling in the leaves drives him away. His nesting places—the activities that are intimately associated with boredom—are already extinct in the cities and are declining in the country as well. With this the gift for listening is lost and the community of listeners disappears. For storytelling is always the art of repeating stories, and this art is lost when the stories are no longer retained. It is lost because there is no more weaving and spinning to go on while they are being listened to. The more self-forgetful the listener is, the more deeply is what he listens to impressed upon his memory. When the rhythm of work has seized him, he listens to the tales in such a way that the gift of retelling them comes to him all by itself. This, then, is the nature of the web in which the gift of storytelling is cradled. This is how today it is becoming unraveled at all its ends after being woven thousands of years ago in the ambience of the oldest forms of craftsmanship.

PEN

Conclusion pure transmission by passes ego

IX

The storytelling that thrives for a long time in the milieu of work—the rural, the maritime, and the urban—is itself an artisan form of communication, as it were. It does not aim to convey the pure essence of the thing, like information or a report. It sinks the thing into the life of the storyteller, in order to bring it out

Paradoxical

of him again. Thus traces of the storyteller cling to the story the way the handprints of the potter cling to the clay vessel. Storytellers tend to begin their story with a presentation of the circumstances in which they themselves have learned what is to follow, unless they simply pass it off as their own experience. Leskov begins his "Deception" with the description of a train trip on which he supposedly heard from a fellow passenger the events which he then goes on to relate; or he thinks of Dostoevsky's funeral, where he sets his acquaintance with the heroine of his story "À Propos of the Kreutzer Sonata"; or he evokes a gathering of a reading circle in which we are told the events that he reproduces for us in his "Interesting Men." Thus his tracks are frequently evident in his narratives, if not as those of the one who experienced it, then as those of the one who reports it.

This craftsmanship, storytelling, was actually regarded as a craft by Leskov himself. "Writing," he says in one of his letters, "is to me no liberal art, but a craft." It cannot come as a surprise that he felt bonds with craftsmanship, but faced industrial technology as a stranger. Tolstoy, who must have understood this, occasionally touches this nerve of Leskov's storytelling talent when he calls him the first man "who pointed out the inadequacy of economic progress. . . . It is strange that Dostoevsky is so widely read. . . . But I simply cannot comprehend why Leskov is not read. He is a truthful writer." In his artful and high-spirited story "The Steel Flea," which is midway between legend and farce, Leskov glorifies native craftsmanship through the silversmiths of Tula. Their masterpiece, the steel flea, is seen by Peter the Great and convinces him that the Russians need not be ashamed before the English.

The intellectual picture of the atmosphere of craftsmanship from which the storyteller comes has perhaps never been sketched in such a significant way as by Paul Valéry. "He speaks of the perfect things in nature, flawless pearls, full-bodied, matured wines, truly developed creatures, and calls them 'the precious product of a long chain of causes similar to one another.'" The accumulation of such causes has its temporal limit only at perfection. "This patient process of Nature," Valéry continues, "was once imitated by men. Miniatures, ivory carvings, elaborated to the point of greatest perfection, stones that are perfect in polish and engraving, lacquer work or paintings in which a series of thin, transparent layers are placed one on top of the other—all these products of sustained, sacrificing effort are vanishing, and the time is past in which time did not matter. Modern man no longer works at what cannot be abbreviated."

In point of fact, he has succeeded in abbreviating even storytelling. We have witnessed the evolution of the "short story," which has removed itself from oral tradition and no longer permits that slow piling one on top of the other of thin, transparent layers which constitutes the most appropriate picture of the way in which the perfect narrative is revealed through the layers of a variety of retellings.

It is just this I taught
density/compression everyword
working so hard/day so many
things

x

Valéry concludes his observations with this sentence: "It is almost as if the decline of the idea of eternity coincided with the increasing aversion to sustained effort." The idea of eternity has ever had its strongest source in death. If this idea declines, so we reason, the face of death must have changed. It turns out that this change is identical with the one that has diminished the communicability of experience to the same extent as the art of storytelling has declined.

It has been observable for a number of centuries how in the general consciousness the thought of death has declined in omnipresence and vividness. In its last stages this process is accelerated. And in the course of the nineteenth century bourgeois society has, by means of hygienic and social, private and public institutions, realized a secondary effect which may have been its subconscious main purpose: to make it possible for people to avoid the sight of the dying. Dying was once a public process in the life of the individual and a most exemplary one; think of the medieval pictures in which the deathbed has turned into a throne toward which the people press through the wide-open doors of the death house. In the course of modern times dying

DECIINE of telling (EVITED
to invisibility of modern DEATH
AND VICE VERSA

has been pushed further and further out of the perceptual world of the living. There used to be no house, hardly a room, in which someone had not once died. (The Middle Ages also felt spatially what makes that inscription on a sun dial of Ibiza, *Ultima multis* [the last day for many], significant as the temper of the times.) Today people live in rooms that have never been touched by death, dry dwellers of eternity, and when their end approaches they are stowed away in sanatoria or hospitals by their heirs. It is, however, characteristic that not only a man's knowledge or wisdom, but above all his real life—and this is the stuff that stories are made of—first assumes transmissible form at the moment of his death. Just as a sequence of images is set in motion inside a man as his life comes to an end—unfolding the views of himself under which he has encountered himself without being aware of it—suddenly in his expressions and looks the unforgettable emerges and imparts to everything that concerned him that authority which even the poorest wretch in dying possesses for the living around him. This authority is at the very source of the story.

XI

ENGAGEDNESS / CULMINATION
BEING / AT MOMENT of EXPIRATION
A SUMMING-UP

Death is the sanction of everything that the storyteller can tell. He has borrowed his authority from death. In other words, it is natural history to which his stories refer back. This is expressed in exemplary form in one of the most beautiful stories we have by the incomparable Johann Peter Hebel. It is found in the *Schatzkästlein des rheinischen Hausfreundes*, is entitled "Unexpected Reunion," and begins with the betrothal of a young lad who works in the mines of Falun. On the eve of his wedding he dies a miner's death at the bottom of his tunnel. His bride keeps faith with him after his death, and she lives long enough to become a wizened old woman; one day a body is brought up from the abandoned tunnel which, saturated with iron vitriol, has escaped decay, and she recognizes her betrothed. After this reunion she too is called away by death. When Hebel, in the course of this story, was confronted with the necessity of making

This > READING of the FOLLING PASSAGE is HIGHLY DEBATABLE

this long period of years graphic, he did so in the following sentences: "In the meantime the city of Lisbon was destroyed by an earthquake, and the Seven Years' War came and went, and Emperor Francis I died, and the Jesuit Order was abolished, and Poland was partitioned, and Empress Maria Theresa died, and Struensee was executed. America became independent, and the united French and Spanish forces were unable to capture Gibraltar. The Turks locked up General Stein in the Veteraner Cave in Hungary, and Emperor Joseph died also. King Gustavus of Sweden conquered Russian Finland, and the French Revolution and the long war began, and Emperor Leopold II went to his grave too. Napoleon captured Prussia, and the English bombarded Copenhagen, [and the peasants sowed and harvested.] The millers ground, the smiths hammered, and the miners dug for veins of ore in their underground workshops. But when in 1809 the miners at Falun . . ." *THIS PASSAGE IS NOT DEMOCRATIC*

Never has a storyteller embedded his report deeper in natural history than Hebel manages to do in this chronology. Read it carefully. Death appears in it with the same regularity as the Reaper does in the processions that pass around the cathedral clock at noon.

SEEMS MORE ABOUT A DIVIDED SOCIETY THAN ANYTHING WHILE PEASANTS KEEP ON WORKING   *MORE TO DO W/ PASSAGE OF TIME THAN AUTHORITY*

XII *DRAMA/CONFLICT/UPHEAVAL FROM ON HIGH*

Any examination of a given epic form is concerned with the relationship of this form to historiography. In fact, one may go even further and raise the question whether historiography does *META 'S REFRACTION* not constitute the common ground of all forms of the epic. Then written history would be in the same relationship to the epic forms as white light is to the colors of the spectrum. However this may be, among all forms of the epic there is not one whose incidence in the pure, colorless light of written history is more certain than the chronicle. And in the broad spectrum of the chronicle the ways in which a story can be told are graduated like shadings of one and the same color. The chronicler is the history-teller. If we think back to the passage from Hebel, which has the tone of a chronicle throughout, it will take no effort to gauge the difference between the writer of history, the historian, and the teller of it, the chronicler. The historian is bound to explain in one way or another the happenings with which he deals; under no circumstances can he content himself with displaying them as models of the course of the world. But this is precisely what the chronicler does, especially in his classical representatives, the chroniclers of the Middle Ages, the precursors of the historians of today. By basing their historical tales on a divine plan of salvation—an inscrutable one—they have from the very start lifted the burden of demonstrable explanation from their own shoulders. Its place is taken by interpretation, which is not concerned with an accurate concatenation of definite events, but with the way these are embedded in the great inscrutable course of the world.

Whether this course is eschatologically determined or is a natural one makes no difference. In the storyteller the chronicler is preserved in changed form, secularized, as it were. Leskov is among those whose work displays this with particular clarity. Both the chronicler with his eschatological orientation and the storyteller with his profane outlook are so represented in his works that in a number of his stories it can hardly be decided whether the web in which they appear is the golden fabric of a religious view of the course of things, or the multicolored fabric of a worldly view.

Consider the story "The Alexandrite," which transports the reader into "that old time when the stones in the womb of the earth and the planets at celestial heights were still concerned with the fate of men, and not today when both in the heavens and beneath the earth everything has grown indifferent to the fates of the sons of men and no voice speaks to them from anywhere, let alone does their bidding. None of the undiscovered planets play any part in horoscopes any more, and there are a lot of new stones, all measured and weighed and examined for their specific weight and their density, but they no longer proclaim anything to us, nor do they bring us any benefit. Their time for speaking with men is past."

As is evident, it is hardly possible unambiguously to charac-

terize the course of the world that is illustrated in this story of
Leskov's. Is it determined eschatologically or naturalistically?
The only certain thing is that in its very nature it is by definition
outside all real historical categories. Leskov tells us that the
epoch in which man could believe himself to be in harmony with
nature has expired. Schiller called this epoch in the history of the
world the period of naïve poetry. The storyteller keeps faith with
it, and his eyes do not stray from that dial in front of which
there moves the procession of creatures of which, depending on
circumstances, Death is either the leader or the last wretched
straggler.

XIII

It has seldom been realized that the listener's naïve relationship to the storyteller is controlled by his interest in retaining
what he is told. The cardinal point for the unaffected listener is
to assure himself of the possibility of reproducing the story.
Memory is the epic faculty *par excellence*. Only by virtue of a
comprehensive memory can epic writing absorb the course of
events on the one hand and, with the passing of these, make its
peace with the power of death on the other. It is not surprising
that to a simple man of the people, such as Leskov once invented,
the Czar, the head of the sphere in which his stories take place,
has the most encyclopedic memory at his command. "Our Emperor," he says, "and his entire family have indeed a most astonishing memory."

Mnemosyne, the rememberer, was the Muse of the epic art
among the Greeks. This name takes the observer back to a part-
ing of the ways in world history. For if the record kept by memory—historiography—constitutes the creative matrix of the various epic forms (as great prose is the creative matrix of the
various metrical forms), its oldest form, the epic, by virtue of
being a kind of common denominator includes the story and the
novel. When in the course of centuries the novel began to emerge
from the womb of the epic, it turned out that in the novel the
element of the epic mind that is derived from the Muse—that is,

memory—manifests itself in a form quite different from the way it manifests itself in the story.

Memory creates the chain of tradition which passes a happening on from generation to generation. It is the Muse-derived element of the epic art in a broader sense and encompasses its varieties. In the first place among these is the one practiced by the storyteller. It starts the web which all stories together form in the end. One ties on to the next, as the great storytellers, particularly the Oriental ones, have always readily shown. In each of them there is a Scheherazade who thinks of a fresh story whenever her tale comes to a stop. This is epic remembrance and the Muse-inspired element of the narrative. But this should be set against another principle, also a Muse-derived element in a narrower sense, which as an element of the novel in its earliest form—that is, in the epic—lies concealed, still undifferentiated from the similarly derived element of the story. It can, at any rate, occasionally be divined in the epics, particularly at moments of solemnity in the Homeric epics, as in the invocations to the Muse at their beginning. What announces itself in these passages is the perpetuating remembrance of the novelist as contrasted with the short-lived reminiscences of the storyteller. The first is dedicated to *one* hero, *one* odyssey, *one* battle; the second, to *many* diffuse occurrences. It is, in other words, *remembrance* which, as the Muse-derived element of the novel, is added to reminiscence, the corresponding element of the story, the unity of their origin in memory having disappeared with the decline of the epic.

XIV

"No one," Pascal once said, "dies so poor that he does not leave something behind." Surely it is the same with memories too—although these do not always find an heir. The novelist takes charge of this bequest, and seldom without profound melancholy. For what Arnold Bennett says about a dead woman in one of his novels—that she had had almost nothing in the way of real life—is usually true of the sum total of the estate which the novelist administers. Regarding this aspect of the matter we owe the most important elucidation to Georg Lukács, who sees in the novel "the form of transcendental homelessness." According to Lukács, the novel is at the same time the only art form which includes time among its constitutive principles.

"Time," he says in his *Theory of the Novel*, "can become constitutive only when connection with the transcendental home has been lost. Only in the novel are meaning and life, and thus the essential and the temporal, separated; one can almost say that the whole inner action of a novel is nothing else but a struggle against the power of time. . . . And from this . . . arise the genuinely epic experiences of time: hope and memory. . . . Only in the novel . . . does there occur a creative memory which transfixes the object and transforms it. . . . The duality of inwardness and outside world can here be overcome for the subject 'only' when he sees the . . . unity of his entire life . . . out of the past life-stream which is compressed in memory. . . . The insight which grasps this unity . . . becomes the divinatory-intuitive grasping of the unattained and therefore inexpressible meaning of life."

The "meaning of life" is really the center about which the novel moves. But the quest for it is no more than the initial expression of perplexity with which its reader sees himself living this written life. Here "meaning of life"—there "moral of the story": with these slogans novel and story confront each other, and from them the totally different historical co-ordinates of these art forms may be discerned. If *Don Quixote* is the earliest perfect specimen of the novel, its latest exemplar is perhaps the *Éducation sentimentale.*

In the final words of the last-named novel, the meaning which the bourgeois age found in its behavior at the beginning of its decline has settled like sediment in the cup of life. Frédéric and Deslauriers, the boyhood friends, think back to their youthful friendship. This little incident then occurred: one day they showed up in the bordello of their home town, stealthily and timidly, doing nothing but presenting the *patronne* with a bouquet of flowers which they had picked in their own gardens.

"This story was still discussed three years later. And now they told it to each other in detail, each supplementing the recollection of the other. 'That may have been,' said Frédéric when they had finished, 'the finest thing in our lives.' 'Yes, you may be right,' said Deslauriers, 'that was perhaps the finest thing in our lives.' "

With such an insight the novel reaches an end which is more proper to it, in a stricter sense, than to any story. Actually there is no story for which the question as to how it continued would not be legitimate. The novelist, on the other hand, cannot hope to take the smallest step beyond that limit at which he invites the reader to a divinatory realization of the meaning of life by writing "Finis."

XV

A man listening to a story is in the company of the storyteller; even a man reading one shares this companionship. The reader of a novel, however, is isolated, more so than any other reader. (For even the reader of a poem is ready to utter the words, for the benefit of the listener.) In this solitude of his, the reader of a novel seizes upon his material more jealously than anyone else. He is ready to make it completely his own, to devour it, as it were. Indeed, he destroys, he swallows up the material as the fire devours logs in the fireplace. The suspense which permeates the novel is very much like the draft which stimulates the flame in the fireplace and enlivens its play.

It is a dry material on which the burning interest of the reader feeds. "A man who dies at the age of thirty-five," said Moritz Heimann once, "is at every point of his life a man who dies at the age of thirty-five." Nothing is more dubious than this sentence—but for the sole reason that the tense is wrong. A man—so says the truth that was meant here—who died at thirty-five will appear to *remembrance* at every point in his life as a man who dies at the age of thirty-five. In other words, the statement that makes no sense for real life becomes indisputable for remembered life. The nature of the character in a novel cannot be presented any better than is done in this statement, which says that the "meaning" of his life is revealed only in his death. But the reader of a novel actually does look for human beings from whom he derives the "meaning of life." Therefore he must, no matter what, know in advance that he will share their experience of death: if need be their figurative death—the end of the novel—but preferably their actual one. How do the characters make him understand that death is already waiting for them—a very definite death and at a very definite place? That is the question which feeds the reader's consuming interest in the events of the novel.

The novel is significant, therefore, not because it presents someone else's fate to us, perhaps didactically, but because this stranger's fate by virtue of the flame which consumes it yields us the warmth which we never draw from our own fate. What draws the reader to the novel is the hope of warming his shivering life with a death he reads about.

XVI

"Leskov," writes Gorky, "is the writer most deeply rooted in the people and is completely untouched by any foreign influences." A great storyteller will always be rooted in the people, primarily in a milieu of craftsmen. But just as this includes the rural, the maritime, and the urban elements in the many stages of their economic and technical development, there are many gradations in the concepts in which their store of experience comes down to us. (To say nothing of the by no means insignificant share which traders had in the art of storytelling; their task was less to increase its didactic content than to refine the tricks with which the attention of the listener was captured. They have left deep traces in the narrative cycle of *The Arabian Nights*.) In short, despite the primary role which storytelling plays in the household of humanity, the concepts through which the yield of the stories may be garnered are manifold. What may most readily be put in religious terms in Leskov seems almost automatically to fall into place in the pedagogical perspectives of the Enlightenment in Hebel, appears as hermetic tradition in Poe, finds a last refuge in Kipling in the life of British seamen and colonial soldiers. All great storytellers have in common the freedom with which they move up and down the rungs of their experience as on a ladder. A ladder extending downward to the interior of the earth and disappearing into the clouds is the image for a collective experience to which even the deepest shock of every individual experience, death, constitutes no impediment or barrier.

"And they lived happily ever after," says the fairy tale. The fairy tale, which to this day is the first tutor of children because it was once the first tutor of mankind, secretly lives on in the story. The first true storyteller is, and will continue to be, the teller of fairy tales. Whenever good counsel was at a premium, the fairy tale had it, and where the need was greatest, its aid was nearest. This need was the need created by the myth. The fairy tale tells us of the earliest arrangements that mankind made to shake off the nightmare which the myth had placed upon its chest. In the figure of the fool it shows us how mankind "acts dumb" toward the myth; in the figure of the youngest brother it shows us how one's chances increase as the mythical primitive times are left behind; in the figure of the man who sets out to learn what fear is it shows us that the things we are afraid of can be seen through; in the figure of the wiseacre it shows us that the questions posed by the myth are simple-minded, like the riddle of the Sphinx; in the shape of the animals which come to the aid of the child in the fairy tale it shows that nature not only is subservient to the myth, but much prefers to be aligned with man. The wisest thing—so the fairy tale taught mankind in olden times, and teaches children to this day—is to meet the forces of the mythical world with cunning and with high spirits. (This is how the fairy tale polarizes *Mut*, courage, dividing it dialectically into *Untermut*, that is, cunning, and *Übermut*, high spirits.) The liberating magic which the fairy tale has at its disposal does not bring nature into play in a mythical way, but points to its complicity with liberated man. A mature man feels this complicity only occasionally, that is, when he is happy; but the child first meets it in fairy tales, and it makes him happy.

XVII

Few storytellers have displayed so profound a kinship with the spirit of the fairy tale as did Leskov. This involves tendencies that were promoted by the dogmas of the Greek Orthodox Church. As is well known, Origen's speculation about *apokatastasis*—the entry of all souls into Paradise—which was rejected by the Roman Church plays a significant part in these dogmas. Leskov was very much influenced by Origen and planned to translate his work *On First Principles*. In keeping with Russian folk belief he interpreted the Resurrection less as a transfiguration than as a disenchantment, in a sense akin to the fairy tale. Such an interpretation of Origen is at the bottom of "The Enchanted Pilgrim." In this, as in many other tales by Leskov, a hybrid between fairy tale and legend is involved, not unlike that hybrid which Ernst Bloch mentions in a connection in which he utilizes our distinction between myth and fairy tale in his fashion.

"A hybrid between fairy tale and legend," he says, "contains figuratively mythical elements, mythical elements whose effect is certainly captivating and static, and yet not outside man. In the legend there are Taoist figures, especially very old ones, which are 'mythical' in this sense. For instance, the couple Philemon and Baucis: magically escaped though in natural repose. And surely there is a similar relationship between fairy tale and legend in the Taoist climate of Gotthelf, which, to be sure, is on a much lower level. At certain points it divorces the legend from the locality of the spell, rescues the flame of life, the specifically human flame of life, calmly burning, within as without."

"Magically escaped" are the beings that lead the procession of Leskov's creations: the righteous ones. Pavlin, Figura, the toupee artiste, the bear keeper, the helpful sentry—all of them embodiments of wisdom, kindness, comfort the world, crowd about the storyteller. They are unmistakably suffused with the *imago* of his mother.

This is how Leskov describes her: "She was so thoroughly good that she was not capable of harming any man, nor even an animal. She ate neither meat nor fish, because she had such pity for living creatures. Sometimes my father used to reproach her with this. But she answered: 'I have raised the little animals myself, they are like my children to me. I can't eat my own children, can I?' She would not eat meat at a neighbor's house either. 'I have seen them alive,' she would say; 'they are my acquaintances. I can't eat my acquaintances, can I?' "

The righteous man is the advocate for created things and at the same time he is their highest embodiment. In Leskov he has a maternal touch which is occasionally intensified into the mythical (and thus, to be sure, endangers the purity of the fairy tale). Typical of this is the protagonist of his story "Kotin the Provider and Platonida." This figure, a peasant named Pisonski, is a hermaphrodite. For twelve years his mother raised him as a girl. His male and female organs mature simultaneously, and his bisexuality "becomes the symbol of God incarnate."

In Leskov's view, the pinnacle of creation has been attained with this, and at the same time he presumably sees it as a bridge established between this world and the other. For these earthily powerful, maternal male figures which again and again claim Leskov's skill as a storyteller have been removed from obedience to the sexual drive in the bloom of their strength. They do not, however, really embody an ascetic ideal; rather, the continence of these righteous men has so little privative character that it becomes the elemental counterpoise to uncontrolled lust which the storyteller has personified in *Lady Macbeth of Mzensk*. If the range between a Pavlin and this merchant's wife covers the breadth of the world of created beings, in the hierarchy of his characters Leskov has no less plumbed its depth.

XVIII

The hierarchy of the world of created things, which has its apex in the righteous man, reaches down into the abyss of the inanimate by many gradations. In this connection one particular has to be noted. This whole created world speaks not so much with the human voice as with what could be called "the voice of Nature" in the title of one of Leskov's most significant stories.

This story deals with the petty official Philip Philipovich who leaves no stone unturned to get the chance to have as his house guest a field marshal passing through his little town. He manages to do so. The guest, who is at first surprised at the clerk's urgent invitation, gradually comes to believe that he recognizes in him someone he must have met previously. But who is he? He cannot remember. The strange thing is that the host, for his part, is not willing to reveal his identity. Instead, he puts off the high personage from day to day, saying that the "voice of Nature" will not fail to speak distinctly to him one day. This goes on until finally the guest, shortly before continuing on his journey, must grant the host's public request to let the "voice of Nature" resound. Thereupon the host's wife withdraws. She "returned with a big, brightly polished, copper hunting horn which she gave to her husband. He took the horn, put it to his lips, and was at the same instant as though transformed. Hardly had he inflated his cheeks and produced a tone as powerful as the rolling of thunder when the field marshal cried: 'Stop, I've got it now, brother. This makes me recognize you at once! You are the bugler from the regiment of jaegers, and because you were so honest I sent you to keep an eye on a crooked supplies supervisor.' 'That's it, Your Excellency,' answered the host. 'I didn't want to remind you of this myself, but wanted to let the voice of Nature speak.'"

The way the profundity of this story is hidden beneath its silliness conveys an idea of Leskov's magnificent humor. This humor is confirmed in the same story in an even more cryptic way. We have heard that because of his honesty the official was assigned to watch a crooked supplies supervisor. This is what we are told at the end, in the recognition scene. At the very beginning of the story, however, we learn the following about the host: "All the inhabitants of the town were acquainted with the man, and they knew that he did not hold a high office, for he was neither a state official nor a military man, but a little supervisor at the tiny supply depot, where together with the rats he chewed on the state rusks and boot soles, and in the course of time had chewed himself together a nice little frame house." It is evident that this story reflects the traditional sympathy which storytellers have for rascals and crooks. All the literature of farce bears witness to it. Nor is it denied on the heights of art; of all Hebel's characters, the Brassenheim Miller, Tinder Frieder, and Red Dieter have been his most faithful companions. And yet for Hebel, too, the righteous man has the main role in the *theatrum mundi*. But because no one is actually up to this role, it keeps changing hands. Now it is the tramp, now the haggling Jewish peddler, now the man of limited intelligence who steps in to play this part. In every single case it is a guest performance, a moral improvisation. Hebel is a casuist. He will not for anything take a stand with any principle, but he does not reject it either, for any principle can at some time become the instrument of the righteous man. Compare this with Leskov's attitude. "I realize," he writes in his story "À Propos of the Kreutzer Sonata," "that my thinking is based much more on a practical view of life than on abstract philosophy or lofty morality; but I am nevertheless used to thinking the way I do." To be sure, the moral catastrophes that appear in Leskov's world are to the moral incidents in Hebel's world as the great, silent flowing of the Volga is to the babbling, rushing little millstream. Among Leskov's historical tales there are several in which passions are at work as destructively as the wrath of Achilles or the hatred of Hagen. It is astonishing how fearfully the world can darken for this author and with what majesty evil can raise its scepter. Leskov has evidently known moods—and this is probably one of the few characteristics he shares with Dostoevsky—in which he was close to antinomian ethics. The elemental natures in his *Tales from Olden Times* go to the limit in their ruthless passion. But it is precisely the mystics who have been inclined to see this limit as the point at which utter depravity turns into saintliness.

XIX

The lower Leskov descends on the scale of created things the more obviously does his way of viewing things approach the mystical. Actually, as will be shown, there is much evidence that in this, too, a characteristic is revealed which is inherent in the nature of the storyteller. To be sure, only a few have ventured into the depths of inanimate nature, and in modern narrative literature there is not much in which the voice of the anonymous storyteller, who was prior to all literature, resounds so clearly as it does in Leskov's story "The Alexandrite." It deals with a semi-precious stone, the chrysoberyl. The mineral is the lowest stratum of created things. For the storyteller, however, it is directly joined to the highest. To him it is granted to see in this chrysoberyl a natural prophecy of petrified, lifeless nature concerning the historical world in which he himself lives. This world is the world of Alexander II. The storyteller—or rather, the man to whom he attributes his own knowledge—is a gem engraver named Wenzel who has achieved the greatest conceivable skill in his art. One can juxtapose him with the silversmiths of Tula and say that—in the spirit of Leskov—the perfect artisan has access to the innermost chamber of the realm of created things. He is an incarnation of the devout. We are told of this gem cutter: "He suddenly squeezed my hand on which was the ring with the alexandrite, which is known to sparkle red in artificial light, and cried: 'Look, here it is, the prophetic Russian stone! O crafty Siberian. It was always green as hope and only toward evening was it suffused with blood. It was that way from the beginning of the world, but it concealed itself for a long time, lay hidden in the earth, and permitted itself to be found only on the day when Czar Alexander was declared of age, when a great sorcerer had come to Siberia to find the stone, a magician. . . .' 'What nonsense are you talking,' I interrupted him; 'this stone wasn't found by a magician at all, it was a scholar named Nordenskjöld!' 'A magician! I tell you, a magician!' screamed Wenzel in a loud voice. 'Just look; what a stone! A green morning is in it and a bloody evening . . . This is fate, the fate of noble Czar Alexander!' With these words old Wenzel turned to the wall, propped his head on his elbows, and . . . began to sob."

One can hardly come any closer to the meaning of this significant story than by some words which Paul Valéry wrote in a very remote context. "Artistic observation," he says in reflections on a woman artist whose work consisted in the silk embroidery of figures, "can attain an almost mystical depth. The objects on which it falls lose their names. Light and shade form very particular systems, present very individual questions which depend upon no knowledge and are derived from no practice, but get their existence and value exclusively from a certain accord of the soul, the eye, and the hand of someone who was born to perceive them and evoke them in his own inner self."

With these words, soul, eye, and hand are brought into connection. Interacting with one another, they determine a practice. We are no longer familiar with this practice. The role of the hand in production has become more modest, and the place it filled in storytelling lies waste. (After all, storytelling, in its sensory aspect, is by no means a job for the voice alone. Rather, in genuine storytelling the hand plays a part which supports what is expressed in a hundred ways with its gestures trained by work.) That old co-ordination of the soul, the eye, and the hand which emerges in Valéry's words is that of the artisan which we encounter wherever the art of storytelling is at home. In fact, one can go on and ask oneself whether the relationship of the storyteller to his material, human life, is not in itself a craftsman's relationship, whether it is not his very task to fashion the raw material of experience, his own and that of others, in a solid, useful, and unique way. It is a kind of procedure which may perhaps most adequately be exemplified by the proverb if one thinks of it as an ideogram of a story. A proverb, one might say, is a ruin which stands on the site of an old story and in which a moral twines about a happening like ivy around a wall.

Seen in this way, the storyteller joins the ranks of the teachers and sages. He has counsel—not for a few situations, as the proverb does, but for many, like the sage. For it is granted to him to reach back to a whole lifetime (a life, incidentally, that comprises not only his own experience but no little of the experience of others; what the storyteller knows from hearsay is added to his own). His gift is the ability to relate his life; his distinction, to be able to tell his entire life. The storyteller: he is the man who could let the wick of his life be consumed completely by the gentle flame of his story. This is the basis of the incomparable aura about the storyteller, in Leskov as in Hauff, in Poe as in Stevenson. The storyteller is the figure in which the righteous man encounters himself.

Franz Kafka

On the Tenth Anniversary of His Death

POTEMKIN

It is related that Potemkin suffered from states of depression which recurred more or less regularly. At such times no one was allowed to go near him, and access to his room was strictly forbidden. This malady was never mentioned at court, and in particular it was known that any allusion to it incurred the disfavor of Empress Catherine. One of the Chancellor's depressions lasted for an extraordinary length of time and brought about serious difficulties; in the offices documents piled up that required Potemkin's signature, and the Empress pressed for their completion. The high officials were at their wits' end. One day an unimportant little clerk named Shuvalkin happened to enter the anteroom of the Chancellor's palace and found the councillors of state assembled there, moaning and groaning as usual. "What is the matter, Your Excellencies?" asked the obliging Shuvalkin. They explained things to him and regretted that they could not use his services. "If that's all it is," said Shuvalkin, "I beg you to let me have those papers." Having nothing to lose, the councillors of state let themselves be persuaded to do so, and with the sheaf of documents under his arm, Shuvalkin set out, through galleries and corridors, for Potemkin's bedroom. Without stopping or bothering to knock, he turned the door-handle; the room was not locked. In semidarkness Potemkin was sitting on his bed in a threadbare nightshirt, biting his nails. Shuvalkin stepped up to the writing desk, dipped a pen in ink, and without saying a word pressed it into Potemkin's hand while putting one of the documents on his knees. Potemkin gave the intruder a vacant stare; then, as though in his sleep, he started to sign—first one paper, then a second, finally all of them. When the last signature had been affixed, Shuvalkin took the papers under his arm and left the room without further ado, just as he had entered it. Waving the papers triumphantly, he stepped into the anteroom. The councillors of state rushed toward him and tore the documents out of his hands. Breathlessly they bent over them. No one spoke a word; the whole group seemed paralyzed. Again Shuvalkin came closer and solicitously asked why the gentlemen seemed so upset. At that point he noticed the signatures. One document after another was signed Shuvalkin . . . Shuvalkin . . . Shuvalkin. . . .

This story is like a herald racing two hundred years ahead of Kafka's work. The enigma which beclouds it is Kafka's enigma. The world of offices and registries, of musty, shabby, dark rooms, is Kafka's world. The obliging Shuvalkin, who makes light of everything and is finally left empty-handed, is Kafka's K. Potemkin, who vegetates, somnolent and unkempt, in a remote, inaccessible room, is an ancestor of those holders of power in Kafka's works who live in the attics as judges or in the castle as secretaries; no matter how highly placed they may be, they are always fallen or falling men, although even the lowest and seediest of them, the doorkeepers and the decrepit officials, may abruptly and strikingly appear in the fullness of their power. Why do they vegetate? Could they be the descendants of the figures of Atlas that support globes with their shoulders? Perhaps that is why each has his head "so deep on his chest that one can hardly see his eyes," like the Castellan in his portrait, or Klamm when he is alone. But it is not the globe they are carrying; it is just that even the most commonplace things have their weight. "His fatigue is that of the gladiator after the fight; his job was the whitewashing of a corner in the office!" Georg Lukács once said that in order to make a decent table nowadays, a man must have the architectural genius of a Michelangelo. If Lukács thinks in terms of ages, Kafka thinks in terms of cosmic epochs. The man who whitewashes has epochs to move, even in his most insignificant movement. On many occasions and often for strange reasons Kafka's figures clap their hands. Once the casual remark is made that these hands are "really steam hammers."

We encounter these holders of power in constant, slow movement, rising or falling. But they are at their most terrible when they rise from the deepest decay—from the fathers. The son calms his spiritless, senile father whom he has just gently put to bed: " 'Don't worry, you are well covered up.' 'No,' cried his father, cutting short the answer, threw the blanket off with such strength that it unfolded fully as it flew, and stood up in bed. Only one hand lightly touched the ceiling to steady him. 'You wanted to cover me up, I know, my little scamp, but I'm not all covered up yet. And even if this is all the strength I have left, it's enough for you, too much for you. . . . But thank goodness a father does not need to be taught how to see through his son.' . . . And he stood up quite unsupported and kicked his legs out. He beamed with insight. . . . 'So now you know what else there was in the world besides yourself; until now you have known only about yourself! It is true, you were an innocent child, but it is even more true that you have been a devilish person!' " As the father throws off the burden of the blanket, he also throws off a cosmic burden. He has to set cosmic ages in motion in order to turn the age-old father-son relationship into a living and consequential thing. But what consequences! He sentences his son to death by drowning. The father is the one who punishes; guilt attracts him as it does the court officials. There is much to indicate that the world of the officials and the world of the fathers are the same to Kafka. The similarity does not redound to this world's credit; it consists of dullness, decay, and dirt. The father's uniform is stained all over; his underwear is dirty. Filth is the element of the officials. "She could not understand why there were office hours for the public in the first place. 'To get some dirt on the front staircase'—this is how her question was once answered by an official, who was probably annoyed, but it made a lot of sense to her." Uncleanness is so much the attribute of officials that one could almost regard them as enormous parasites. This, of course, does not refer to the economic context, but to the forces of reason and humanity from which this clan makes a living. In the same way the fathers in Kafka's strange families batten on their sons, lying on top of them like giant parasites. They not only prey upon their strength, but gnaw away at the sons' right to exist. The fathers punish, but they are at the same time the accusers. The sin of which they accuse their sons seems to be a kind of original sin. The definition of it which Kafka has given applies to the sons more than to anyone else: "Original sin, the old injustice committed by man, consists in the complaint unceasingly made by man that he has been the victim of an injustice, the victim of original sin." But who is accused of this inherited sin—the sin of having produced an heir—if not the father by the son? Accordingly the son would be the sinner. But one must not conclude from Kafka's definition that the accusation is sinful because it is false. Nowhere does Kafka say that it is made wrongfully. A never-ending process is at work here, and no cause can appear in a worse light than the one for which the father enlists the aid of these officials and court offices. A boundless corruptibility is not their worst feature, for their essence is such that their venality is the only hope held out to the human spirit facing them. The courts, to be sure, have lawbooks at their disposal, but people are not allowed to see them. "It is characteristic of this legal system," conjectures K., "that one is sentenced not only in innocence but also in ignorance." Laws and definite norms remain unwritten in the prehistoric world. A man can transgress them without suspecting it and thus become subject to atonement. But no matter how hard it may hit the unsuspecting, the transgression in the sense of the law is not accidental but fated, a destiny which appears here in all its ambiguity. In a cursory investigation of the idea of fate in antiquity Hermann Cohen came to a "conclusion that becomes inescapable": "the very rules of fate seem to be what causes and brings about the breaking away from them, the defection." It is the same way with the legal authorities whose proceedings are directed against K. It takes us back far beyond the time of the giving of the Law on twelve tablets to a prehistoric world, written law being one of the first victories scored over this world. In Kafka the written law is contained in books, but these are secret; by basing itself on them the prehistoric world exerts its rule all the more ruthlessly.

In Kafka's works, the conditions in offices and in families have multifarious points of contact. In the village at the foot of Castle Hill people use an illuminating saying. " 'We have a saying here that you may be familiar with: Official decisions are as shy as young girls.' 'That's a sound observation,' said K., 'a sound observation. Decisions may have even other characteristics in common with girls.' " The most remarkable of these qualities is the willingness to lend oneself to anything, like the shy girls whom K. meets in *The Castle* and *The Trial*, girls who indulge in unchastity in the bosom of their family as they would in a bed. He encounters them at every turn; the rest give him as little trouble as the conquest of the barmaid. "They embraced each other; her little body burned in K.'s hands; in a state of unconsciousness which K. tried to master constantly but fruitlessly, they rolled a little way, hit Klamm's door with a thud, and then lay in the little puddles of beer and the other refuse that littered the floor. Hours passed . . . in which K. constantly had the feeling that he was losing his way or that he had wandered farther than anyone had ever wandered before, to a place where even the air had nothing in common with his native air, where all this strangeness might choke one, yet a place so insanely enchanting that one could not help but go on and lose oneself even further." We shall have more to say about this strange place. The remarkable thing is that these whorelike women never seem to be beautiful. Rather, beauty appears in Kafka's world only in the most obscure places—among the accused persons, for example. "This, to be sure, is a strange phenomenon, a natural law, as it were. . . .

It cannot be guilt that makes them attractive . . . nor can it be the just punishment which makes them attractive in anticipation . . . so it must be the mere charges brought against them that somehow show on them."

From *The Trial* it may be seen that these proceedings usually are hopeless for those accused—hopeless even when they have hopes of being acquitted. It may be this hopelessness that brings out the beauty in them—the only creatures in Kafka thus favored. At least this would be very much in keeping with a conversation which Max Brod has related. "I remember," Brod writes, "a conversation with Kafka which began with present-day Europe and the decline of the human race. 'We are nihilistic thoughts, suicidal thoughts that come into God's head,' Kafka said. This reminded me at first of the Gnostic view of life: God as the evil demiurge, the world as his Fall. 'Oh no,' said Kafka, 'our world is only a bad mood of God, a bad day of his.' 'Then there is hope outside this manifestation of the world that we know.' He smiled. 'Oh, plenty of hope, an infinite amount of hope—but not for us.'" These words provide a bridge to those extremely strange figures in Kafka, the only ones who have escaped from the family circle and for whom there may be hope. These are not the animals, not even those hybrids or imaginary creatures like the Cat Lamb or Odradek; they all still live under the spell of the family. It is no accident that Gregor Samsa wakes up as a bug in his parental home and not somewhere else, and that the peculiar animal which is half kitten, half lamb, is inherited from the father; Odradek likewise is the concern of the father of the family. The "assistants," however, are outside this circle.

These assistants belong to a group of figures which recurs through Kafka's entire work. Their tribe includes the confidence man who is unmasked in "Meditation"; the student who appears on the balcony at night as Karl Rossmann's neighbor; and the fools who live in that town in the south and never get tired. The twilight in which they exist is reminiscent of the uncertain light in which the figures in the short prose pieces of Robert Walser appear [the author of *Der Gehülfe*, The Assistant, a novel Kafka was very fond of]. In Indian mythology there are the *gandharvas,* celestial creatures, beings in an unfinished state. Kafka's assistants are of that kind: neither members of, nor strangers to, any of the other groups of figures, but, rather, messengers from one to the other. Kafka tells us that they resemble Barnabas, who is a messenger. They have not yet been completely released from the womb of nature, and that is why they have "settled down on two old women's skirts on the floor in a corner. It was . . . their ambition . . . to use up as little space as possible. To that end they kept making various experiments, folding their arms and legs, huddling close together; in the darkness all one could see in their corner was one big ball." It is for them and their kind, the unfinished and the bunglers, that there is hope.

What may be discerned, subtly and informally, in the activities of these messengers is law in an oppressive and gloomy way for this whole group of beings. None has a firm place in the world, firm, inalienable outlines. There is not one that is not either rising or falling, none that is not trading qualities with its enemy or neighbor, none that has not completed its period of time and yet is unripe, none that is not deeply exhausted and yet is only at the beginning of a long existence. To speak of any order or hierarchy is impossible here. Even the world of myth of which we think in this context is incomparably younger than Kafka's world, which has been promised redemption by the myth. But if we can be sure of one thing, it is this: Kafka did not succumb to its temptation. A latter-day Ulysses, he let the Sirens go by "his gaze which was fixed on the distance, the Sirens disappeared as it were before his determination, and at the very moment when he was closest to them he was no longer aware of them." Among Kafka's ancestors in the ancient world, the Jews and the Chinese, whom we shall encounter later, this Greek one should not be forgotten. Ulysses, after all, stands at the dividing line between myth and fairy tale. Reason and cunning have inserted tricks into myths; their forces cease to be invincible. Fairy tales are the traditional stories about victory over these forces, and fairy tales for dialecticians are what Kafka wrote when he went to work on legends. He inserted little tricks into them; then he used them as proof "that inadequate, even childish measures may also serve to rescue one." With these words he begins his story about the "Silence of the Sirens." For Kafka's Sirens are silent; they have "an even more terrible weapon than their song . . . their silence." This they used on Ulysses. But he, so Kafka tells us, "was so full of guile, was such a fox that not even the goddess of fate could pierce his armor. Perhaps he had really noticed, although here the human understanding is beyond its depths, that the Sirens were silent, and opposed the afore-mentioned pretense to them and the gods merely as a sort of shield."

Kafka's Sirens are silent. Perhaps because for Kafka music and singing are an expression or at least a token of escape, a token of hope which comes to us from that intermediate world—at once unfinished and commonplace, comforting and silly—in which the assistants are at home. Kafka is like the lad who set out to learn what fear was. He has got into Potemkin's palace and finally, in the depths of its cellar, has encountered Josephine, the singing mouse, whose tune he describes: "Something of our poor, brief childhood is in it, something of lost happiness which can never be found again, but also something of active present-day life, of its small gaieties, unaccountable and yet real and unquenchable."

A CHILDHOOD PHOTOGRAPH

There is a childhood photograph of Kafka, a rarely touching portrayal of the "poor, brief childhood." It was probably made in one of those nineteenth-century studios whose draperies and palm trees, tapestries and easels placed them somewhere between a torture chamber and a throne room. At the age of approximately six the boy is presented in a sort of greenhouse setting, wearing a tight, heavily lace-trimmed, almost embarrassing child's suit. Palm branches loom in the background. And as if to make these upholstered tropics still more sultry and sticky, the model holds in his left hand an oversized, wide-brimmed hat of the type worn by Spaniards. Immensely sad eyes dominate the landscape prearranged for them, and the auricle of a big ear seems to be listening for its sounds.

The ardent "wish to become a Red Indian" may have consumed this great sadness at some point. "If one were only an Indian, instantly alert, and on a racing horse, leaning against the wind, kept on quivering briefly over the quivering ground, until one shed one's spurs, for there were no spurs, threw away the reins, for there were no reins, and barely saw the land before one as a smoothly mown heath, with the horse's neck and head already gone." A great deal is contained in this wish. Its fulfillment, which he finds in America, yields up its secret. That *Amerika* is a very special case is indicated by the name of its hero. While in the earlier novels the author never addressed himself otherwise than with a mumbled initial, here he experiences a rebirth on a new continent with a full name. He has this experience in the Nature Theater of Oklahoma. "At a street corner Karl saw a poster with the following announcement: The Oklahoma Theater will engage members for its company today at Clayton Racetrack from 6 a.m. until midnight. The great Theater of Oklahoma calls you! The one and only call is today! If you miss your chance now, you miss it forever! If you think of your future, you should be one of us! Everyone is welcome! If you want to be an artist, come forward! Our Theater can use everyone and find the right place for everyone! If you decide to join us, we congratulate you here and now! But hurry, so that you get in before midnight! At twelve o'clock the doors will be shut and never opened again! A curse on those who do not believe in us! Set out for Clayton!" The reader of this announcement is Karl Rossmann, the third and happier incarnation of K., the hero of Kafka's novels. Happiness awaits him at the Nature Theater of Oklahoma, which is really a racetrack, just as "unhappiness" had once beset him on the narrow rug in his room on which he ran about "as on a racetrack." Ever since Kafka wrote his "reflections for gentleman jockeys," ever since he made the "new attorney" mount the courthouse steps, lifting his legs high, with a tread that made the marble ring, ever since he made his "children on a country road" amble through the countryside with large steps and folded arms, this figure had been familiar to him; and even Karl Rossmann, "distracted by his sleepiness," may often make "too high, time-consuming, and useless leaps." Thus it can only be a racetrack on which he attains the object of his desire.

This racetrack is at the same time a theater, and this poses a puzzle. The mysterious place and the entirely unmysterious, transparent, pure figure of Karl Rossmann are congruous, however. For Karl Rossmann is transparent, pure, without character as it were in the same sense in which Franz Rosenzweig says in his *Star of Redemption* that in China people, in their spiritual aspects, are "as it were devoid of individual character; the idea of the wise man, of which Confucius is the classic incarnation, blurs any individuality of character; he is the truly characterless man, namely, the average man. . . . What distinguishes a Chinese is something quite different from character: a very elemental purity of feeling." No matter how one may convey it intellectually, this purity of feeling may be a particularly sensitive measurement of gestic behavior; the Nature Theater of Oklahoma in any case harks back to the Chinese theater, which is a gestic theater. One of the most significant functions of this theater is to dissolve happenings into their gestic components. One can go even further and say that a good number of Kafka's shorter studies and stories are seen in their full light only when they are, so to speak, put on as acts in the "Nature Theater of Oklahoma." Only then will one recognize with certainty that Kafka's entire work constitutes a code of gestures which surely had no definite symbolic meaning for the author from the outset; rather, the author tried to derive such a meaning from them in ever-changing contexts and experimental groupings. The theater is the logical place for such groupings. In an unpublished commentary on "A Fratricide," Werner Kraft perceptively identified the events in this little story as scenic events. "The play is ready to begin, and it is actually announced by a bell. This comes about in a very natural way. Wese leaves the building in which his office is located. But this doorbell, so we are expressly told, is 'too loud for a doorbell; it rings out over the town and up to heaven.'" Just as this bell, which is too loud for a doorbell, rings out toward heaven, the gestures of Kafka's figures are too powerful for our accustomed surroundings and break out into wider areas. The greater Kafka's mastery became, the more frequently did he eschew adapting these gestures to common situations or explaining them. "It is strange behavior," we read in "The Metamorphosis," "to sit on the desk and talk down at the employee, who, furthermore, must come quite close because his boss is hard of hearing." *The Trial* has already left such motivations far behind. In the penultimate chapter, K. stops at the first rows in the Cathedral, "but the priest seemed to consider the distance still too great; he stretched out an arm and pointed with his sharply bent forefinger to a spot right in front of the pulpit. K. followed this direction too; at that place he had to bend his head far back to see the priest at all."

Max Brod has said: "The world of those realities that were important for him was invisible." What Kafka could see least of all was the *gestus*. Each gesture is an event—one might even say, a drama—in itself. The stage on which this drama takes place is the World Theater which opens up toward heaven. On the other hand, this heaven is only background; to explore it according to its own laws would be like framing the painted backdrop of the stage and hanging it in a picture gallery. Like El Greco, Kafka tears open the sky behind every gesture; but as with El Greco—who was the patron saint of the Expressionists—the gesture remains the decisive thing, the center of the event. The people who have assumed responsibility for the knock at the manor gate walk doubled up with fright. This is how a Chinese actor would portray terror, but no one would give a start. Elsewhere K. himself does a bit of acting. Without being fully conscious of it, "slowly . . . with his eyes not looking down but cautiously raised upwards he took one of the papers from the desk, put it on the palm of his hand and gradually raised it up to the gentlemen while getting up himself. He had nothing definite in mind, but acted only with the feeling that this was what he would have to do once he had completed the big petition which was to exonerate him completely." This animal gesture combines the utmost mysteriousness with the utmost simplicity. It is possible to read Kafka's animal stories for quite a while without realizing that they are not about human beings at all. When one encounters the name of the creature—monkey, dog, mole—one looks up in fright and realizes that one is already far away from the continent of man. But it is always Kafka; he divests the human gesture of its traditional supports and then has a subject for reflection without end.

Strangely enough, these reflections are endless even when their point of departure is one of Kafka's philosophical tales. Take, for example, the parable "Before the Law." The reader who read it in *A Country Doctor* may have been struck by the cloudy spot in it. But would it have led him to the never-ending series of reflections traceable to this parable at the place where Kafka undertakes to interpret it? This is done by the priest in *The Trial*, and at such a significant moment that it looks as if the novel were nothing but the unfolding of the parable. The word "unfolding" has a double meaning. A bud unfolds into a blossom, but the boat which one teaches children to make by folding paper unfolds into a flat sheet of paper. This second kind of "unfolding" is really appropriate to the parable; it is the reader's pleasure to smooth it out so that he has the meaning on the palm of his hand. Kafka's parables, however, unfold in the first sense, the way a bud turns into a blossom. That is why their effect resembles poetry. This does not mean that his prose pieces belong entirely in the tradition of Western prose forms; they have, rather, a similar relationship to doctrine as the Haggadah does to the Halakah. They are not parables, and yet they do not want to be taken at their face value; they lend themselves to quotation and can be told for purposes of clarification. But do we have the doctrine which Kafka's parables interpret and which K.'s postures and the gestures of his animals clarify? It does not exist; all we can say is that here and there we have an allusion to it. Kafka might have said that these are relics transmitting the doctrine, although we could regard them just as well as precursors preparing the doctrine. In every case it is a question of how life and work are organized in human society. This question increasingly occupied Kafka as it became impenetrable to him. If Napoleon, in his famous conversation with Goethe at Erfurt, substituted politics for fate, Kafka, in a variation of this statement, could have defined organization as destiny. He faces it not only in the extensive hierarchy of officialdom in *The Trial* and *The Castle*, but even more concretely in the difficult and incalculable construction plans whose venerable model he dealt with in *The Great Wall of China.*

"The wall was to be a protection for centuries; accordingly, the most scrupulous care in the construction, the application of the architectural wisdom of all known ages and peoples, a constant sense of personal responsibility on the part of the builders were indispensable prerequisites for the work. To be sure, for the menial tasks ignorant day laborers from the populace, men, women, and children, whoever offered his services for good money, could be used; but for the supervision even of every four day laborers a man trained in the building trade was required. . . . We—and here I speak in the name of many people—did not really know ourselves until we had carefully scrutinized the decrees of the high command; then we discovered that without this leadership neither our book learning nor our common sense would have sufficed for the humble tasks which we performed in the great whole." This organization resembles fate. Metchnikoff, who has outlined this in his famous book *La Civilisation et les grands fleuves historiques* [Civilization and the Great Historical Rivers], uses language that could be Kafka's. "The canals of the Yangtze and the dams of the Yellow River," he writes, "are in all likelihood the result of the skillfully organized joint labor of . . . generations. The slightest carelessness in the digging of a ditch or the buttressing of a dam, the least bit of negligence or selfish behavior on the part of an individual or a group of men in the maintenance of the common hydraulic wealth becomes, under such unusual circumstances, the source of social evils and far-reaching social calamity. Consequently, a life-giving river requires on pain of death a close and permanent solidarity between groups of people that frequently are alien or even hostile to one another; it sentences everyone to labors whose common usefulness is revealed only by time and whose design quite often remains utterly incomprehensible to an ordinary man."

Kafka wished to be numbered among ordinary men. He was pushed to the limits of understanding at every turn, and he liked to push others to them as well. At times he seems to come close to saying with Dostoevsky's Grand Inquisitor: "So we have before us a mystery which we cannot comprehend. And precisely because it is a mystery we have had the right to preach it, to teach the people that what matters is neither freedom nor love, but the riddle, the secret, the mystery to which they have to bow—without reflection and even against their conscience." Kafka did not always evade the temptations of mysticism. There is a diary entry concerning his encounter with Rudolf Steiner; in its published form at least it does not reflect Kafka's attitude toward him. Did he avoid taking a stand? His way with his own writings certainly does not exclude this possibility. Kafka had a rare capacity for creating parables for himself. Yet his parables are never exhausted by what is explainable; on the contrary, he took all conceivable precautions against the interpretation of his writings. One has to find one's way in them circumspectly, cautiously, and warily. One must keep in mind Kafka's way of reading as exemplified in his interpretation of the above-mentioned parable. His testament is another case in point. Given its background, the directive in which Kafka ordered the destruction of his literary remains is just as unfathomable, to be weighed just as carefully as the answers of the doorkeeper before the law. Perhaps Kafka, whose every day on earth brought him up against insoluble behavior problems and undecipherable communications, in death wished to give his contemporaries a taste of their own medicine.

Kafka's world is a world theater. For him, man is on the stage from the very beginning. The proof of the pudding is the fact that everyone is accepted by the Nature Theater of Oklahoma. What the standards for admission are cannot be determined. Dramatic talent, the most obvious criterion, seems to be of no importance. But this can be expressed in another way: all that is expected of the applicants is the ability to play themselves. It is no longer within the realm of possibility that they could, if necessary, be what they claim to be. With their roles these people look for a position in the Nature Theater just as Pirandello's six characters sought an author. For all of them this place is the last refuge, which does not preclude it from being their salvation. Salvation is not a premium on existence, but the last way out for a man whose path, as Kafka puts it, is "blocked . . . by his own frontal bone." The law of this theater is contained in a sentence tucked away in "A Report to an Academy": "I imitated people because I was looking for a way out, and for no other reason." Before the end of his trial, K. seems to have an intimation of these things. He suddenly turns to the two gentlemen wearing top hats who have come for him and asks them: " 'What theater are you playing at?' 'Theater?' asked one, the corners of his mouth twitching as he looked for advice to the other, who acted as if he were a mute struggling to overcome a stubborn disability." The men do not answer this question, but there is much to indicate that it has hit home.

At a long bench which has been covered with a white cloth all those who will henceforth be with the Nature Theater are fed. "They were all happy and excited." By way of celebration, extras act as angels. They stand on high pedestals that are covered with flowing raiments and have stairs inside—the makings of a country church fair, or maybe a children's festival, which may have eliminated the sadness from the eyes of the tightly laced, dressed-up boy we discussed above. But for the fact that their wings are tied on, these angels might be real. They have forerunners in Kafka's works. One of them is the impresario who climbs up on the luggage rack next to the trapeze artist beset by his "first sorrow," caresses him and presses his face against the artist's, "so that he was bathed by the trapeze artist's tears." Another, a guardian angel or guardian of the law, takes care of Schmar the murderer following the "fratricide" and leads him away, stepping lightly, with Schmar's "mouth pressed against the policeman's shoulder." Kafka's *Amerika* ends with the rustic ceremonies of Oklahoma. "In Kafka," said Soma Morgenstern, "there is the air of a village, as with all great founders of religions." Lao-tse's presentation of piousness is all the more pertinent here because Kafka has supplied its most perfect description in "The Next Village." "Neighboring countries may be within sight, so that the sounds of roosters and dogs may be heard in the distance. And yet people are said to die at a ripe old age without having traveled far." Thus Lao-tse. Kafka was a writer of parables, but he did not found a religion.

Let us consider the village at the foot of Castle Hill whence K.'s alleged employment as a land surveyor is so mysteriously and unexpectedly confirmed. In his Postscript to *The Castle* Brod mentioned that in depicting this village at the foot of Castle Hill Kafka had in mind a specific place, Zürau in the Erz Gebirge. We may, however, also recognize another village in it. It is the village in a Talmudic legend told by a rabbi in answer to the question why Jews prepare a festive evening meal on Fridays. The legend is about a princess languishing in exile, in a village whose language she does not understand, far from her compatriots. One day this princess receives a letter saying that her fiancé has not forgotten her and is on his way to her. The fiancé, so says the rabbi, is the Messiah; the princess is the soul; the village in which she lives in exile is the body. She prepares a meal for him because this is the only way in which she can express her joy in a village whose language she does not know. This village of the Talmud is right in Kafka's world. For just as K. lives in the village on Castle Hill, modern man lives in his body; the body slips away from him, is hostile toward him. It may happen that a man wakes up one day and finds himself transformed into vermin. Exile—his exile—has gained control over him. The air of this village blows about Kafka, and that is why he was not tempted to found a religion. The pigsty which houses the country doctor's horses; the stuffy back room in which Klamm, a cigar in his mouth, sits over a glass of beer; the manor gate, to knock against which brings ruin—all these are part of this village. The air in this village is not free of all the abortive and overripe elements that form such a putrid mixture. This is the air that Kafka had to breathe all his life. He was neither mantic nor the founder of a religion. How was he able to survive in this air?

THE LITTLE HUNCHBACK

Some time ago it became known that Knut Hamsun was in the habit of expressing his views in an occasional letter to the editor of the local paper in the small town near which he lived. Years ago that town was the scene of the jury trial of a maid who had killed her infant child. She was sentenced to a prison term. Soon thereafter the local paper printed a letter from Hamsun in which he announced his intention of leaving a town which did not visit the supreme punishment on a mother who killed her newborn child—the gallows, or at least a life term of hard labor. A few years passed. *Growth of the Soil* appeared, and it contained the story of a maid who committed the same crime, suffered the same punishment, and, as is made clear to the reader, surely deserved no more severe one.

Kafka's posthumous reflections, which are contained in *The Great Wall of China*, recall this to mind. Hardly had this volume appeared when the reflections served as the basis for a Kafka criticism which concentrated on an interpretation of these reflections to the neglect of his real works. There are two ways to miss the point of Kafka's works. One is to interpret them naturally, the other is the supernatural interpretation. Both the psychoanalytic and the theological interpretations equally miss the essential points. The first kind is represented by Hellmuth Kaiser; the second, by numerous writers, such as H. J. Schoeps, Bernhard Rang, and Bernhard Groethuysen. To these last also belongs Willy Haas, although he has made revealing comments on Kafka in other contexts which we shall discuss later; such insights did not prevent him from interpreting Kafka's work after a theological pattern. "The powers above, the realm of grace," so Haas writes, "Kafka has depicted in his great novel *The Castle*; the powers below, the realm of the courts and of damnation, he has dealt with in his equally great novel *The Trial*. The earth between the two, earthly fate and its arduous demands, he attempted to present in strictly stylized form in a third novel, *Amerika*." The first third of this interpretation has, since Brod, become the common property of Kafka criticism. Bernhard Rang writes in a similar vein: "To the extent that one may regard the Castle as the seat of grace, precisely these vain efforts and attempts mean, theologically speaking, that God's grace cannot be attained or forced by man at will and deliberately. Unrest and impatience only impede and confound the exalted stillness of the divine." This interpretation is a convenient one; but the further it is carried, the clearer it becomes that it is untenable. This is perhaps seen most clearly in a statement by Willy Haas. "Kafka goes back . . . to Kierkegaard as well as to Pascal; one may call him the only legitimate heir of these two. In all three there is an excruciatingly harsh basic religious theme: man is always in the wrong before God. . . . Kafka's upper world, his so-called Castle, with its immense, complex staff of petty and rather lecherous officials, his strange heaven plays a horrible game with people . . . and yet man is very much in the wrong even before this god." This theology falls far behind the doctrine of justification of St. Anselm of Canterbury into barbaric speculations which do not even seem consistent with the text of Kafka's works. "Can an individual official forgive?" we read in *The Castle*. "This could only be a matter for the over-all authorities, but even they can probably not forgive but only judge." This road has soon led into a blind alley. "All this," says Denis de Rougemont, "is not the wretched situation of man without a god, but the wretched state of a man who is bound to a god he does not know, because he does not know Christ."

It is easier to draw speculative conclusions from Kafka's posthumous collection of notes than to explore even one of the motifs that appear in his stories and novels. Yet only these give some clue to the prehistoric forces that dominated Kafka's creativeness, forces which, to be sure, may justifiably be regarded as belonging to our world as well. Who can say under what names they appeared to Kafka himself? Only this much is certain: he did not know them and failed to get his bearings among them. In the mirror which the prehistoric world held before him in the form of guilt he merely saw the future emerging in the form of judgment. Kafka, however, did not say what it was like. Was it not the Last Judgment? Does it not turn the judge into the defendant? Is the trial not the punishment? Kafka gave no answer. Did he expect anything of this punishment? Or was he not rather concerned to postpone it? In the stories which Kafka left us, narrative art regains the significance it had in the mouth of Scheherazade: to postpone the future. In *The Trial* postponement is the hope of the accused man only if the proceedings do not gradually turn into the judgment. The patriarch himself is to benefit by postponement, even though he may have to trade his place in tradition for it. "I could conceive of another Abraham—to be sure, he would never get to be a patriarch or even an old-clothes dealer—, an Abraham who would be prepared to satisfy the demand for a sacrifice immediately, with the promptness of a waiter, but would be unable to bring it off because he cannot get away, being indispensable; the household needs him, there is always something or other to take care of, the house is never ready; but without having his house ready, without having something to fall back on, he cannot leave—this the Bible also realized, for it says: 'He set his house in order.'"

This Abraham appears "with the promptness of a waiter." Kafka could understand things only in the form of a *gestus*, and this *gestus* which he did not understand constitutes the cloudy part of the parables. Kafka's writings emanate from it. The way he withheld them is well known. His testament orders their destruction. This document, which no one interested in Kafka can disregard, says that the writings did not satisfy their author, that he regarded his efforts as failures, that he counted himself among those who were bound to fail. He did fail in his grandiose attempt to convert poetry into doctrine, to turn it into a parable and restore to it that stability and unpretentiousness which, in the face of reason, seemed to him to be the only appropriate thing for it. No other writer has obeyed the commandment "Thou shalt not make unto thee a graven image" so faithfully.

"It was as if the shame of it was to outlive him." With these words *The Trial* ends. Corresponding as it does to his "elemental purity of feeling," shame is Kafka's strongest gesture. It has a dual aspect, however. Shame is an intimate human reaction, but at the same time it has social pretensions. Shame is not only shame in the presence of others, but can also be shame one feels for them. Kafka's shame, then, is no more personal than the life and thought which govern it and which he has described thus: "He does not live for the sake of his own life, he does not think for the sake of his own thought. He feels as though he were living and thinking under the constraint of a family. . . . Because of this unknown family . . . he cannot be released." We do not know the make-up of this unknown family, which is composed of human beings and animals. But this much is clear: it is this family that forces Kafka to move cosmic ages in his writings. Doing this family's bidding, he moves the mass of historical happenings as Sisyphus rolled the stone. As he does so, its nether side comes to light; it is not a pleasant sight, but Kafka is capable of bearing it. "To believe in progress is not to believe that progress has already taken place. That would be no belief." Kafka did not consider the age in which he lived as an advance over the beginnings of time. His novels are set in a swamp world. In his works, created things appear at the stage which Bachofen has termed the hetaeric stage. The fact that it is now forgotten does not mean that it does not extend into the present. On the contrary: it is actual by virtue of this very oblivion. An experience deeper than that of an average person can make contact with it. "I have experience," we read in one of Kafka's earliest notes, "and I am not joking when I say that it is a seasickness on dry land." It is no accident that the first "Meditation" was made on a swing. And Kafka does not tire of expressing himself on the fluctuating nature of experiences. Each gives way and mingles with its opposite. "It was summer, a hot day," so begins "The Knock at the Manor Gate." "With my sister I was passing the gate of a great house on our way home. I don't remember whether she knocked on the gate out of mischief or in a fit of absent-mindedness, or merely shook her fist at it and did not knock at all." The very possibility of the third alternative puts the other two, which at first seemed harmless, in a different light. It is from the swampy soil of such experiences that Kafka's female characters rise. They are swamp creatures like Leni, "who stretches out the middle and ring fingers of her right hand between which the connecting web of skin reached almost to the top joint, short as the fingers were." "Fine times," so the ambivalent Frieda reminisces about her earlier life; "you never asked me about my past." This past takes us back to the dark, deep womb, the scene of the mating "whose untrammeled voluptuousness," to quote Bachofen, "is hateful to the pure forces of heavenly light and which justifies the term used by Arnobius, *luteae voluptates* [dirty voluptuousness]."

Only from this vantage point can the technique of Kafka the storyteller be comprehended. Whenever figures in the novels have anything to say to K., no matter how important or surprising it may be, they do so casually and with the implication that he must really have known it all along. It is as though nothing new was being imparted, as though the hero was just being subtly invited to recall to mind something that he had forgotten. This is how Willy Haas has interpreted the course of events in *The Trial*, and justifiably so. "The object of the trial," he writes, "indeed, the real hero of this incredible book is forgetting, whose main characteristic is the forgetting of itself. . . . Here it has actually become a mute figure in the shape of the accused man, a figure of the most striking intensity." It probably cannot be denied that "this mysterious center . . . derives from the Jewish religion." "Memory plays a very mysterious role as piousness. It is not an ordinary, but . . . the most profound quality of Jehovah that he remembers, that he retains an infallible memory 'to the third and fourth, even to the hundredth generation.' The most sacred . . . act of the . . . ritual is the erasing of sins from the book of memory."

What has been forgotten—and this insight affords us yet another avenue of access to Kafka's work—is never something purely individual. Everything forgotten mingles with what has been forgotten of the prehistoric world, forms countless, uncertain, changing compounds, yielding a constant flow of new, strange products. Oblivion is the container from which the inexhaustible intermediate world in Kafka's stories presses toward the light. "Here the very fullness of the world is considered as the only reality. All spirit must be concrete, particularized in order to have its place and *raison d'être*. The spiritual, if it plays a role at all, turns into spirits. These spirits become definite individuals, with names and a very special connection with the name of the worshiper. . . . Without any scruples their fullness is crammed into the fullness of the world. . . . The crowd of spirits is swelled without any concern . . . new ones are constantly added to the old ones, and all are distinguished from the others by their own names." All this does not refer to Kafka, but to—China. This is how Franz Rosenzweig describes the Chinese ancestor cult in his *Star of Redemption*. To Kafka, the world of his ancestors was as unfathomable as the world of realities was important for him, and we may be sure that, like the totem poles of primitive peoples, the world of ancestors took him down to the animals. Incidentally, Kafka is not the only writer for whom animals are the receptacles of the forgotten. In Tieck's profound story "Fair Eckbert," the forgotten name of a little dog, Strohmi, stands for a mysterious guilt. One can understand, then, that Kafka did not tire of picking up the forgotten from animals. They are not the goal, to be sure, but one cannot do without them. A case in point is the "hunger artist" who, "strictly speaking, was only an impediment on the way to the menagerie." Can one not see the animals in "The Burrow" or "The Giant Mole" ponder as they dig in? And yet this thinking is extremely flighty. Irresolutely it flits from one worry to the next, it nibbles at every anxiety with the fickleness of despair. Thus there are butterflies in Kafka, too. The guilt-ridden "Hunter Gracchus," who refuses to acknowledge his guilt, "has turned into a butterfly." "Don't laugh," says the hunter Gracchus. This much is certain: of all of Kafka's creatures, the animals have the greatest opportunity for reflection. What corruption is in the law, anxiety is in their thinking. It messes a situation up, yet it is the only hopeful thing about it. However, because the most forgotten alien land is one's own body, one can understand why Kafka called the cough that erupted from within him "the animal." It was the most advanced outpost of the great herd.

The strangest bastard which the prehistoric world has begotten with guilt in Kafka is Odradek [in "The Cares of a Family

Man"]. "At first sight it looks like a flat, star-shaped spool for thread, and it really seems to have thread wound around it; to be sure, they probably are only old, broken-off bits of thread that are knotted and tangled together, of all sorts and colors. But it is not just a spool, for a small wooden cross-bar sticks out of the middle of the star, and another small rod is joined to it at a right angle. With the aid of this latter rod on one side and one of the extensions of the star on the other, the whole thing can stand upright as if on two legs." Odradek "stays alternately in the attic, on the staircase, in the corridors, and in the hall." So it prefers the same places as the court of law which investigates guilt. Attics are the places of discarded, forgotten objects. Perhaps the necessity to appear before a court of justice gives rise to a feeling similar to that with which one approaches trunks in the attic which have been locked up for years. One would like to put off this chore till the end of time, just as K. regards his written defense as suitable "for occupying one's senile mind some day during retirement."

Odradek is the form which things assume in oblivion. They are distorted. The "cares of a family man," which no one can identify, are distorted; the bug, of which we know all too well that it represents Gregor Samsa, is distorted; the big animal, half lamb, half kitten, for which "the butcher's knife" might be "a release," is distorted. These Kafka figures are connected by a long series of figures with the prototype of distortion, the hunchback. Among the images in Kafka's stories, none is more frequent than that of the man who bows his head far down on his chest: the fatigue of the court officials, the noise affecting the doormen in the hotel, the low ceiling facing the visitors in the gallery. In the *Penal Colony* those in power use an archaic apparatus which engraves letters with curlicues on the backs of guilty men, multiplying the stabs and piling up the ornaments to the point where the back of the guilty man becomes clairvoyant and is able to decipher the writing from which he must derive the nature of his unknown guilt. It is the back on which this is incumbent. It was always this way with Kafka. Compare this early diary entry: "In order to be as heavy as possible, which I believe to be an aid to falling asleep, I had crossed my arms and put my hands on my shoulders, so that I lay there like a soldier with his pack." Quite palpably, being loaded down is here equated with forgetting, the forgetting of a sleeping man. The same symbol occurs in the folksong "The Little Hunchback." This little man is at home in distorted life; he will disappear with the coming of the Messiah, of whom a great rabbi once said that he did not wish to change the world by force, but would only make a slight adjustment in it.

> When I come into my room,
> My little bed to make,
> A little hunchback is in there,
> With laughter does he shake.

This is the laughter of Odradek, which is described as sounding "something like the rustling in falling leaves."

> When I kneel upon my stool
> And I want to pray,
> A hunchbacked man is in the room
> And he starts to say:
> My dear child, I beg of you,
> Pray for the little hunchback too.

So ends the folksong. In his depth Kafka touches the ground which neither "mythical divination" nor "existential theology" supplied him with. It is the core of folk tradition, the German as well as the Jewish. Even if Kafka did not pray—and this we do not know—he still possessed in the highest degree what Malebranche called "the natural prayer of the soul": attentiveness. And in this attentiveness he included all living creatures, as saints include them in their prayers.

SANCHO PANZA

In a Hasidic village, so the story goes, Jews were sitting together in a shabby inn one Sabbath evening. They were all local people, with the exception of one person no one knew, a very poor, ragged man who was squatting in a dark corner at the back of the room. All sorts of things were discussed, and then it was suggested that everyone should tell what wish he would make if one were granted him. One man wanted money; another wished for a son-in-law; a third dreamed of a new carpenter's bench; and so everyone spoke in turn. After they had finished, only the beggar in his dark corner was left. Reluctantly and hesitantly he answered the question. "I wish I were a powerful king reigning over a big country. Then, some night while I was asleep in my palace, an enemy would invade my country, and by dawn his horsemen would penetrate to my castle and meet with no resistance. Roused from my sleep, I wouldn't have time even to dress and I would have to flee in my shirt. Rushing over hill and dale and through forests day and night, I would finally arrive safely right here at the bench in this corner. This is my wish." The others exchanged uncomprehending glances. "And what good would this wish have done you?" someone asked. "I'd have a shirt," was the answer.

This story takes us right into the milieu of Kafka's world. No one says that the distortions which it will be the Messiah's mission to set right someday affect only our space; surely they are distortions of our time as well. Kafka must have had this in mind, and in this certainty he made the grandfather in "The Next Village" say: "Life is astonishingly short. As I look back over it, life seems so foreshortened to me that I can hardly understand, for instance, how a young man can decide to ride over to the next village without being afraid that, quite apart from accidents, even the span of a normal life that passes happily may be totally insufficient for such a ride." This old man's brother is the beggar whose "normal" life that "passes happily" does not even leave him time for a wish, but who is exempted from this wish in the abnormal, unhappy life, that is, the flight which he attempts in his story, and exchanges the wish for its fulfillment.

Among Kafka's creatures there is a clan which reckons with the brevity of life in a peculiar way. It comes from the "city in the south . . . of which it was said: 'People live there who—imagine!—don't sleep!'—'And why not?'—'Because they don't get tired.'—'Why don't they?'—'Because they are fools.'—'Don't fools get tired?'—'How could fools get tired?'" One can see that the fools are akin to the indefatigable assistants. But there is more to this clan. It is casually remarked of the faces of the assistants that they seem to be those of "grown-ups, perhaps even students." Actually, the students who appear in the strangest places in Kafka's works are the spokesmen for and leaders of this clan. "'But when do you sleep?' asked Karl, looking at the student in surprise. 'Oh, sleep!' said the student. 'I'll get some sleep when I'm finished with my studies.'" This reminds one of the reluctance with which children go to bed; after all, while they are asleep, something might happen that concerns them. "Don't forget the best!" We are familiar with this remark from a nebulous bunch of old stories, although it may not occur in any of them. But forgetting always involves the best, for it involves the possibility of redemption. "The idea of helping me is an illness and requires bed rest for a cure," ironically says the restlessly wandering ghost of the hunter Gracchus. While they study, the students are awake, and perhaps their being kept awake is the best thing about these studies. The hunger artist fasts, the doorkeeper is silent, and the students are awake. This is the veiled way in which the great rules of asceticism operate in Kafka.

Their crowning achievement is studying. Reverently Kafka unearths it from long-lost boyhood. "Not very unlike this—a long time ago—Karl had sat at home at his parents' table writing his homework, while his father read the newspaper or did bookkeeping and correspondence for some organization and his mother was busy sewing, drawing the thread high out of the material in her hand. To avoid disturbing his father, Karl used to put only his exercise book and his writing materials on the table, while he arranged the books he needed on chairs to the right and left of him. How quiet it had been there! How seldom strangers had entered that room!" Perhaps these studies had amounted to nothing. But they are very close to that nothing which alone makes it possible for something to be useful—that is, to the Tao. This is what Kafka was after with his desire "to hammer a table together with painstaking craftsmanship and, at the same time, to do nothing—not in such a way that someone could say 'Hammering is nothing to him,' but 'To him, hammering is real hammering and at the same time nothing,' which would have made the hammering even bolder, more determined, more real, and, if you like, more insane." This is the resolute, fanatical mien which students have when they study; it is the strangest mien imaginable. The scribes, the students, are out of breath; they fairly race along. "Often the official dictates in such a low voice that the scribe cannot even hear it sitting down; then he has to jump up, catch the dictation, quickly sit down again and write it down, then jump up again and so forth. How strange that is! It is almost incomprehensible!" It may be easier to understand this if one thinks of the actors in the Nature Theater. Actors have to catch their cues in a flash, and they resemble those assiduous people in other ways as well. Truly, for them "hammering is real hammering and at the same time nothing"—provided that this is part of their role. They study this role, and only a bad actor would forget a word or a movement. For the members of the Oklahoma troupe, however, the role is their earlier life; hence the "nature" in this Nature Theater. Its actors have been redeemed, but not so the student whom Karl watches silently on the balcony as he reads his book, "turning the pages, occasionally looking something up in another book which he always snatched up quick as a flash, and frequently making notes in a notebook, which he always did with his face surprisingly close to the paper."

Kafka does not grow tired of representing the *gestus* in this fashion, but he invariably does so with astonishment. K. has rightly been compared with the Good Soldier Schweik; the one is astonished at everything, the other at nothing. The invention of the film and the phonograph came in an age of maximum alienation of men from one another, of unpredictably intervening relationships which have become their only ones. Experiments have proved that a man does not recognize his own walk on the screen or his own voice on the phonograph. The situation of the subject in such experiments is Kafka's situation; this is what directs him to learning, where he may encounter fragments of his own existence, fragments that are still within the context of the role. He might catch hold of the lost *gestus* the way Peter

Schlemihl caught hold of the shadow he had sold. He might understand himself, but what an enormous effort would be required! It is a tempest that blows from the land of oblivion, and learning is a cavalry attack against it. Thus the beggar on the corner bench rides toward his past in order to catch hold of himself in the figure of the fleeing king. This ride, which is long enough for a life, corresponds to life, which is too short for a ride—". . . until one shed one's spurs, for there were no spurs, threw away the reins, for there were no reins, and barely saw the land before one as a smoothly mown heath, with the horse's neck and head already gone." This is the fulfillment of the fantasy about the blessed horseman who rushes toward the past on an untrammeled, happy journey, no longer a burden on his race horse. But accursed is the rider who is chained to his nag because he has set himself a goal for the future, even though it is as close as the coal cellar—accursed his animal, accursed both of them. "Seated on the bucket, my hands up on the handle, with the simplest kind of bridle, I propel myself with difficulty down the stairs; but once down below, my bucket ascends, superbly, superbly; camels lying flat on the ground do not rise any more handsomely as they shake themselves under the sticks of their drivers." There is no more hopeless vista than that of "the regions of the ice mountains" in which the bucket rider drops out of sight forever. From the "nethermost regions of death" blows the wind that is favorable to him, the same wind which so often blows from the prehistoric world in Kafka's works, and which also propels the boat of the hunter Gracchus. "At mysteries and sacrifices, among Greeks as well as barbarians," writes Plutarch, "it is taught that there must be two primary essences and two opposing forces, one of which points to the right and straight ahead, whereas the other turns around and drives back." Reversal is the direction of learning which transforms existence into writing. Its teacher is Bucephalus, "the new attorney," who takes the road back without the powerful Alexander—which means, rid of the onrushing conqueror. "His flanks free and unhampered by the thighs of a rider, under a quiet lamp far from the din of

Alexander's battles, he reads and turns the pages of our old books."

Werner Kraft once wrote an interpretation of this story. After giving careful attention to every detail of the text, Kraft notes: "Nowhere else in literature is there such a powerful and penetrating criticism of the myth in its full scope." According to Kraft, Kafka does not use the word "justice," yet it is justice which serves as the point of departure for his critique of the myth. But once we have reached this point, we are in danger of missing Kafka by stopping here. Is it really the law which could thus be invoked against the myth in the name of justice? No, as a legal scholar Bucephalus remains true to his origins, except that he does not seem to be practicing law—and this is probably something new, in Kafka's sense, for both Bucephalus and the bar. The law which is studied and not practiced any longer is the gate to justice.

The gate to justice is learning. And yet Kafka does not dare attach to this learning the promises which tradition has attached to the study of the Torah. His assistants are sextons who have lost their house of prayer, his students are pupils who have lost the Holy Writ. Now there is nothing to support them on their "untrammeled, happy journey." Kafka, however, has found the law of his journey—at least on one occasion he succeeded in bringing its breath-taking speed in line with the slow narrative pace that he presumably sought all his life. He expressed this in a little prose piece which is his most perfect creation not only because it is an interpretation.

"Without ever boasting of it, Sancho Panza succeeded in the course of years, by supplying a lot of romances of chivalry and adventure for the evening and night hours, in so diverting from him his demon, whom he later called Don Quixote, that his demon thereupon freely performed the maddest exploits, which, however, lacking a preordained object, which Sancho Panza himself was supposed to have been, did no one any harm. A free man, Sancho Panza philosophically followed Don Quixote on his crusades, perhaps out of a sense of responsibility, and thus enjoyed a great and profitable entertainment to the end of his days."

Sancho Panza, a sedate fool and clumsy assistant, sent his rider on ahead; Bucephalus outlived his. Whether it is a man or a horse is no longer so important, if only the burden is removed from the back.

Some Reflections on Kafka*

Kafka's work is an ellipse with foci that are far apart and are determined, on the one hand, by mystical experience (in particular, the experience of tradition) and, on the other, by the experience of the modern big-city dweller. In speaking of the experience of the big-city dweller, I have a variety of things in mind. On the one hand, I think of the modern citizen who knows that he is at the mercy of a vast machinery of officialdom whose functioning is directed by authorities that remain nebulous to the executive organs, let alone to the people they deal with. (It is known that one level of meaning in the novels, particularly in *The Trial*, is encompassed by this.) When I refer to the modern big-city dweller, I am speaking also of the contemporary of today's physicists. If one reads the following passage from Eddington's *The Nature of the Physical World*, one can virtually hear Kafka speak.

I am standing on the threshold about to enter a room. It is a com-

---

* This text is contained in a letter to Gerhard Scholem, dated June 12, 1938.

plicated business. In the first place I must shove against an atmosphere pressing with a force of fourteen pounds on every square inch of my body. I must make sure of landing on a plank travelling at twenty miles a second round the sun—a fraction of a second too early or too late, the plank would be miles away. I must do this whilst hanging from a round planet head outward into space, and with a wind of aether blowing at no one knows how many miles a second through every interstice of my body. The plank has no solidity of substance. To step on it is like stepping on a swarm of flies. Shall I not slip through? No, if I make the venture one of the flies hits me and gives a boost up again; I fall again and am knocked upwards by another fly; and so on. I may hope that the net result will be that I remain about steady; but if unfortunately I should slip through the floor or be boosted too violently up to the ceiling, the occurrence would be, not a violation of the laws of Nature, but a rare coincidence. . . .

Verily, it is easier for a camel to pass through the eye of a needle than for a scientific man to pass through a door. And whether the door be barn door or church door it might be wiser that he should consent to be an ordinary man and walk in rather than wait till all the difficulties involved in a really scientific ingress are resolved.*

In all of literature I know no passage which has the Kafka stamp to the same extent. Without any effort one could match almost every passage of this physical perplexity with sentences from Kafka's prose pieces, and there is much to indicate that in so doing many of the most "incomprehensible" passages would be accommodated. Therefore, if one says—as I have just said— that there was a tremendous tension between those of Kafka's experiences that correspond to present-day physics and his mystical ones, only a half-truth is stated. What is actually and in a very literal sense wildly incredible in Kafka is that this most recent world of experience was conveyed to him precisely by this mystical tradition. This, of course, could not have happened without devastating processes (to be discussed presently) within this tradition. The long and the short of it is that apparently an appeal had to be made to the forces of this tradition if an individual (by the name of Franz Kafka) was to be confronted with that reality of ours which realizes itself theoretically, for example, in modern

---

* Arthur Stanley Eddington, *The Nature of the Physical World*, New York–Cambridge, 1929, p. 342. Quoted by Benjamin in German translation.

physics, and practically in the technology of modern warfare. What I mean to say is that this reality can virtually no longer be experienced by an *individual,* and that Kafka's world, frequently of such playfulness and interlaced with angels, is the exact complement of his era which is preparing to do away with the inhabitants of this planet on a considerable scale. The experience which corresponds to that of Kafka, the private individual, will probably not become accessible to the masses until such time as they are being done away with.

Kafka lives in a *complementary* world. (In this he is closely related to Klee, whose work in painting is just as essentially *solitary* as Kafka's work is in literature.) Kafka offered the complement without being aware of what surrounded him. If one says that he perceived what was to come without perceiving what exists in the present, one should add that he perceived it essentially as an *individual* affected by it. His gestures of terror are given scope by the marvelous *margin* which the catastrophe will not grant us. But his experience was based solely on the tradition to which Kafka surrendered; there was no far-sightedness or "prophetic vision." Kafka listened to tradition, and he who listens hard does not see.

The main reason why this listening demands such effort is that only the most indistinct sounds reach the listener. There is no doctrine that one could absorb, no knowledge that one could preserve. The things that want to be caught as they rush by are not meant for anyone's ears. This implies a state of affairs which negatively characterizes Kafka's works with great precision. (Here a negative characterization probably is altogether more fruitful than a positive one.) Kafka's work presents a sickness of tradition. Wisdom has sometimes been defined as the epic side of truth. Such a definition stamps wisdom as inherent in tradition; it is truth in its haggadic consistency.

It is this consistency of truth that has been lost. Kafka was far from being the first to face this situation. Many had accommodated themselves to it, clinging to truth or whatever they happened to regard as truth and, with a more or less heavy heart, forgoing its transmissibility. Kafka's real genius was that he tried

something entirely new: he sacrificed truth for the sake of clinging to its transmissibility, its haggadic element. Kafka's writings
are by their nature parables. But it is their misery and their
beauty that they had to become *more* than parables. They do not
modestly lie at the feet of the doctrine, as the Haggadah lies at
the feet of the Halakah. Though apparently reduced to sub-
mission, they unexpectedly raise a mighty paw against it.

This is why, in regard to Kafka, we can no longer speak of
wisdom. Only the products of its decay remain. There are two:
one is the rumor about the true things (a sort of theological whis-
pered intelligence dealing with matters discredited and obsolete);
the other product of this diathesis is folly—which, to be sure, has
utterly squandered the substance of wisdom, but preserves its at-
tractiveness and assurance, which rumor invariably lacks. Folly
lies at the heart of Kafka's favorites—from Don Quixote via the
assistants to the animals. (Being an animal presumably meant to
him only to have given up human form and human wisdom from
a kind of shame—as shame may keep a gentleman who finds himself in a disreputable tavern from wiping his glass clean.) This
much Kafka was absolutely sure of: first, that someone must be
a fool if he is to help; second, that only a fool's help is real help.
The only uncertain thing is whether such help can still do a human being any good. It is more likely to help the angels (compare the passage about the angels who get something to do) who
could do without help. Thus, as Kafka puts it, there is an infinite amount of hope, but not for us. This statement really contains Kafka's hope; it is the source of his radiant serenity.

I transmit to you this somewhat dangerously compressed
image—in the manner of perspective reduction—with all the more
ease as you may sharpen it by means of the views I have developed from different aspects in my Kafka essay in the *Jüdische
Rundschau.** My main criticism of that study today is its apologetic character. To do justice to the figure of Kafka in its purity
and its peculiar beauty one must never lose sight of one thing:

* See the preceding essay.

it is the purity and beauty of a failure. The circumstances of this failure are manifold. One is tempted to say: once he was certain of eventual failure, everything worked out for him *en route* as in a dream. There is nothing more memorable than the fervor with which Kafka emphasized his failure.

What Is Epic Theater?

"There is nothing more pleasant than to lie on a sofa and read a novel," wrote a nineteenth-century narrator, indicating the great extent to which a work of fiction can relax the reader who is enjoying it. The common image of a man attending a theatrical performance is the opposite: one pictures a man who follows the action with every fiber of his being at rapt attention. The concept of the epic theater, originated by Brecht as the theoretician of his poetic practice, indicates above all that this theater desires an audience that is relaxed and follows the action without strain. This audience, to be sure, always appears as a collective, and this differentiates it from the reader, who is alone with his text. Also, this audience, being a collective, will usually feel impelled to react promptly. This reaction, according to Brecht, ought to be a well-considered and therefore a relaxed one—in short, the reaction of people who have an interest in the matter. Two objects are provided for this interest. The first is the action; it has to be such that the audience can keep a check on it at crucial places on the basis of its own experience. The second is the performance; it should be mounted artistically in a pellucid manner. (This manner of presentation is anything but artless; actually, it presupposes artistic sophistication and acumen on the part of the director.) Epic theater appeals to an interest group who "do not think without reason." Brecht does not lose sight of the masses, whose limited practice of thinking is probably described by this phrase. In the endeavor to interest the audience in the theater expertly, but definitely not by way of mere cultural involvement, a political will has prevailed.

THE PLOT

The epic theater purposes to "deprive the stage of its sensation derived from subject matter." Thus an old story will often do more for it than a new one. Brecht has considered the question of whether the incidents that are presented by the epic theater should not already be familiar. The theater would have the same relationship to the plot as a ballet teacher has to his pupil: his first task would be to loosen her joints to the greatest possible extent. This is how the Chinese theater actually proceeds. In his essay "The Fourth Wall of China" (*Life and Letters Today*, Vol. XV, No. 6, 1936), Brecht states what he owes to this theater. If the theater is to cast about for familiar events, "historical incidents would be the most suitable." Their epic extension through the style of acting, the placards and captions, is intended to purge them of the sensational.

In this vein Brecht takes the life of Galileo as the subject of his latest play. Brecht presents Galileo primarily as a great teacher who not only teaches a new physics, but does so in a new way. In his hands, experiments are not only an achievement of science, but a tool of pedagogy as well. The main emphasis of this play is not on Galileo's recantation; rather, the truly epic process must be sought in what is evident from the labeling of the penultimate scene: "1633 to 1642. As a prisoner of the Inquisition, Galileo continues his scientific work until his death. He succeeds in smuggling his main works out of Italy."

Epic theater is in league with the course of time in an entirely different way from that of the tragic theater. Because suspense belongs less to the outcome than to the individual events, this theater can cover the greatest spans of time. (The same is true of the earlier mystery plays. The dramaturgy of *Oedipus* or *The Wild Duck* constitutes the counterpole of epic dramaturgy.)

THE UNTRAGIC HERO

The French classical theater made room in the midst of the players for persons of rank, who had their armchairs on the open stage. To us this seems inappropriate. According to the concept of the "dramatic element" with which we are familiar, it seemed inappropriate to attach to the action on the stage a nonparticipating third party as a dispassionate observer or "thinker." Yet Brecht often had something like that in mind. One can go even further and say that Brecht made an attempt to make the thinker, or even the wise man, the hero of the drama. From this very point of view one can define his theater as epic theater. This attempt is taken furthest in the character of Galy Gay, the packer. Galy Gay, the protagonist of the play *A Man's a Man*, is nothing but an exhibit of the contradictions which make up our society. It may not be too bold to regard the wise man in the Brechtian sense as the perfect showcase of its dialectics. In any case, Galy Gay is a wise man. Plato already recognized the undramatic quality of that most excellent man, the sage. In his Dialogues he took him to the threshold of the drama; in his *Phaidon*, to the threshold of the passion play. The medieval Christ, who also represented the wise man (we find this in the Early Fathers), is the untragic hero *par excellence*. But in the secular drama of the West, too, the search for the untragic hero has never ceased. In always new ways, and frequently in conflict with its theoreticians, this drama has differed from the authentic—that is, the Greek—form of tragedy. This important but poorly marked road, which may here serve as the image of a tradition, went via Roswitha and the mystery plays in the Middle Ages, via Gryphius and Calderón in the Baroque age; later we may trace it in Lenz and Grabbe, and finally in Strindberg. Scenes in Shakespeare are its roadside monuments, and Goethe crosses it in the second part of *Faust.* It is a European road, but a German one as well—provided that we may speak of a road and not of a secret smugglers' path by which the legacy of the medieval and the Baroque drama has reached us. It is this mule track, neglected and overgrown, which comes to light today in the dramas of Brecht.

THE INTERRUPTION

Brecht differentiates his epic theater from the dramatic theater in the narrower sense, whose theory was formulated by Aristotle. Appropriately, Brecht introduces his art of the drama as non-Aristotelian, just as Riemann introduced a non-Euclidian geometry. This analogy may bring out the fact that it is not a matter of competition between the theatrical forms in question. Riemann eliminated the parallel postulate; Brecht's drama eliminated the Aristotelian catharsis, the purging of the emotions through empathy with the stirring fate of the hero.

The special character of the relaxed interest of the audience for which the performances of the epic theater are intended is the fact that hardly any appeal is made to the empathy of the spectators. Instead, the art of the epic theater consists in producing astonishment rather than empathy. To put it succinctly: instead of identifying with the characters, the audience should be educated to be astonished at the circumstances under which they function.

The task of the epic theater, according to Brecht, is not so much the development of actions as the representation of conditions. This presentation does not mean reproduction as the theoreticians of Naturalism understood it. Rather, the truly important thing is to discover the conditions of life. (One might say just as well: to alienate [*verfremden*] them.) This discovery (alienation) of conditions takes place through the interruption of happenings. The most primitive example would be a family scene. Suddenly a stranger enters. The mother was just about to seize a bronze bust and hurl it at her daughter; the father was in the act of opening the window in order to call a policeman. At that moment the stranger appears in the doorway. This means that the stranger is confronted with the situation as with a startling picture: troubled faces, an open window, the furniture in disarray. But there are eyes to which even more ordinary scenes of middle-class life look almost equally startling.

THE QUOTABLE GESTURE

In one of his didactic poems on dramatic art Brecht says: "The effect of every sentence was waited for and laid bare. And the waiting lasted until the crowd had carefully weighed our sentence." In short, the play was interrupted. One can go even further and remember that interruption is one of the fundamental devices of all structuring. It goes far beyond the sphere of art. To give only one example, it is the basis of quotation. To quote a text involves the interruption of its context. It is therefore understandable that the epic theater, being based on interruption, is, in a specific sense, a quotable one. There is nothing special about the quotability of its texts. It is different with the gestures which fit into the course of the play.

"Making gestures quotable" is one of the substantial achievements of the epic theater. An actor must be able to space his gestures the way a typesetter produces spaced type. This effect may be achieved, for instance, by an actor's quoting his own gesture on the stage. Thus we saw in *Happy End* how Carola Neher, acting a sergeant in the Salvation Army, sang, by way of proselytizing, a song in a sailors' tavern that was more appropriate there than it would have been in a church, and then had to quote this song and act out the gestures before a council of the Salvation Army. Similarly, in *The Measure Taken* the party tribunal is given not only the report of the comrades, but also the acting out of some of the gestures of the comrade they are accusing. What is a device of the subtlest kind in the epic theater generally becomes an immediate purpose in the specific case of the didactic play. Epic theater is by definition a gestic theater. For the more frequently we interrupt someone in the act of acting, the more gestures result.

THE DIDACTIC PLAY

In every instance, the epic theater is meant for the actors as much as for the spectators. The didactic play is a special case largely because it facilitates and suggests the interchange between audience and actors and vice versa through the extreme paucity of the mechanical equipment. Every spectator is enabled to become a participant. And it is indeed easier to play the "teacher" than the "hero."

In the first version of *Lindberghflug* (Lindbergh's Flight), which appeared in a periodical, the flier was still presented as a hero. That version was intended as his glorification. The second version—and this is revealing—owes its origin to the fact that Brecht revised himself. What enthusiasm there was on both continents on the days following this flight! But this enthusiasm petered out as a mere sensation. In *The Flight of the Lindberghs* Brecht endeavors to refract the spectrum of the "thrill" (*Erlebnis*) in order to derive from it the hues of "experience" (*Erfahrung*)—the experience that could be obtained only from Lindbergh's effort, not from the excitement of the public, and which was to be conveyed to "the Lindberghs."

T. E. Lawrence, the author of *The Seven Pillars of Wisdom*, wrote to Robert Graves when he joined the air force that such a step was for modern man what entering a monastery was for medieval man. In this remark we perceive the same tension that we find in *The Flight of the Lindberghs* and the later didactic plays. A clerical sternness is applied to instruction in a modern technique—here, that of aviation; later, that of the class struggle. This second application may be seen most fully in *Mother*. It was a particularly daring undertaking to keep a social drama free of the effects which empathy produces and which the audience was accustomed to. Brecht knew this and expressed it in an epistolary poem that he sent to a New York workingmen's theater when *Mother* was produced there. "We have been asked: Will a worker understand this? Will he be able to do without his accustomed opiate, his mental participation in someone else's uprising, the rise of others; the illusion which whips him up for a few hours and leaves him all the more exhausted, filled with vague memories and even vaguer hopes?"

THE ACTOR

Like the pictures in a film, epic theater moves in spurts. Its basic form is that of the shock with which the single, well-defined situations of the play collide. The songs, the captions, the lifeless conventions set off one situation from another. This brings about intervals which, if anything, impair the illusion of the audience and paralyze its readiness for empathy. These intervals are reserved for the spectators' critical reaction—to the actions of the players and to the way in which they are presented. As to the manner of presentation, the actor's task in the epic theater is to demonstrate through his acting that he is cool and relaxed. He too has hardly any use for empathy. For this kind of acting the "player" of the dramatic theater is not always fully prepared. Perhaps the most open-minded approach to epic theater is to think of it in terms of "putting on a show."

Brecht wrote: "The actor must show his subject, and he must show himself. Of course, he shows his subject by showing himself, and he shows himself by showing his subject. Although the two coincide, they must not coincide in such a way that the difference between the two tasks disappears." In other words: an actor should reserve for himself the possibility of stepping out of character artistically. At the proper moment he should insist on portraying a man who reflects about his part. It would be erroneous to think at such a moment of Romantic Irony, as employed by Tieck in his *Puss in Boots.* This irony has no didactic aim. Basically, it demonstrates only the philosophic sophistication of the author who, in writing his plays, always remembers that in the end the world may turn out to be a theater.

To what extent artistic and political interests coincide on the scene of epic theater will become manifest in the style of acting appropriate to this genre. A case in point is Brecht's cycle *The Private Life of the Master Race.* It is easy to see that if a German actor in exile were assigned the part of an SS man or a member of the People's Court, his feelings about it would be quite different from those of a devoted father and husband asked to portray Molière's Don Juan. For the former, empathy can hardly be regarded as an appropriate method, since he presumably cannot identify with the murderers of his fellow fighters. Another mode of performance, which calls for detachment, would in such cases be right and fitting and particularly successful. This is the epic stagecraft.

THEATER ON A DAIS

The aims of the epic theater can be defined more easily in terms of the stage than of a new drama. Epic theater allows for a circumstance which has been too little noticed. It may be called the filling in of the orchestra pit. The abyss which separates the players from the audience as it does the dead from the living; the abyss whose silence in a play heightens the sublimity, whose resonance in an opera heightens the intoxication—this abyss, of all elements of the theater the one that bears the most indelible traces of its ritual origin, has steadily decreased in significance. The stage is still raised, but it no longer rises from an unfathomable depth; it has become a dais. The didactic play and the epic theater are attempts to sit down on a dais.

On Some Motifs in Baudelaire

Baudelaire envisaged readers to whom the reading of lyric poetry would present difficulties. The introductory poem of the *Fleurs du mal* is addressed to these readers. Will power and the ability to concentrate are not their strong points; what they prefer is sensual pleasures; they are familiar with the "spleen" which kills interest and receptiveness. It is strange to come across a lyric poet who addresses himself to this, the least rewarding type of audience. There is of course a ready explanation for it. Baudelaire was anxious to be understood; he dedicates his book to kindred spirits. The poem addressed to the reader ends with the salutation: "*Hypocrite lecteur,—mon semblable,—mon frère!*" It might be more fruitful to put it another way and say: Baudelaire wrote a book which from the very beginning had little prospect of becoming an immediate popular success. The kind of reader he envisaged is described in the introductory poem, and this turned out to have been a far-sighted judgment. He was eventually to find the reader at whom his work was aimed. This situation, the fact, in other words, that the climate for lyric poetry has become increasingly inhospitable, is attested to, among other things, by three factors. In the first place, the lyric poet has ceased to represent the poet *per se*. He no longer is a "minstrel," as Lamartine still was; he has become a representative of a genre. (Verlaine is a concrete example of this specialization; Rimbaud must already be regarded as an esoteric figure, a poet who maintained an *ex officio* distance between his public and his work.) Secondly, there has been no success on a mass scale in lyric poetry since Baudelaire. (The lyric poetry of Victor Hugo was still able to set off powerful reverberations when it first appeared. In Germany, Heine's *Buch der Lieder* marks a watershed.) As a result, a third factor was the greater coolness of the public even toward the lyric poetry that had been handed down as part of its own cultural heritage. The period in question dates back roughly to the middle of the last century. Throughout it the fame of the *Fleurs du mal* has constantly spread. This book, which was expected to be read by the least indulgent of readers and which was at first read by few indulgent ones, has, over the decades, acquired the stature of a classic and become one of the most widely printed ones as well.

If conditions for a positive reception of lyric poetry have become less favorable, it is reasonable to assume that only in rare instances is lyric poetry in rapport with the experience of its readers. This may be due to a change in the structure of their experience. Even though one may approve of this development, one may be all the more hard put to it to say precisely in what respect there may have been a change. Thus one turns to philosophy for an answer, which brings one up against a strange situation. Since the end of the last century, philosophy has made a series of attempts to lay hold of the "true" experience as opposed to the kind that manifests itself in the standardized, denatured life of the civilized masses. It is customary to classify these efforts under the heading of a philosophy of life. Their point of departure, understandably enough, was not man's life in society. What they invoked was poetry, preferably nature, and, most recently, the age of myths. Dilthey's book *Das Erlebnis und die Dichtung* represents one of the earliest of these efforts which end with Klages and Jung; both made common cause with Fascism.

Towering above this literature is Bergson's early monumental work, *Matière et mémoire*. More than the others, it preserves links with empirical research. It is oriented toward biology. The title suggests that it regards the structure of memory as decisive for the philosophical pattern of experience. Experience is indeed a matter of tradition, in collective existence as well as private life. It is less the product of facts firmly anchored in memory than of a convergence in memory of accumulated and frequently unconscious data. It is, however, not at all Bergson's intention to attach any specific historical label to memory. On the contrary, he rejects any historical determination of memory. He thus manages above all to stay clear of that experience from which his own philosophy evolved or, rather, in reaction to which it arose. It was the inhospitable, blinding age of big-scale industrialism. In shutting out this experience the eye perceives an experience of a complementary nature in the form of its spontaneous afterimage, as it were. Bergson's philosophy represents an attempt to give the details of this afterimage and to fix it as a permanent record. His philosophy thus indirectly furnishes a clue to the experience which presented itself to Baudelaire's eyes in its undistorted version in the figure of his reader.

II

Matière et mémoire defines the nature of experience in the *durée* in such a way that the reader is bound to conclude that only a poet can be the adequate subject of such an experience. And it was indeed a poet who put Bergson's theory of experience to the test. Proust's work *À la Recherche du temps perdu* may be regarded as an attempt to produce experience synthetically, as Bergson imagines it, under today's conditions, for there is less and less hope that it will come into being naturally. Proust, incidentally, does not evade the question in his work. He even introduces a new factor, one that involves an immanent critique of Bergson. Bergson emphasized the antagonism between the *vita activa* and the specific *vita contemplativa* which arises from memory. But he leads us to believe that turning to the contemplative actualization of the stream of life is a matter of free choice. From the start Proust indicates his divergent view terminologically. To him, the *mémoire pure* of Bergson's theory becomes a *mémoire involontaire*. Proust immediately confronts this involuntary memory with a voluntary memory, one that is in the service of the intellect. The first pages of his great work are charged with making this relationship clear. In the reflection which introduces the term Proust tells us how poorly, for many years, he remembered the town of Combray in which, after all, he spent part of his childhood. One afternoon the taste of a kind of pastry called *madeleine* (which he later mentions often) transported him back to the past, whereas before then he had been limited to the promptings of a memory which obeyed the call of attentiveness. This he calls the *mémoire volontaire*, and it is its characteristic that the information which it gives about the past retains no trace of it. "It is the same with our own past. In vain we try to conjure it up again; the efforts of our intellect are futile." Therefore Proust, summing up, says that the past is "somewhere beyond the reach of the intellect, and unmistakably present in some material object (or in the sensation which such an object arouses in us), though we have no idea which one it is. As for that object, it depends entirely on chance whether we come upon it before we die or whether we never encounter it."

According to Proust, it is a matter of chance whether an individual forms an image of himself, whether he can take hold of his experience. It is by no means inevitable to be dependent on chance in this matter. Man's inner concerns do not have their issueless private character by nature. They do so only when he is increasingly unable to assimilate the data of the world around him by way of experience. Newspapers constitute one of many evidences of such an inability. If it were the intention of the press to have the reader assimilate the information it supplies as part of his own experience, it would not achieve its purpose. But its intention is just the opposite, and it is achieved: to isolate what happens from the realm in which it could affect the experience of the reader. The principles of journalistic information (freshness of the news, brevity, comprehensibility, and, above all, lack of connection between the individual news items) contribute as much to this as does the make-up of the pages and the paper's style. (Karl Kraus never tired of demonstrating the great extent to which the linguistic usage of newspapers paralyzed the imagination of their readers.) Another reason for the isolation of information from experience is that the former does not enter "tradition." Newspapers appear in large editions. Few readers can boast of any information which another reader may require of him.

Historically, the various modes of communication have competed with one another. The replacement of the older narration by information, of information by sensation, reflects the increasing atrophy of experience. In turn, there is a contrast between all these forms and the story, which is one of the oldest forms of communication. It is not the object of the story to convey a happening *per se*, which is the purpose of information; rather, it embeds it in the life of the storyteller in order to pass it on as experience to those listening. It thus bears the marks of the storyteller much as the earthen vessel bears the marks of the potter's hand.

Proust's eight-volume work conveys an idea of the efforts it took to restore the figure of the storyteller to the present generation. Proust undertook this assignment with magnificent consistency. From the outset this involved him in the primary task of resurrecting his own childhood. In saying that it was a matter of chance whether the problem could be solved at all, he gave the full measure of its difficulty. In connection with these reflections he coined the phrase *mémoire involontaire*. This concept bears the marks of the situation which gave rise to it; it is part of the inventory of the individual who is isolated in many ways. Where there is experience in the strict sense of the word, certain contents of the individual past combine with material of the collective past. The rituals with their ceremonies, their festivals (quite probably nowhere recalled in Proust's work) kept producing the amalgamation of these two elements of memory over and over again. They triggered recollection at certain times and remained handles of memory for a lifetime. In this way, voluntary and involuntary recollection lose their mutual exclusiveness.

I I I

In seeking a more substantial definition of what appears in Proust's *mémoire de l'intelligence* as a by-product of Bergson's theory, it is well to go back to Freud. In 1921 Freud published his essay *Beyond the Pleasure Principle*, which presents a correlation between memory (in the sense of the *mémoire involontaire*) and consciousness in the form of a hypothesis. The following remarks based on it are not intended to confirm it; we shall have to content ourselves with investigating the fruitfulness of this hypothesis in situations far removed from those which Freud had in mind when he wrote. Freud's pupils are more likely to have encountered such situations. Some of Reik's writings on his own theory of memory are in line with Proust's distinction between involuntary and voluntary recollection. "The function of remembrance [*Gedächtnis*]," Reik writes, "is the protection of impressions; memory [*Erinnerung*] aims at their disintegration. Remembrance is essentially conservative, memory is destructive." Freud's fundamental thought, on which these remarks are based, is formulated by the assumption that "consciousness comes into being at the site of a memory trace." (For our purposes, there is no substantial difference between the concepts *Erinnerung* and *Gedächtnis*, as used in Freud's essay.) Therefore, "it would be the special characteristic of consciousness that, unlike what happens in all other psychical systems, the excitatory process does not leave behind a permanent change in its elements, but expires, as it were, in the phenomenon of becoming conscious." The basic formula of this hypothesis is that "becoming conscious and leaving behind a memory trace are processes incompatible with each other within one and the same system." Rather, memory fragments are "often most powerful and most enduring when the incident which left them behind was one that never entered consciousness." Put in Proustian terms, this means that only what has not been experienced explicitly and consciously, what has not happened to the subject as an experience, can become a component of the *mémoire involontaire*. According to Freud, the attribution of "permanent traces as the basis of memory" to processes of stimulation is reserved for "other systems," which must be thought of as different from consciousness. In Freud's view, consciousness as such receives no memory traces whatever, but has another important function: protection against stimuli. "For a living organism, protection against stimuli is an almost more important function than the reception of stimuli; the protective shield is equipped with its own store of energy and must above all strive to preserve the special forms of conversion of energy operating in it against the effects of the excessive energies at work in the external world, effects which tend toward an equalization of potential and hence toward destruction." The threat from these energies is one of shocks. The more readily consciousness registers these shocks, the less likely are they to have a traumatic effect. Psychoanalytic theory strives to understand the nature of these traumatic shocks "on the basis of their breaking through the protective shield against stimuli." According to this theory, fright has "significance" in the "absence of any preparedness for anxiety."

Freud's investigation was occasioned by a dream characteristic of accident neuroses which reproduce the catastrophe in which the patient was involved. Dreams of this kind, according to Freud, "endeavor to master the stimulus retroactively, by developing the anxiety whose omission was the cause of the traumatic neurosis." Valéry seems to have had something similar in mind. The coincidence is worth noting, for Valéry was among those interested in the special functioning of psychic mechanisms under present-day conditions. (Moreover, Valéry was able to reconcile this interest with his poetic production, which remained exclusively lyric. He thus emerges as the only author who goes back directly to Baudelaire.) "The impressions and sense perceptions of man," Valéry writes, "actually belong in the category of surprises; they are evidence of an insufficiency in man. . . . Recollection is . . . an elemental phenomenon which aims at giving us the time for organizing the reception of stimuli which we initially lacked." The acceptance of shocks is facilitated by training in coping with stimuli, and, if need be, dreams as well as recollection may be enlisted. As a rule, however—so Freud assumes—this training devolves upon the wakeful consciousness, located in a part of the cortex which is "so blown out by the effect of the stimulus" that it offers the most favorable situation for the reception of stimuli. That the shock is thus cushioned, parried by consciousness, would lend the incident that occasions it the character of having been lived in the strict sense. If it were incorporated directly in the registry of conscious memory, it would sterilize this incident for poetic experience.

The question suggests itself how lyric poetry can have as its basis an experience for which the shock experience has become the norm. One would expect such poetry to have a large measure of consciousness; it would suggest that a plan was at work in its composition. This is indeed true of Baudelaire's poetry; it establishes a connection between him and Poe, among his predecessors, and with Valéry, among his successors. Proust's and Valéry's reflections concerning Baudelaire complement each other providentially. Proust wrote an essay about Baudelaire the significance of which is even exceeded by certain reflections in his novels. In his "Situation de Baudelaire" Valéry supplies the classical introduction to the *Fleurs du mal.* There he says: "The problem for Baudelaire was bound to be this: to become a great poet, yet neither Lamartine nor Hugo nor Musset. I do not claim that this ambition was a conscious one in Baudelaire; but it was bound to be present in him, it was his reason of state." There is something odd about speaking of a reason of state in the case of a poet; there is something remarkable about it: the emancipation from experiences. Baudelaire's poetic output is assigned a mission. He envisioned blank spaces which he filled in with his poems. His work cannot merely be categorized as historical, like anyone else's, but it intended to be so and understood itself as such.

IV

The greater the share of the shock factor in particular impressions, the more constantly consciousness has to be alert as a screen against stimuli; the more efficiently it does so, the less do these impressions enter experience (*Erfahrung*), tending to remain in the sphere of a certain hour in one's life (*Erlebnis*). Perhaps the special achievement of shock defense may be seen in its function of assigning to an incident a precise point in time in consciousness at the cost of the integrity of its contents. This would be a peak achievement of the intellect; it would turn the incident into a moment that has been lived (*Erlebnis*). Without reflection there would be nothing but the sudden start, usually the sensation of fright which, according to Freud, confirms the failure of the shock defense. Baudelaire has portrayed this condition in a harsh image. He speaks of a duel in which the artist, just before being beaten, screams in fright. This duel is the creative process itself. Thus Baudelaire placed the shock experience at the very center of his artistic work. This self-portrait, which is corroborated by evidence from several contemporaries, is of great significance. Since he is himself exposed to fright, it is not unusual for Baudelaire to occasion fright. Vallès tells us about his eccentric grimaces; on the basis of a portrait by Nargeot, Pontmartin establishes Baudelaire's alarming appearance; Claudel stresses the cutting quality he could give to his speech; Gautier speaks of the italicizing Baudelaire indulged in when reciting poetry; Nadar describes his jerky gait.

Psychiatry knows traumatophile types. Baudelaire made it his business to parry the shocks, no matter where they might come from, with his spiritual and his physical self. This shock defense is depicted graphically in an attitude of combat. Baudelaire describes his friend Constantin Guys, whom he visits when Paris is asleep: ". . . how he stands there, bent over his table, scrutinizing the sheet of paper just as intently as he does the objects around him by day; how he *stabs away* with his pencil, his pen, his brush; how he spurts water from his glass to the ceiling and tries his pen on his shirt; how he pursues his work swiftly and intensely, as though he were afraid that his images might escape him; thus he is combative, even when alone, and parries his own blows." In the opening stanza of his poem "Le Soleil" Baudelaire has pictured himself engaged in such a fantastic combat; this is probably the only place in *Les Fleurs du mal* that shows the poet at work.

> Le long du vieux faubourg, où pendent aux masures
> Les persiennes, abri des secrètes luxures,
> Quand le soleil cruel frappe à traits redoublés
> Sur la ville et les champs, sur les toits et les blés,
> Je vais m'exercer seul à ma fantasque escrime,
> Flairant dans tous les coins les hasards de la rime,
> Trébuchant sur les mots comme sur les pavés,
> Heurtant parfois des vers depuis longtemps rêvés.*

Shock is among those experiences that have assumed decisive importance for Baudelaire's personality. Gide has dealt with the interstices between image and idea, word and thing, which are the real site of Baudelaire's poetic excitation. Rivière has pointed to the subterranean shocks by which Baudelaire's poetry is shaken; it is as though they caused words to collapse. Rivière has indicated such collapsing words.

> Et qui sait si les fleurs nouvelles que je rêve
> Trouveront dans ce sol lavé comme une grève
> Le mystique aliment qui *ferait* leur vigueur.†

Or:

> Cybèle, qui les aime, *augmente ses verdures.*‡

* Along the old faubourg where the masonry is tented by
  Shutters, sheltering secret pleasures,
  When the cruel sun's redoubled beams
  Are lashing city and field, roofs and grain,
  I go, alone, to practice my curious fencing,
  In every corner smelling out the dodges of rhyme,
  Stumbling over words as over cobblestones,
  Colliding now and then with long-dreamed-of verses.

† And who knows whether my dreams' new flowers
  Will find within this soil, washed like a shore,
  The mystic nourishment that would give them strength?

‡ Cybele, who loves them, augments her verdure.

Another example is this famous first line:

La servante au grand coeur dont vous étiez *jalouse*.*

To give these covert laws their due outside his verses as well was Baudelaire's intention in his *Spleen de Paris*, his prose poems. In the dedication of his collection to the editor-in-chief of *La Presse*, Arsène Houssaye, Baudelaire wrote: "Who among us has not dreamt, in his ambitious days, of the miracle of a poetic prose? It would have to be musical without rhythm and rhyme, supple and resistant enough to adapt itself to the lyrical stirrings of the soul, the wave motions of dreaming, the shocks of consciousness. This ideal, which can turn into an *idée fixe*, will grip especially those who are at home in the giant cities and the web of their numberless interconnecting relationships."

This passage suggests two insights. For one thing, it tells us about the close connection in Baudelaire between the figure of shock and contact with the metropolitan masses. For another, it tells us what is really meant by these masses. They do not stand for classes or any sort of collective; rather, they are nothing but the amorphous crowd of passers-by, the people in the street.[1] This crowd, of whose existence Baudelaire is always aware, has not served as the model for any of his works, but it is imprinted on his creativity as a hidden figure, just as it constitutes the figure concealed in the fragment quoted before. We may discern the image of the fencer in it; the blows he deals are designed to open a path through the crowd for him. To be sure, the *faubourgs* through which the poet of "Le Soleil" makes his way are deserted. But the meaning of the hidden configuration (which reveals the beauty of that stanza to its very depth) probably is this: it is the phantom crowd of the words, the fragments, the beginnings of lines from which the poet, in the deserted streets, wrests the poetic booty.

* That magnanimous servant of whom you were jealous.

V

The crowd—no subject was more entitled to the attention of nineteenth-century writers. It was getting ready to take shape as a public in broad strata who had acquired facility in reading. It became a customer; it wished to find itself portrayed in the contemporary novel, as the patrons did in the paintings of the Middle Ages. The most successful author of the century met this demand out of inner necessity. To him, crowd meant—almost in the ancient sense—the crowd of the clients, the public. Victor Hugo was the first to address the crowd in his titles: *Les Misérables, Les Travailleurs de la mer*. In France, Hugo was the only writer able to compete with the serial novel. As is generally known, Eugène Sue was the master of this genre, which began to be the source of revelation for the man in the street. In 1850 an overwhelming majority elected him to Parliament as representative of the city of Paris. It is no accident that the young Marx chose Sue's *Les Mystères de Paris* for an attack. He early recognized it as his task to forge the amorphous mass, which was then being wooed by an aesthetic socialism, into the iron of the proletariat. Engels' description of these masses in his early writings may be regarded as a prelude, however modest, to one of Marx's themes. In his book *The Condition of the Working Class in England*, Engels writes: "A city like London, where one can roam about for hours without reaching the beginning of an end, without seeing the slightest indication that open country is nearby, is really something very special. This colossal centralization, this agglomeration of three and a half million people on a single spot has multiplied the strength of these three and a half million inhabitants a hundredfold. . . . But the price that has been paid is not discovered until later. Only when one has tramped the pavements of the main streets for a few days does one notice that these Londoners have had to sacrifice what is best in human nature in order to create all the wonders of civilization with which their city teems, that a hundred creative faculties that lay dormant in them remained inactive and were suppressed. . . . There is something distasteful about the very bustle of the streets, something that is abhorrent to human nature itself. Hundreds of thousands of people of all classes and ranks of society jostle past one another; are they not all human beings with the same characteristics and potentialities, equally interested in the pursuit of happiness? . . . And yet they rush past one another as if they had nothing in common or were in no way associated with one another. Their only agreement is a tacit one: that everyone should keep to the right of the pavement, so as not to impede the stream of people moving in the opposite direction. No one even bothers to spare a glance for the others. The greater the number of people that are packed into a tiny space, the more repulsive and offensive becomes the brutal indifference, the unfeeling concentration of each person on his private affairs."

This description differs markedly from those to be found in minor French masters, such as Gozlan, Delvau, or Lurine. It lacks the skill and ease with which the *flâneur* moves among the crowd and which the journalist eagerly learns from him. Engels is dismayed by the crowd; he responds with a moral reaction, and an aesthetic one as well; the speed with which people rush past one another unsettles him. The charm of his description lies in the intersecting of unshakable critical integrity with an old-fashioned attitude. The writer came from a Germany that was still provincial; he may never have faced the temptation to lose himself in a stream of people. When Hegel went to Paris for the first time not long before his death, he wrote to his wife: "When I walk through the streets, people look just as they do in Berlin; they wear the same clothes and the faces are about the same—the same aspect, but in a large crowd." To move in this crowd was natural for a Parisian. No matter how great the distance which an individual cared to keep from it, he still was colored by it and, unlike Engels, was not able to view it from without. As regards Baudelaire, the masses were anything but external to him; indeed, it is easy to trace in his works his defensive reaction to their attraction and allure.

The masses had become so much a part of Baudelaire that it is rare to find a description of them in his works. His most important subjects are hardly ever encountered in descriptive form.

As Dujardin so aptly put it, he was "more concerned with implanting the image in the memory than with adorning and elaborating it." It is futile to search in *Les Fleurs du mal* or in *Spleen de Paris* for any counterpart to the portrayals of the city which Victor Hugo did with such mastery. Baudelaire describes neither the Parisians nor their city. Forgoing such descriptions enables him to invoke the ones in the form of the other. His crowd is always the crowd of a big city, his Paris is invariably overpopulated. It is this that makes him so superior to Barbier, whose descriptive method caused a rift between the masses and the city.[2] In *Tableaux parisiens* the secret presence of a crowd is demonstrable almost everywhere. When Baudelaire takes the dawn as his theme, the deserted streets emanate something of that "silence of a throng" which Hugo senses in nocturnal Paris. As Baudelaire looks at the plates in the anatomical works for sale on the dusty banks of the Seine, the mass of the departed takes the place of the singular skeletons on these pages. In the figures of the *danse macabre*, he sees a compact mass on the move. The heroism of the wizened old women whom the cycle "Les petites vieilles" follows on their rounds, consists in their standing apart from the crowd, unable to keep its pace, no longer participating with their thoughts in the present. The mass was the agitated veil; through it Baudelaire saw Paris. The presence of the mass determines one of the most famous components of *Les Fleurs du mal*.

In the sonnet "À une passante" the crowd is nowhere named in either word or phrase. And yet the whole happening hinges on it, just as the progress of a sailboat depends on the wind.

> La rue assourdissante autour de moi hurlait.
> Longue, mince, en grand deuil, douleur majestueuse,
> Une femme passa, d'une main fastueuse
> Soulevant, balançant le feston et l'ourlet;
>
> Agile et noble, avec sa jambe de statue.
> Moi, je buvais, crispé comme un extravagant,
> Dans son oeil, ciel livide où germe l'ouragan,
> La douceur qui fascine et le plaisir qui tue.

Un éclair . . . puis la nuit!—Fugitive beauté
Dont le regard m'a fait soudainement renaître,
Ne te verrai-je plus que dans l'éternité?

Ailleurs, bien loin d'ici! Trop tard! *Jamais* peut-être!
Car j'ignore où tu fuis, tu ne sais où je vais,
O toi que j'eusse aimée, ô toi qui le savais! *

In a widow's veil, mysteriously and mutely borne along by
the crowd, an unknown woman comes into the poet's field of
vision. What this sonnet communicates is simply this: Far from
experiencing the crowd as an opposed, antagonistic element, this
very crowd brings to the city dweller the figure that fascinates.
The delight of the urban poet is love—not at first sight, but at
last sight. It is a farewell forever which coincides in the poem
with the moment of enchantment. Thus the sonnet supplies the
figure of shock, indeed of catastrophe. But the nature of the
poet's emotions has been affected as well. What makes his body
contract in a tremor—*crispé comme un extravagant*, Baudelaire
says—is not the rapture of a man whose every fiber is suffused
with *eros*; it is, rather, like the kind of sexual shock that can
beset a lonely man. The fact that "these verses could only have
been written in a big city," as Thibaudet put it, is not very meaningful. They reveal the stigmata which life in a metropolis in-
flicts upon love. Proust read the sonnet in this light, and that is
why he gave his later echo of the woman in mourning, which

* The deafening street was screaming all around me.
  Tall, slender, in deep mourning—majestic grief—
  A woman made her way, with fastidious hand
  Raising and swaying festoon and hem;

  Agile and noble, with her statue's limbs.
  And there was I, who drank, contorted like a madman,
  Within her eyes—that livid sky where hurricane is born—
  Gentleness that fascinates, pleasure that kills.

  A lightning-flash . . . then night!—O fleeting beauty
  Whose glance all of a sudden gave me new birth,
  Shall I see you again only in eternity?

  Far, far from here! Too late! or maybe, *never?*
  For I know not where you flee, you know not where I go,
  O you I would have loved (o you who knew it too!)

appeared to him one day in the form of Albertine, the evocative caption "La Parisienne." "When Albertine came into my room again, she wore a black satin dress. It made her pale, and she resembled the type of the fiery and yet pale Parisian woman, the woman who is not used to fresh air and has been affected by living among masses and possibly in an atmosphere of vice, the kind that can be recognized by a certain glance which seems unsteady if there is no rouge on her cheeks." This is the look—even as late as Proust—of the object of a love which only a city dweller experiences, which Baudelaire captured for poetry, and of which one might not infrequently say that it was spared, rather than denied, fulfillment.[3]

V I

A story by Poe which Baudelaire translated may be regarded as the classic example among the older versions of the motif of the crowd. It is marked by certain peculiarities which, upon closer inspection, reveal aspects of social forces of such power and hidden depth that we may count them among those which alone are capable of exerting both a subtle and a profound effect upon artistic production. The story is entitled "The Man of the Crowd." Set in London, its narrator is a man who, after a long illness, ventures out again for the first time into the hustle and bustle of the city. In the late afternoon hours of an autumn day he installs himself behind a window in a big London coffeehouse. He looks over the other guests, pores over advertisements in the paper, but his main focus of interest is the throng of people surging past his window in the street. "The latter is one of the principal thoroughfares of the city, and had been very much crowded during the whole day. But, as the darkness came on, the throng momently increased; and by the time the lamps were well lighted, two dense and continuous tides of population were rushing past the door. At this particular period of the evening I had never before been in a similar situation, and the tumultuous sea of human heads filled me, therefore, with a delicious novelty of emotion. I gave up, at length, all care of things within the hotel, and became absorbed in contemplation of the scene without." Important as it is, let us disregard the narrative to which this is the prelude and examine the setting.

The appearance of the London crowd as Poe describes it is as gloomy and fitful as the light of the gas lamps overhead. This applies not only to the riffraff that is "brought forth from its den" as night falls. The employees of higher rank, "the upper clerks of staunch firms," Poe describes as follows: "They had all slightly bald heads, from which the right ears, long used to pen-holding, had an odd habit of standing off on end. I observed that they always removed or settled their hats with both hands, and wore watches, with short gold chains of a substantial and ancient pattern." Even more striking is his description of the crowd's movements. "By far the greater number of those who went by had a satisfied business-like demeanour, and seemed to be thinking only of making their way through the press. Their brows were knit, and their eyes rolled quickly; when pushed against by fellow-wayfarers they evinced no symptom of impatience, but adjusted their clothes and hurried on. Others, still a numerous class, were restless in their movements, had flushed faces, and talked and gesticulated to themselves, as if feeling in solitude on account of the very denseness of the company around. When impeded in their progress, these people suddenly ceased muttering, but redoubled their gesticulations, and awaited, with an absent and overdone smile upon the lips, the course of the persons impeding them. If jostled, they bowed profusely to the jostlers, and appeared overwhelmed with confusion." [4] One might think he was speaking of half-drunken wretches. Actually, they were "noblemen, merchants, attorneys, tradesmen, stock-jobbers." [5]

Poe's manner of presentation cannot be called realism. It shows a purposely distorting imagination at work, one that removes the text far from what is commonly advocated as the model of social realism. Barbier, perhaps one of the best examples of this type of realism that come to mind, describes things in a less eccentric way. Moreover, he chose a more transparent subject: the oppressed masses. Poe is not concerned with these; he deals with "people," pure and simple. For him, as for Engels, there was something menacing in the spectacle they presented. It is precisely this image of big-city crowds that became decisive for Baudelaire. If he succumbed to the force by which he was drawn to them and, as a *flâneur*, was made one of them, he was nevertheless unable to rid himself of a sense of their essentially inhuman make-up. He becomes their accomplice even as he dissociates himself from them. He becomes deeply involved with them, only to relegate them to oblivion with a single glance of contempt. There is something compelling about this ambivalence where he cautiously admits to it. Perhaps the charm of his "Crépuscule du soir," so difficult to account for, is bound up with this.

VII

Baudelaire saw fit to equate the man of the crowd, whom Poe's narrator follows throughout the length and breadth of nocturnal London, with the *flâneur*. It is hard to accept this view. The man of the crowd is no *flâneur*. In him, composure has given way to manic behavior. Hence he exemplifies, rather, what had to become of the *flâneur* once he was deprived of the milieu to which he belonged. If London ever provided it for him, it was certainly not the setting described by Poe. In comparison, Baudelaire's Paris preserved some features that dated back to the happy old days. Ferries were still crossing the Seine at points that would later be spanned by the arch of a bridge. In the year of Baudelaire's death it was still possible for some entrepreneur to cater to the comfort of the well-to-do with a fleet of five hundred sedan chairs circulating about the city. Arcades where the *flâneur* would not be exposed to the sight of carriages that did not recognize pedestrians as rivals were enjoying undiminished popularity.[6] There was the pedestrian who would let himself be jostled by the crowd, but there was also the *flâneur* who demanded elbow room and was unwilling to forgo the life of a gentleman of leisure. Let the many attend to their daily affairs; the man of leisure can indulge in the perambulations of the *flâneur* only if as such he is already out of place. He is as much

out of place in an atmosphere of complete leisure as in the fever-
ish turmoil of the city. London has its man of the crowd. His
counterpart, as it were, is the boy Nante [Ferdinand], of the
street corner, a popular figure in Berlin before the March Revolution of 1848; the Parisian *flâneur* might be said to stand midway between them.[7]

How the man of leisure looks upon the crowd is revealed in
a short piece by E. T. A. Hoffmann, the last that he wrote, entitled "The Cousin's Corner Window." It antedates Poe's story
by fifteen years and probably is one of the earliest attempts to
capture the street scene of a large city. The differences between
the two pieces are worth noting. Poe's narrator observes from
behind the window of a public coffeehouse, whereas the cousin
is installed at home. Poe's observer succumbs to the fascination
of the scene, which finally lures him outside into the whirl of the
crowd. Hoffmann's cousin, looking out from his corner window,
is immobilized as a paralytic; he would not be able to follow the
crowd even if he were in the midst of it. His attitude toward the
crowd is, rather, one of superiority, inspired as it is by his observation post at the window of an apartment building. From
this vantage point he scrutinizes the throng; it is market day, and
they all feel in their element. His opera glasses enable him to
pick out individual genre scenes. The employment of this instrument is thoroughly in keeping with the inner disposition of its
user. He would like, as he admits, to initiate his visitor into the
"principles of the art of seeing." [8] This consists of an ability to
enjoy *tableaux vivants*—a favorite pursuit of the Biedermeier period. Edifying sayings provide the interpretation.[9] One can look
upon the narrative as an attempt which was then due to be
made. But it is obvious that the conditions under which it was
made in Berlin prevented it from being a complete success. If
Hoffmann had ever set foot in Paris or London, or if he had been
intent upon depicting the masses as such, he would not have
focused on a market place; he would not have portrayed the
scene as being dominated by women; he would perhaps have
seized on the motifs that Poe derives from the swarming crowds
under the gas lamps. Actually, there would have been no need

for these motifs in order to bring out the uncanny elements that other students of the physiognomy of the big city have felt. A thoughtful observation by Heine is relevant here: "Heine's eyesight," wrote a correspondent in a letter to Varnhagen in 1838, "caused him acute trouble in the spring. On the last such occasion I was walking down one of the boulevards with him. The magnificence, the life of this in its way unique thoroughfare roused me to boundless admiration, something that prompted Heine this time to make a significant point in stressing the horror with which this center of the world was tinged."

VIII

Fear, revulsion, and horror were the emotions which the big-city crowd aroused in those who first observed it. For Poe it has something barbaric; discipline just barely manages to tame it. Later, James Ensor tirelessly confronted its discipline with its wildness; he liked to put military groups in his carnival mobs, and both got along splendidly—as the prototype of totalitarian states, in which the police make common cause with the looters. Valéry, who had a fine eye for the cluster of symptoms called "civilization," has characterized one of the pertinent facts. "The inhabitant of the great urban centers," he writes, "reverts to a state of savagery—that is, of isolation. The feeling of being dependent on others, which used to be kept alive by need, is gradually blunted in the smooth functioning of the social mechanism. Any improvement of this mechanism eliminates certain modes of behavior and emotions." Comfort isolates; on the other hand, it brings those enjoying it closer to mechanization. The invention of the match around the middle of the nineteenth century brought forth a number of innovations which have one thing in common: one abrupt movement of the hand triggers a process of many steps. This development is taking place in many areas. One case in point is the telephone, where the lifting of a receiver has taken the place of the steady movement that used to be required to crank the older models. Of the countless movements of switching, inserting, pressing, and the like, the "snapping" of the photographer has had the greatest consequences. A touch of the finger now sufficed to fix an event for an unlimited period of time. The camera gave the moment a posthumous shock, as it were. Haptic experiences of this kind were joined by optic ones, such as are supplied by the advertising pages of a newspaper or the traffic of a big city. Moving through this traffic involves the individual in a series of shocks and collisions. At dangerous intersections, nervous impulses flow through him in rapid succession, like the energy from a battery. Baudelaire speaks of a man who plunges into the crowd as into a reservoir of electric energy. Circumscribing the experience of the shock, he calls this man "a *kaleidoscope* equipped with consciousness." Whereas Poe's passers-by cast glances in all directions which still appeared to be aimless, today's pedestrians are obliged to do so in order to keep abreast of traffic signals. Thus technology has subjected the human sensorium to a complex kind of training. There came a day when a new and urgent need for stimuli was met by the film. In a film, perception in the form of shocks was established as a formal principle. That which determines the rhythm of production on a conveyor belt is the basis of the rhythm of reception in the film.

Marx had good reason to stress the great fluidity of the connection between segments in manual labor. This connection appears to the factory worker on an assembly line in an independent, objectified form. Independently of the worker's volition, the article being worked on comes within his range of action and moves away from him just as arbitrarily. "It is a common characteristic of all capitalist production . . . ," wrote Marx, "that the worker does not make use of the working conditions. The working conditions make use of the worker; but it takes machinery to give this reversal a technically concrete form." In working with machines, workers learn to co-ordinate "their own movements with the uniformly constant movements of an automaton." These words shed a peculiar light on the absurd kind of uniformity with which Poe wants to saddle the crowd—uniformities of attire and behavior, but also a uniformity of facial expression. Those smiles provide food for thought. They are probably the

familiar kind, as expressed in the phrase "keep smiling"; in that
context they function as a mimetic shock absorber. "All machine
work," it is said in the above context, "requires early drilling of
the worker." This drill must be differentiated from practice.
Practice, which was the sole determinant in craftsmanship, still
had a function in manufacturing. With it as the basis, "each particular area of production finds its appropriate technical form
in *experience* and *slowly* perfects it." To be sure, it quickly crys-
tallizes it, "as soon as a certain degree of maturity has been attained." On the other hand, this same manufacturing produces
"in every handicraft it seizes a class of so-called unskilled laborers which the handicraft system strictly excluded. In developing
the greatly simplified specialty to the point of virtuosity at the
cost of the work capacity as a whole, it starts turning the lack of
any development into a specialty. In addition to ranks we get
the simple division of workers into the skilled and the unskilled."
The unskilled worker is the one most deeply degraded by the
drill of the machines. His work has been sealed off from experience; practice counts for nothing there.[10] What the Fun Fair
achieves with its Dodgem cars and other similar amusements is
nothing but a taste of the drill to which the unskilled laborer is
subjected in the factory—a sample which at times was for him
the entire menu; for the art of being off center, in which the
little man could acquire training in places like the Fun Fair, flour-
ished concomitantly with unemployment. Poe's text makes us
understand the true connection between wildness and discipline.
His pedestrians act as if they had adapted themselves to the machines and could express themselves only automatically. Their
behavior is a reaction to shocks. "If jostled, they bowed profusely to the jostlers."

IX

The shock experience which the passer-by has in the crowd
corresponds to what the worker "experiences" at his machine.
This does not entitle us to the assumption that Poe knew anything about industrial work processes. Baudelaire, at any rate,

did not have the faintest notion of them. He was, however, captivated by a process whereby the reflecting mechanism which the machine sets off in the workman can be studied closely, as in a mirror, in the idler. If we say that this process is the game of chance, the statement may appear to be paradoxical. Where would one find a more evident contrast than the one between work and gambling? Alain puts it convincingly when he writes: "It is inherent in the concept of gambling . . . that no game is dependent on the preceding one. Gambling cares about no assured position. . . . Winnings secured earlier are not taken into account, and in this it differs from work. Gambling gives short shrift to the weighty past on which work bases itself." The work which Alain has in mind here is the highly specialized kind (which, like intellectual effort, probably retains certain features of handicraft); it is not that of most factory workers, least of all the work of the unskilled. The latter, to be sure, lacks any touch of adventure, of the mirage that lures the gambler. But it certainly does not lack the futility, the emptiness, the inability to complete something which is inherent in the activity of a wage slave in a factory. Gambling even contains the workman's gesture that is produced by the automatic operation, for there can be no game without the quick movement of the hand by which the stake is put down or a card is picked up. The jolt in the movement of a machine is like the so-called *coup* in a game of chance. The manipulation of the worker at the machine has no connection with the preceding operation for the very reason that it is its exact repetition. Since each operation at the machine is just as screened off from the preceding operation as a *coup* in a game of chance is from the one that preceded it, the drudgery of the laborer is, in its own way, a counterpart to the drudgery of the gambler. The work of both is equally devoid of substance.

There is a lithograph by Senefelder which represents a gambling club. Not one of those depicted is pursuing the game in the customary fashion. Each man is dominated by an emotion: one shows unrestrained joy; another, distrust of his partner; a third, dull despair; a fourth evinces belligerence; another is getting ready to depart from the world. All these modes of conduct share a concealed characteristic: the figures presented show us how the mechanism to which the participants in a game of chance entrust themselves seizes them body and soul, so that even in their private sphere, and no matter how agitated they may be, they are capable only of a reflex action. They behave like the pedestrians in Poe's story. They live their lives as automatons and resemble Bergson's fictitious characters who have completely liquidated their memories.

Baudelaire does not appear to have been a devotee of gambling, although he had words of friendly understanding, even homage, for those addicted to it. The motif which he treated in his night piece "Le Jeu" was part of his view of modern times, and he considered it as part of his mission to write this poem. The image of the gambler became in Baudelaire the characteristically modern complement to the archaic image of the fencer; both are heroic figures to him. Ludwig Börne looked at things through Baudelaire's eyes when he wrote: "If all the energy and passion . . . that are expended every year at Europe's gambling tables . . . were saved, they would suffice to fashion a Roman people and a Roman history from them. But that is just it. Because every man is born a Roman, bourgeois society seeks to de-Romanize him, and that is why there are games of chance and parlor games, novels, Italian operas, and fashionable newspapers." Gambling became a stock diversion of the bourgeoisie only in the nineteenth century; in the eighteenth, only the aristocracy gambled. Games of chance were disseminated by the Napoleonic armies, and they now became part of "fashionable living and the thousands of unsettled lives that are lived in the basements of a large city," part of the spectacle in which Baudelaire claimed he saw the heroic—"as it is characteristic of our epoch."

If one wants to examine gambling from the psychological as well as the technical point of view, Baudelaire's conception of it appears even more significant. It is obvious that the gambler is out to win. Yet one will not want to call his desire to win and make money a wish in the strict sense of the word. He may be inwardly motivated by greed or by some sinister determination. At any rate, his frame of mind is such that he cannot make much use of experience.[11] A wish, however, is a kind of experience. "What one wishes for in one's youth, one has in abundance in old age," said Goethe. The earlier in life one makes a wish, the greater one's chances that it will be fulfilled. The further a wish reaches out in time, the greater the hopes for its fulfillment. But it is experience that accompanies one to the far reaches of time, that fills and divides time. Thus a wish fulfilled is the crowning of experience. In folk symbolism, distance in space can take the place of distance in time; that is why the shooting star, which plunges into the infinite distance of space, has become the symbol of a fulfilled wish. The ivory ball which rolls into the *next* compartment, the *next* card which lies on top are the very antithesis of a falling star. The period of time encompassed by the instant in which the light of a shooting star flashes for a man is of the kind that Joubert has described with his customary assurance. "Time," he says, "is found even in eternity; but it is not earthly, worldly time. . . . That time does not destroy; it merely completes." It is the antithesis of time in hell, the province of those who are not allowed to complete anything they have started. The disrepute of games of chance is actually based on the fact that the player himself has a hand in it. (An incorrigible patron of a lottery will not be proscribed in the same way as the gambler in a stricter sense.)

This starting all over again is the regulative idea of the game, as it is of work for wages. Thus it is highly meaningful if in Baudelaire the second-hand—"la Seconde"—appears as partner of the gambler:

Souviens-toi que le Temps est un joueur avide
Qui gagne sans tricher, à tout coup! c'est la loi! *

In another place, Satan himself takes the place of this second. The taciturn corner of the cave to which the poem "Le Jeu" relegates those who are addicted to gambling undoubtedly is part of his realm.

* Keep in mind that Time's a rabid gambler
Who wins always without cheating—it's the law!

Voilà le noir tableau qu'en un rêve nocturne
Je vis se dérouler sous mon oeil clairvoyant,
Moi-même, dans un coin de l'antre taciturne,
Je me vis accoudé, froid, muet, enviant,
Enviant de ces gens la passion tenace.*

The poet does not participate in the game. He stands in his corner, no happier than those who are playing. He too has been cheated out of his experience—a modern man. The only difference is that he rejects the narcotics with which the gamblers seek to submerge the consciousness that has delivered them to the march of the second-hand.[12]

Et mon coeur s'effraya d'envier maint pauvre homme
Courant avec ferveur à l'abîme béant,
Et qui, soûl de son sang, préférerait en somme
La douleur à la mort et l'enfer au néant! †

In this last stanza Baudelaire presents impatience as the substratum of the passion for gambling. He found it in himself in its purest form. His violent temper had the expressiveness of Giotto's *Iracundia* at Padua.

X

It is—if one follows Bergson—the actualization of the *durée* which rids man's soul of obsession with time. Proust shared this belief, and from it he developed the lifelong exercises in which he strove to bring to light past things saturated with all the reminiscences that had worked their way into his pores during his sojourn in the unconscious. Proust was an incomparable reader of the *Fleurs du mal*, for he sensed that it contained kin-

* Here you see the hellish picture that one night in a dream
  I saw unfolding before my clairvoyant eyes;
  And, over in a corner of this silent cave,
  Myself I saw, hunched up, cold, mute, and envying,
  Envying these people their tenacious passion.

† And my heart took fright—to envy some poor man
  Who ran in frenzy to the sheer abyss,
  Who, drunk with the pulsing of his blood, preferred
  Grief to death, and hell to nothingness.

dred elements. Familiarity with Baudelaire must include Proust's experience with him. Proust writes: "Time is peculiarly chopped up in Baudelaire; only a very few days open up, they are significant ones. Thus it is understandable why turns of phrases like 'one evening' occur frequently in his works." These significant days are days of completing time, to paraphrase Joubert. They are days of recollection, not marked by any experience. They are not connected with the other days, but stand out from time. As for their substance, Baudelaire has defined it in the notion of the *correspondances*, a concept that in Baudelaire stands side by side and unconnected with the notion of "modern beauty."

Disregarding the scholarly literature on the *correspondances* (the common property of the mystics; Baudelaire encountered them in Fourier's writings), Proust no longer fusses about the artistic variations on the situation which are supplied by synaesthesia. The important thing is that the *correspondances* record a concept of experience which includes ritual elements. Only by appropriating these elements was Baudelaire able to fathom the full meaning of the breakdown which he, a modern man, was witnessing. Only in this way was he able to recognize in it the challenge meant for him alone, a challenge which he incorporated in the *Fleurs du mal*. If there really is a secret architecture in this book—and many speculations have been devoted to it—the cycle of poems that opens the volume probably is devoted to something irretrievably lost. This cycle includes two sonnets whose motif is the same. The first, entitled "Correspondances," begins with these lines:

> La Nature est un temple où de vivants piliers
> Laissent parfois sortir de confuses paroles;
> L'homme y passe à travers des forêts de symboles
> Qui l'observent avec des regards familiers.
>
> Comme de longs échos qui de loin se confondent
> Dans une ténébreuse et profonde unité,
> Vaste comme la nuit et comme la clarté,
> Les parfums, les couleurs et les sons se répondent.*

* Nature is a temple whose living pillars
Sometimes give forth a babel of words;

What Baudelaire meant by *correspondances* may be described as an experience which seeks to establish itself in crisis-proof form. This is possible only within the realm of the ritual. If it transcends this realm, it presents itself as the beautiful. In the beautiful the ritual value of art appears.[13]

The *correspondances* are the data of remembrance—not historical data, but data of prehistory. What makes festive days great and significant is the encounter with an earlier life. Baudelaire recorded this in a sonnet entitled "La Vie antérieure." The images of caves and vegetation, of clouds and waves which are evoked at the beginning of this second sonnet rise from the warm vapor of tears, tears of homesickness. "The wanderer looks into the tear-veiled distance, and hysterical tears [*sic*] well up in his eyes," writes Baudelaire in his review of the poems of Marceline Desbordes-Valmore. There are no simultaneous correspondences, such as were cultivated by the symbolists later. The murmur of the past may be heard in the correspondences, and the canonical experience of them has its place in a previous life:

> Les houles, en roulant les images des cieux,
> Mêlaient d'une façon solennelle et mystique
> Les tout-puissants accords de leur riche musique
> Aux couleurs du couchant reflété par mes yeux.
>
> C'est là que j'ai vécu. . . .*

The fact that Proust's restorative will remains within the limits of earthly existence, whereas Baudelaire's transcends it, may be regarded as symptomatic of the incomparably more elemental and powerful counterforces that Baudelaire faced. And prob-

---

> Man wends his way through forests of symbols
> Which look at him with their familiar glances.
>
> As long-resounding echoes from afar
> Are mingling in a deep, dark unity,
> Vast as the night or as the orb of day,
> Perfumes, colors, and sounds commingle.

> * The breakers, rolling the images of the sky,
> Mixed, in a mystical and solemn way,
> The powerful chords of their rich music
> With the colors of the sunset reflected in my eyes.
>
> There did I live. . . .

ably he nowhere achieved greater perfection than when he seems resigned to being overcome by them. "Recueillement" traces the allegories of the old years against the deep sky:

> . . . Vois se pencher les défuntes Années
> Sur les balcons du ciel, en robes surannées.*

In these verses Baudelaire resigns himself to paying homage to times out of mind that escaped him in the guise of the outdated. When Proust in the last volume of his work reverts to the sensation that suffused him at the taste of a *madeleine,* he imagines the years which appear on the balcony as being loving sisters of the years of Combray. "In Baudelaire . . . these reminiscences are even more numerous. It is apparent that they are not occasioned by chance, and this, to my mind, is what gives them crucial importance. There is no one else who pursues the interconnected *correspondances* with such leisurely care, fastidiously and yet nonchalantly—in a woman's smell, for instance, in the fragrance of her hair or her breasts—*correspondances* which then yield him lines like 'the azure of the vast, vaulted sky' or 'a harbor full of flames and masts.'" These words are a confessional motto for Proust's work. It bears a relationship to Baudelaire's work, which has assembled the days of remembrance into a spiritual year.

But the *Fleurs du mal* would not be what it is if all it contained were this success. It is unique because it was able to wrest from the inefficacy of the same consolation, the breakdown of the same fervor, the failure of the same effort poems that are in no way inferior to those in which the *correspondances* celebrate their triumphs. "Spleen et idéal" is the first of the cycles in *Les Fleurs du mal.* The *idéal* supplies the power of remembrance; the *spleen* musters the multitude of the seconds against it. It is their commander, just as the devil is the lord of the flies. One of the *Spleen* poems, "Le Goût du néant," says: *"Le Printemps adorable a perdu son odeur!"* † In this line Baudelaire expresses

* . . . See the dead departed Years in antiquated
  Dress leaning over heaven's balconies.

† Spring, the Beloved, has lost its scent.

something extreme with extreme discretion; this makes it unmistakably his. The word *"perdu"* acknowledges the present state of collapse of that experience which he once shared. The scent is the inaccessible refuge of the *mémoire involontaire*. It is unlikely that it will associate itself with a visual image; of all sensual impressions it will ally itself only with the same scent. If the recognition of a scent is more privileged to provide consolation than any other recollection, this may be so because it deeply drugs the sense of time. A scent may drown years in the odor it recalls. This gives a sense of measureless desolation to Baudelaire's verse. For someone who is past experiencing, there is no consolation. Yet it is this very inability to experience that lies at the heart of rage. An angry man "won't listen"; his prototype Timon rages against people indiscriminately; he is no longer capable of telling his proven friend from his mortal enemy. D'Aurevilly very perceptively recognized this condition in Baudelaire, calling him "a Timon with the genius of Archilochus." The outbreaks of rage are timed to the ticking of the seconds to which the melancholy man is slave.

> Et le Temps m'engloutit minute par minute,
> Comme la neige immense un corps pris de roideur.*

These verses follow immediately after those quoted above. In the *spleen*, time becomes palpable; the minutes cover a man like snowflakes. This time is outside history, as is that of the *mémoire involontaire*. But in the *spleen* the perception of time is supernaturally keen; every second finds consciousness ready to intercept its shock.[14]

Even though chronology places regularity above permanence, it cannot prevent heterogeneous, conspicuous fragments from remaining within it. To have combined recognition of a quality with the measurement of the quantity was the work of the calendars in which the places of recollection are left blank, as it were, in the form of holidays. The man who loses his capacity for experiencing feels as though he is dropped from the calendar. The

---

* And, minute by minute, Time engulfs me,
  As the snow's measureless fall covers a motionless body.

big-city dweller knows this feeling on Sundays; Baudelaire has it *avant la lettre* in one of the *Spleen* poems.

> Des cloches tout à coup sautent avec furie
> Et lancent vers le ciel un affreux hurlement,
> Ainsi que des esprits errants et sans patrie
> Qui se mettent à geindre opiniâtrement.*

The bells, which once were part of holidays, have been dropped from the calendar, like the human beings. They are like the poor souls that wander restlessly, but outside of history. If Baudelaire in "Spleen" and "Vie antérieure" holds in his hands the scattered fragments of genuine historical experience, Bergson in his conception of the *durée* has become far more estranged from history. "Bergson the metaphysician suppresses death." The fact that death is eliminated from Bergson's *durée* isolates it effectively from a historical (as well as prehistorical) order. Bergson's concept of *action* is in keeping with this. The "sound common sense" which distinguishes the "practical man" has been its godfather. The *durée* from which death has been eliminated has the miserable endlessness of a scroll. Tradition is excluded from it.[15] It is the quintessence of a passing moment [*Erlebnis*] that struts about in the borrowed garb of experience. The *spleen*, on the other hand, exposes the passing moment in all its nakedness. To his horror, the melancholy man sees the earth revert to a mere state of nature. No breath of prehistory surrounds it: there is no aura. This is how the earth emerges in the verses of "Le Goût du néant" which follow the ones we have quoted.

> Je contemple d'en haut le globe en sa rondeur,
> Et je n'y cherche plus l'abri d'une cahute.†

* Suddenly bells leap forth with fury,
 Hurling a hideous howling to the sky
 Like wandering homeless spirits
 Who break into stubborn wailing.

† And from on high I contemplate the globe in its roundness;
 No longer do I look there for the shelter of a hut.

XI

If we designate as aura the associations which, at home in the *mémoire involontaire,* tend to cluster around the object of a perception, then its analogue in the case of a utilitarian object is the experience which has left traces of the practiced hand. The techniques based on the use of the camera and of subsequent analogous mechanical devices extend the range of the *mémoire volontaire;* by means of these devices they make it possible for an event at any time to be permanently recorded in terms of sound and sight. Thus they represent important achievements of a society in which practice is in decline. To Baudelaire there was something profoundly unnerving and terrifying about daguerreotypy; he speaks of the fascination it exerted as "startling and cruel." Thus he must have sensed, though he certainly did not see through them, the connections of which we have spoken. His willingness always to grant the modern its place and, especially in art, to assign it its specific function also determined his attitude toward photography. Whenever he felt it as a threat, he tried to put it down to its "mistaken developments"; yet he admitted that these were promoted by "the stupidity of the broad masses." "These masses demanded an ideal that would conform to their aspirations and the nature of their temperament. . . . Their prayers were granted by a vengeful god, and Daguerre became his prophet." Nevertheless, Baudelaire tried to take a more conciliatory view. Photography should be free to stake out a claim for ephemeral things, those that have a right "to a place in the archives of our memory," as long as it stops short of the "region of the intangible, imaginative": that of art in which only that is allotted a place "on which man has bestowed the imprint of his soul." This is scarcely a Solomonian judgment. The perpetual readiness of volitional, discursive memory, encouraged by the technique of mechanical reproduction, reduces the scope for the play of the imagination. The latter may perhaps be defined as an ability to give expression to desires of a special kind, with "something beautiful" thought of as their fulfillment. Valéry has set forth the conditions for this fulfillment: "We recognize a work

of art by the fact that no idea it inspires in us, no mode of behavior that it suggests we adopt could exhaust it or dispose of it.
We may inhale the smell of a flower whose fragrance is agree-
able to us for as long as we like; it is impossible for us to rid ourselves of the fragrance by which our senses have been aroused,
and no recollection, no thought, no mode of behavior can ob-
literate its effect or release us from the hold it has on us. He who
has set himself the task of creating a work of art aims at the same
effect." According to this view, the painting we look at reflects
back at us that of which our eyes will never have their fill. What
it contains that fulfills the original desire would be the very same
stuff on which the desire continuously feeds. What distinguishes
photography from painting is therefore clear, and why there
can be no encompassing principle of "creation" applicable to
both: to the eyes that will never have their fill of a painting,
photography is rather like food for the hungry or drink for the
thirsty.

The crisis of artistic reproduction which manifests itself in
this way can be seen as an integral part of a crisis in perception
itself. What prevents our delight in the beautiful from ever being
satisfied is the image of the past, which Baudelaire regards as
veiled by the tears of nostalgia. "*Ach, du warst in abgelebten
Zeiten meine Schwester oder meine Frau!*" *—this declaration of
love is the tribute which the beautiful as such is entitled to claim.
Insofar as art aims at the beautiful and, on however modest a
scale, "reproduces" it, it conjures it up (as Faust does Helen) out
of the womb of time.[16] This no longer happens in the case of
technical reproduction. (The beautiful has no place in it.) Proust,
complaining of the barrenness and lack of depth in the images of
Venice that his *mémoire volontaire* presented to him, notes that
the very word "Venice" made that wealth of images seem to
him as vapid as an exhibition of photographs. If the distinctive
feature of the images that rise from the *mémoire involontaire* is
seen in their aura, then photography is decisively implicated in
the phenomenon of the "decline of the aura." What was inevi-

* "Oh, you were in time gone by my sister or my wife." (Goethe.)

tably felt to be inhuman, one might even say deadly, in daguerreotypy was the (prolonged) looking into the camera, since the
camera records our likeness without returning our gaze. But
looking at someone carries the implicit expectation that our look
will be returned by the object of our gaze. Where this expectation is met (which, in the case of thought processes, can apply
equally to the look of the eye of the mind and to a glance pure
and simple), there is an experience of the aura to the fullest extent. "Perceptibility," as Novalis puts it, "is a kind of attentiveness." The perceptibility he has in mind is none other than that
of the aura. Experience of the aura thus rests on the transposition
of a response common in human relationships to the relationship
between the inanimate or natural object and man. The person we
look at, or who feels he is being looked at, looks at us in turn.
To perceive the aura of an object we look at means to invest it
with the ability to look at us in return.[17] This experience corresponds to the data of the *mémoire involontaire*. (These data, incidentally, are unique: they are lost to the memory that seeks to
retain them. Thus they lend support to a concept of the aura
that comprises the "unique manifestation of a distance." This
designation has the advantage of clarifying the ceremonial character of the phenomenon. The essentially distant is the inap-
proachable: inapproachability is in fact a primary quality of the
ceremonial image.) Proust's great familiarity with the problem of
the aura requires no emphasis. Nevertheless, it is notable that he
alludes to it at times in terms which comprehend its theory:
"Some people who are fond of secrets flatter themselves that
objects retain something of the gaze that has rested on them."
(The ability, it would seem, of returning the gaze.) "They believe that monuments and pictures present themselves only beneath the delicate veil which centuries of love and reverence on
the part of so many admirers have woven about them. This chi-
mera," Proust concludes evasively, "would change into truth if
they related it to the only reality that is valid for the individual,
namely, the world of his emotions." Valéry's characterization of
perception in dreams as aural is akin to this and, by virtue of its
objective orientation, reaches further. "To say, 'Here I see such

and such an object' does not establish an equation between me and the object. . . . In dreams, however, there is an equation. The things I see, see me just as much as I see them." On a level with perception in dreams is the nature of temples, of which Baudelaire said:

> L'homme y passe à travers des forêts de symboles
> Qui l'observent avec des regards familiers.*

The greater Baudelaire's insight into this phenomenon, the more unmistakably did the disintegration of the aura make itself felt in his lyrical poetry. This occurs in the form of a symbol which we encounter in the *Fleurs du mal* almost invariably whenever the look of the human eye is invoked. (That Baudelaire did not follow some preconceived scheme goes without saying.) What is involved here is that the expectation roused by the look of the human eye is not fulfilled. Baudelaire describes eyes of which one is inclined to say that they have lost their ability to look. Yet this lends them a charm which to a large, perhaps predominant, extent serves as a means of defraying the cost of his instinctual desires. It was under the spell of these eyes that *sexus* in Baudelaire detached itself from *eros*. If in "Selige Sehnsucht" the lines

> Keine Ferne macht dich schwierig,
> Kommst geflogen und gebannt †

must be regarded as the classic description of that love which is sated with the experience of the aura, then lyric poetry could hardly offer a greater challenge to those lines than Baudelaire's

> Je t'adore à l'égal de la voûte nocturne,
> O vase de tristesse, o grande taciturne,
> Et t'aime d'autant plus, belle, que tu me fuis,
> Et que tu me parais, ornement de mes nuits,

* Man wends his way through forests of symbols
  Which look at him with their familiar glances.

† No distance makes you difficult; you come flying, and stay under a spell. (Goethe.)

> Plus ironiquement accumuler les lieues
> Qui séparent mes bras des immensités bleues.*

The deeper the remoteness which a glance has to overcome, the stronger will be the spell that is apt to emanate from the gaze. In eyes that look at us with a mirrorlike blankness the remoteness remains complete. It is precisely for this reason that such eyes know nothing of distance. Baudelaire incorporated the smoothness of their stare in a subtle couplet:

> Plonge tes yeux dans des yeux fixes
> Des Satyresses ou des Nixes.†

Female satyrs and nymphs are no longer members of the family of man. Theirs is a world apart. Significantly, Baudelaire injected into his poem the look of the eye encumbered by distance as *regard familier*. The poet who failed to found a family endowed the word *familier* with overtones pervaded by promise and renunciation. He has lost himself to the spell of eyes which do not return his glance and submits to their sway without illusions.

> Tes yeux, illuminés ainsi que des boutiques
> Et des ifs flamboyants dans les fêtes publiques,
> Usent insolemment d'un pouvoir emprunté.‡

"Dullness," says Baudelaire in one of his earliest publications, "is frequently an ornament of beauty. It is to this that we owe it if eyes are sad and translucent like blackish swamps or if their gaze has the oily inertness of tropical seas." When such eyes come alive, it is with the self-protective wariness of a wild ani-

---

* No less than the night's vault do I adore you,
  Vessel of sorrow, O deeply silent one,
  And even more I love you, my lovely one,
  Because you flee from me and, ornament of my nights,
  Ironically you seem to multiply the miles
  That separate my arms from blue immensities.

† Let your eyes look deeply into the fixed stare
  Of Satyresses or of Nymphs.

‡ Your eyes, lit up like shop windows
  And trees illuminated for public celebrations,
  With insolence make use of borrowed power.

mal hunting for prey. (Thus the eye of the prostitute scrutinizing
the passers-by is at the same time on its guard against the police.
Baudelaire found the physiognomic type bred by this kind of life
delineated in Constantin Guys's numerous drawings of prosti-
tutes. "Her eyes, like those of a wild animal, are fixed on the
distant horizon; they have the restlessness of a wild animal . . . ,
but sometimes also the animal's sudden tense vigilance.") That
the eye of the city dweller is overburdened with protective functions is obvious. Georg Simmel refers to some less obvious tasks
with which it is charged. "The person who is able to see but unable to hear is much more . . . troubled than the person who is
able to hear but unable to see. Here is something . . . characteristic of the big city. The interpersonal relationships of people in
big cities are characterized by a markedly greater emphasis on
the use of the eyes than on that of the ears. This can be attrib-
uted chiefly to the institution of public conveyances. Before
buses, railroads, and streetcars became fully established during
the nineteenth century, people were never put in a position of
having to stare at one another for minutes or even hours on end
without exchanging a word."

There is no daydreaming surrender to faraway things in the
protective eye. It may even cause one to feel something like
pleasure in the degradation of such abandonment. This is probably the sense in which the following curious sentences should
be read. In his "Salon of 1859" Baudelaire lets the landscapes pass
in review, concluding with this admission: "I long for the return
of the dioramas whose enormous, crude magic subjects me to the
spell of a useful illusion. I prefer looking at the backdrop paintings of the stage where I find my favorite dreams treated with
consummate skill and tragic concision. Those things, so completely false, are for that very reason much closer to the truth,
whereas the majority of our landscape painters are liars, precisely
because they fail to lie." One is inclined to attach less importance
to the "useful illusion" than to the "*tragic* concision." Baudelaire insists on the magic of distance; he goes so far as to judge
landscapes by the standard of paintings in the booths at fairs.
Does he mean the magic of distance to be pierced, as must needs

happen when the spectator steps too close to the depicted scene?
This is embodied in one of the great verses of the *Fleurs du mal:*

Le Plaisir vaporeux fuira vers l'horizon
Ainsi qu'une sylphide au fond de la coulisse.*

XII

Les Fleurs du mal was the last lyric work that had a European repercussion; no later work penetrated beyond a more or less limited linguistic area. Added to this is the fact that Baudelaire expended his productive capacity almost entirely on this one work. And, finally, it cannot be denied that some of his motifs—and the present study has dealt with them—render the possibility of lyric poetry questionable. These three facts define Baudelaire historically. They show that he imperturbably stuck to his cause and single-mindedly concentrated on his mission. He went so far as to proclaim as his goal "the creation of a cliché." In this he saw the condition of every future poet; he had a low opinion of those who were not up to it. "Do you drink beef tea made of ambrosia? Do you eat cutlets from Paros? How much do they give in the pawnshop for a lyre?" To Baudelaire, the lyric poet with a halo is antiquated. In a prose piece which came to light at a late date, "A Lost Halo," Baudelaire has such a poet appear as a supernumerary. When Baudelaire's literary remains were first examined, this piece was rejected as "unsuitable for publication"; to this day it has been neglected by Baudelaire scholarship.

" 'What do I see, my dear fellow? *You—here?* I find *you* in a place of ill repute—a man who sips quintessences, who consumes ambrosia? Really! I couldn't be more surprised.'

" 'You know, my dear fellow, how afraid I am of horses and carriages. A short while ago I was hurrying across the boulevard, and amidst this moving chaos in which death comes galloping at you from all sides at once I must have made an awkward movement, for the halo slipped off my head and fell onto the muddy asphalt pavement. I didn't have the courage to pick it up, and

* Nebulous Pleasure horizonward will flee,
  Just like a sylph behind the wings.

decided that it hurts less to lose one's insignia than to have one's bones broken. And furthermore, I said to myself, every cloud has a silver lining. Now I can go about incognito, do bad things, and indulge in vulgar behavior like ordinary mortals. So here I am, just like you!'

" 'But you ought to report the loss of your halo or inquire at the lost-and-found office.'

" 'I wouldn't dream of it. I like it here. You are the only person who has recognized me. Besides, dignity bores me. And I enjoy the thought that some bad poet will pick up the halo and won't think twice about adorning himself with it. There is nothing I like better than to make someone happy—especially if the happy man is one I can laugh at. Just picture X. wearing it, or Y.! Won't that be funny?' "

The same motif may be found in the diaries; only the ending is different. The poet quickly picks the halo up; but now he is bothered by the feeling that the incident may be a bad omen.[18]

The man who wrote these pieces was no *flâneur*. They embody, in ironic form, the same experiences which Baudelaire put into this sentence, without any trimmings and in passing: *"Perdu dans ce vilain monde, coudoyé par les foules, je suis comme un homme lassé don't l'oeil ne voit en arrière, dans les années profondes, que désabusement et amertume, et, devant lui, qu'un orage où rien de neuf n'est contenu, ni enseignement ni douleur."* * Of all the experiences which made his life what it was, Baudelaire singled out his having been jostled by the crowd as the decisive, unique experience. The luster of a crowd with a motion and a soul of its own, the glitter that had bedazzled the *flâneur*, had dimmed for him. To impress the crowd's meanness upon himself, he envisaged the day on which even the lost women, the outcasts, would be ready to advocate a well-ordered life, condemn libertinism, and reject everything except money. Having been betrayed by these last allies of his, Baudelaire battled the

---

* "Lost in this mean world, jostled by the crowd, I am like a weary man whose eye, looking backwards, into the depth of the years, sees nothing but disillusion and bitterness, and before him nothing but a tempest which contains nothing new, neither instruction nor pain."

crowd—with the impotent rage of someone fighting the rain or the wind. This is the nature of something lived through (*Erlebnis*) to which Baudelaire has given the weight of an experience (*Erfahrung*). He indicated the price for which the sensation of the modern age may be had: the disintegration of the aura in the experience of shock. He paid dearly for consenting to this disintegration—but it is the law of his poetry, which shines in the sky of the Second Empire as "a star without atmosphere."

1. To endow this crowd with a soul is the very special purpose of the *flâneur*. His encounters with it are the experience that he does not tire of telling about. Certain reflexes of this illusion are an integral part of Baudelaire's work. It has continued to be an active force to this day. Jules Romains's *unanimisme* is an admired late flowering of it.

2. Characteristic of Barbier's method is his poem "Londres" which in 24 lines describes the city, awkwardly closing with the following verses:

> Enfin, dans un amas de choses, sombre, immense,
> Un peuple noir, vivant et mourant en silence.
> Des êtres par milliers, suivant l'instinct fatal,
> Et courant après l'or par le bien et le mal.*

(Auguste Barbier, *Iambes et poèmes*. Paris, 1841.) Barbier's tendentious poems, particularly the London cycle, *Lazare*, influenced Baudelaire more profoundly than people have been willing to admit. Baudelaire's "Crépuscule du soir" concludes as follows:

> . . . ils finissent
> Leur destinée et vont vers le gouffre commun;
> L'hôpital se remplit de leurs soupirs.—Plus d'un
> Ne viendra plus chercher la soupe parfumée,
> Au coin du feu, le soir, auprès d'une âme aimée.†

Compare this with the end of the eighth stanza of Barbier's "Mineurs de Newcastle":

* Finally, within a huge and somber mass of things,
  A blackened people, who live and die in silence.
  Thousands of beings, who follow a fatal instinct,
  Pursuing gold with good and evil means.

† . . . their fate
  Accomplished, they approach the common pit;
  Their sighings fill the ward.—More than one
  Will come no more to get his fragrant soup,
  At night, by the fireside, next to a beloved one.

Et plus d'un qui rêvait dans le fond de son âme
Aux douceurs du logis, à l'oeil bleu de sa femme,
Trouve au ventre du gouffre un éternel tombeau.*

With a little masterful retouching Baudelaire turns a "miner's fate" into the commonplace end of big-city dwellers.

3. The motif of love for a woman passing by occurs in an early poem by Stefan George. The poet has missed the important thing: the stream in which the woman moves past, borne along by the crowd. The result is a self-conscious elegy. The poet's glances—so he must confess to his lady—have "moved away, moist with longing/ before they dared mingle with yours" (". . . *feucht vor sehnen fort-gezogen/eh sie in deine sich zu tauchen trauten.*" Stefan George, *Hymnen. Pilgerfahrten. Algabal.* Berlin, 1922). Baudelaire leaves no doubt that *he* looked deep into the eyes of the passer-by.

4. This passage has a parallel in "Un Jour de pluie." Even though it bears another name, this poem must be ascribed to Baudelaire. The last verse, which gives the poem its extraordinarily somber quality, has an exact counterpart in "The Man of the Crowd." Poe writes: "The rays of the gas lamps, feeble at first in their struggle with the dying day, had now at length gained ascendancy, and threw over everything a fitful and garish luster. All was dark yet splendid—as that ebony to which has been likened the style of Tertullian." This coincidence is all the more astonishing here as the following verses were written in 1843 at the latest, a period when Baudelaire did not know Poe.

Chacun, nous coudoyant sur le trottoir glissant,
Egoïste et brutal, passe et nous éclabousse,
Ou, pour courir plus vite, en s'éloignant nous pousse.
Partout fange, déluge, obscurité du ciel.
Noir tableau qu'eût rêvé le noir Ezéchiel.†

5. There is something demonic about Poe's businessmen. One is reminded of Marx, who blamed the "feverishly youthful pace of ma-

---

* And more than one who in his heart of hearts had dreams
  Of home, sweet home, and of his wife's blue eyes,
  Finds, within the belly of the pit, an everlasting tomb.

† Each one, elbowing us upon the slippery sidewalk,
  Selfish and savage goes by and splashes us,
  Or, to run the faster, gives us a push as he makes off.
  Mud everywhere, deluge, darkness in the sky.
  A somber scene that Ezekiel the somber might have dreamed.

terial production" in the United States for the lack of "either time or opportunity . . . to abolish the old world of the spirit." As darkness descends, Baudelaire has "the harmful demons" awaken in the air "sluggish as a bunch of businessmen." This passage in "Crépuscule du soir" may have been inspired by Poe's text.

6. A pedestrian knew how to display his nonchalance provocatively on certain occasions. Around 1840 it was briefly fashionable to take turtles for a walk in the arcades. The *flâneurs* liked to have the turtles set the pace for them. If they had had their way, progress would have been obliged to accommodate itself to this pace. But this attitude did not prevail; Taylor, who popularized the watchword "Down with dawdling!," carried the day.

7. In Glassbrenner's character the man of leisure appears as a paltry scion of the *citoyen*. Nante, Berlin's street-corner boy, has no reason to bestir himself. He makes himself at home on the street, which naturally does not lead him anywhere, and is as comfortable as the philistine is in his four walls.

8. What leads up to this confession is remarkable. The visitor says that the cousin watches the bustle down below only because he enjoys the changing play of the colors; in the long run, he says, this must be tiring. In a similar vein, and probably not much later, Gogol wrote of a fair in the Ukraine: "So many people were on their way there that it made one's eyes swim." The daily sight of a lively crowd may once have constituted a spectacle to which one's eyes had to adapt first. On the basis of this supposition, one may assume that once the eyes had mastered this task they welcomed opportunities to test their newly acquired faculties. This would mean that the technique of Impressionist painting, whereby the picture is garnered in a riot of dabs of color, would be a reflection of experiences with which the eyes of a big-city dweller have become familiar. A picture like Monet's "Cathedral of Chartres," which is like an ant-heap of stone, would be an illustration of this hypothesis.

9. In his story E. T. A. Hoffmann devotes edifying reflections, for instance, to the blind man who lifts his head toward the sky. In the last line of "Les Aveugles," Baudelaire, who knew this story, modifies Hoffmann's reflections in such a way as to disprove their edifying quality: "*Que cherchent-ils au Ciel, tous ces aveugles?*" [What are all those blind people looking for in the sky?]

10. The shorter the training period of an industrial worker is, the

longer that of a military man becomes. It may be part of society's preparation for total war that training is shifting from the practice of production to the practice of destruction.

11. Gambling invalidates the standards of experience. It may be due to an obscure sense of this that the "vulgar appeal to experience" (Kant) has particular currency among gamblers. A gambler says "my number" in the same way as a man about town says "my type." Toward the end of the Second Empire this attitude prevailed. "On the boulevards it was customary to attribute everything to chance." This disposition is promoted by betting, which is a device for giving events the character of a shock, detaching them from the context of experience. For the bourgeoisie, even political events were apt to assume the form of occurrences at the gambling table.

12. The narcotic effect that is involved here is specified as to time, like the malady that it is supposed to alleviate. Time is the material into which the phantasmagoria of gambling has been woven. In his *Faucheurs de nuits* Gourdon de Genouillac writes: "I claim that the mania for gambling is the noblest of all passions, for it includes all the others. A series of lucky *coups* gives me more pleasure than a non-gambler can have in years. . . . If you think that I see only profit in the gold that falls to my share, you are mistaken. I see in it the pleasures that it gets me, and I enjoy them fully. They come too quickly to make me weary, and there are too many of them for me to get bored. I live a hundred lives in one. When I travel, it is the way that an electric spark travels. . . . If I am stingy and reserve my bank notes for gambling, it is because I know the value of time too well to invest them as other people do. A certain enjoyment that I might permit myself would cost me a thousand other enjoyments. . . . I have intellectual pleasures and want no others." In the fine notes on gambling in his *Jardin d'Épicure*, Anatole France presents a similar view.

13. Beauty can be defined in two ways: in its relationship to history and to nature. In both relationships the semblance, the problematic element in the beautiful, manifests itself. (Let us indicate the first relationship briefly. On the basis of its *historical* existence, beauty is an appeal to join those who admired it at an earlier time. Being moved by beauty is an *ad plures ire*, as the Romans called dying. According to this definition, the semblance of beauty means that the identical object which admiration is courting cannot be found in the work. This admiration harvests what earlier generations have admired

in it. Words of Goethe express here the final conclusion of wisdom: "Everything that has had a great effect can really no longer be evaluated.") Beauty in its relationship to *nature* can be defined as that which "remains true to its essential nature only when veiled." The *correspondances* tell us what is meant by such a veil. We may call it, in a somewhat daring abbreviation, the "reproducing aspect" of the work of art. The *correspondances* constitute the court of judgment before which the object of art is found to be a faithful reproduction—which, to be sure, makes it entirely problematic. If one attempted to reproduce this *aporia* through language, one would define beauty as the object of experience in the state of resemblance. This definition would probably coincide with Valéry's formulation: "Beauty may require the servile imitation of what is indefinable in objects." If Proust so readily returns to this subject (which in his work appears as time recovered), one cannot say that he is telling any secrets. It is, rather, one of the disconcerting features of his technique that he repeatedly and loquaciously builds his reflections around the concept of beauty—in short, the hermetic aspect of art. He writes about the origin and the intentions of his work with a fluency and an urbanity that would befit a refined amateur. This, to be sure, has its counterpart in Bergson. The following passage in which the philosopher indicates all the things that may be expected from a visual actualization of the uninterrupted stream of becoming has a flavor reminiscent of Proust. "We can let our day-to-day existence be permeated with such a visualization and thus, thanks to philosophy, enjoy a satisfaction similar to that of art; but this satisfaction would be more frequent, more regular, and more easily accessible to ordinary mortals." Bergson sees within reach what Valéry's better, Goethean understanding visualizes as the "here" in which the inadequate becomes an actuality.*

14. In the mystical "Colloquy of Monos and Una," Poe has, so to speak, inserted the empty time sequence, to which the man in the mood of "spleen" is abandoned, into the *durée*, and he seems to regard it as bliss that he is now rid of its horrors. It is a "sixth sense" acquired by the departed which takes the form of an ability to derive harmony even from the empty passage of time. To be sure, it is quite easily disrupted by the rhythm of the second-hand. "There seemed to have sprung up in the brain *that* of which no words could

---

* ". . . *in dem das Unzulängliche Ereignis wird*." An allusion to the Chorus Mysticus that ends Goethe's *Faust*, Part Two.—Trans.

convey to the merely human intelligence even an indistinct conception. Let me term it a mental pendulous pulsation. It was the moral embodiment of man's abstract idea of *Time*. By the absolute equalization of this movement—or of such as this—had the cycles of the firmamental orbs themselves been adjusted. By its aid I measured the irregularities of the clock upon the mantel, and of the watches of the attendants. Their tickings came sonorously to my ears. The slightest deviation from the true proportion . . . affected me just as violations of abstract truth are wont, on earth, to affect the moral sense."

15. The deterioration of experience manifests itself in Proust in the complete realization of his ultimate intention. There is nothing more ingenious or more loyal than the way in which he nonchalantly and constantly strives to tell the reader: Redemption is my private show.

16. The moment of such a success is itself marked as something unique. It is the basis of the structural design of Proust's works. Each situation in which the chronicler is touched by the breath of lost time is thereby rendered incomparable and removed from the sequence of the days.

17. This endowment is a wellspring of poetry. Wherever a human being, an animal, or an inanimate object thus endowed by the poet lifts up its eyes, it draws him into the distance. The gaze of nature thus awakened dreams and pulls the poet after its dream. Words, too, can have an aura of their own. This is how Karl Kraus described it: "The closer the look one takes at a word, the greater the distance from which it looks back."

18. It is not impossible that this entry was occasioned by a pathogenic shock. The form which relates it to Baudelaire's work is all the more revealing.

The Image of Proust

The thirteen volumes of Marcel Proust's *À la Recherche du temps perdu* are the result of an unconstruable synthesis in which the absorption of a mystic, the art of a prose writer, the verve of a satirist, the erudition of a scholar, and the self-consciousness of a monomaniac have combined in an autobiographical work. It has rightly been said that all great works of literature found a genre or dissolve one—that they are, in other words, special cases. Among these cases this is one of the most unfathomable. From its structure, which is fiction, autobiography, and commentary in one, to the syntax of endless sentences (the Nile of language, which here overflows and fructifies the regions of truth), everything transcends the norm. The first revealing observation that strikes one is that this great special case of literature at the same time constitutes its greatest achievement of recent decades. The conditions under which it was created were extremely unhealthy: an unusual malady, extraordinary wealth, and an abnormal disposition. This is not a model life in every respect, but everything about it is exemplary. The outstanding literary achievement of our time is assigned a place in the heart of the impossible, at the center—and also at the point of indifference—of all dangers, and it marks this great realization of a "lifework" as the last for a long time. The image of Proust is the highest physiognomic expression which the irresistibly growing discrepancy between literature and life was able to assume. This is the lesson which justifies the attempt to evoke this image.

We know that in his work Proust did not describe a life as it actually was, but a life as it was remembered by the one who had lived it. And yet even this statement is imprecise and far too crude. For the important thing for the remembering author is not what he experienced, but the weaving of his memory, the Penelope work of recollection. Or should one call it, rather, a Penelope work of forgetting? Is not the involuntary recollection, Proust's *mémoire involontaire*, much closer to forgetting than what is usually called memory? And is not this work of spontaneous recollection, in which remembrance is the woof and forgetting the warf, a counterpart to Penelope's work rather than its likeness? For here the day unravels what the night was woven. When we awake each morning, we hold in our hands, usually weakly and loosely, but a few fringes of the tapestry of lived life, as loomed for us by forgetting. However, with our purposeful activity and, even more, our purposive remembering each day unravels the web and the ornaments of forgetting. This is why Proust finally turned his days into nights, devoting all his hours to undisturbed work in his darkened room with artificial illumination, so that none of those intricate arabesques might escape him.

The Latin word *textum* means "web." No one's text is more tightly woven than Marcel Proust's; to him nothing was tight or durable enough. From his publisher Gallimard we know that Proust's proofreading habits were the despair of the typesetters. The galleys always went back covered with marginal notes, but not a single misprint had been corrected; all available space had been used for fresh text. Thus the laws of remembrance were operative even within the confines of the work. For an experienced event is finite—at any rate, confined to one sphere of experience; a remembered event is infinite, because it is only a key to everything that happened before it and after it. There is yet another sense in which memory issues strict weaving regulations. Only the *actus purus* of recollection itself, not the author or the plot, constitutes the unity of the text. One may even say that the intermittence of author and plot is only the reverse of the continuum of memory, the pattern on the back side of the tapestry. This is what Proust meant, and this is how he must be understood, when he said that he would prefer to see his entire work printed in one volume in two columns and without any paragraphs.

What was it that Proust sought so frenetically? What was at the bottom of these infinite efforts? Can we say that all lives, works, and deeds that matter were never anything but the undisturbed unfolding of the most banal, most fleeting, most sentimental, weakest hour in the life of the one to whom they pertain? When Proust in a well-known passage described the hour that was most his own, he did it in such a way that everyone can find it in his own existence. We might almost call it an everyday hour; it comes with the night, a lost twittering of birds, or a breath drawn at the sill of an open window. And there is no telling what encounters would be in store for us if we were less inclined to give in to sleep. Proust did not give in to sleep. And yet—or, rather, precisely for this reason—Jean Cocteau was able to say in a beautiful essay that the intonation of Proust's voice obeyed the laws of night and honey. By submitting to these laws he conquered the hopeless sadness within him (what he once called *"l'imperfection incurable dans l'essence même du présent"* *), and from the honeycombs of memory he built a house for the swarm of his thoughts. Cocteau recognized what really should have been the major concern of all readers of Proust and yet has served no one as the pivotal point of his reflections or his affection. He recognized Proust's blind, senseless, frenzied quest for happiness. It shone from his eyes; they were not happy, but in them there lay fortune as it lies in gambling or in love. Nor is it hard to say why this paralyzing, explosive will to happiness which pervades Proust's writings is so seldom compre-

* ". . . the incurable imperfection in the very essence of the present moment."

hended by his readers. In many places Proust himself made it easy for them to view this *oeuvre*, too, from the time-tested, comfortable perspective of resignation, heroism, asceticism. After all, nothing makes more sense to the model pupils of life than the notion that a great achievement is the fruit of toil, misery, and disappointment. The idea that happiness could have a share in beauty would be too much of a good thing, something that their *ressentiment* would never get over.

There is a dual will to happiness, a dialectics of happiness: a hymnic and an elegiac form. The one is the unheard-of, the unprecedented, the height of bliss; the other, the eternal repetition, the eternal restoration of the original, the first happiness. It is this elegiac idea of happiness—it could also be called Eleatic—which for Proust transforms existence into a preserve of memory. To it he sacrificed in his life friends and companionship, in his works plot, unity of characters, the flow of the narration, the play of the imagination. Max Unold, one of Proust's more discerning readers, fastened on the "boredom" thus created in Proust's writings and likened it to "pointless stories." "Proust managed to make the pointless story interesting. He says: 'Imagine, dear reader, yesterday I was dunking a cookie in my tea when it occurred to me that as a child I spent some time in the country.' For this he uses eighty pages, and it is so fascinating that you think you are no longer the listener but the daydreamer himself." In such stories—"all ordinary dreams turn into pointless stories as soon as one tells them to someone"—Unold has discovered the bridge to the dream. No synthetic interpretation of Proust can disregard it. Enough inconspicuous gates lead into it—Proust's frenetically studying resemblances, his impassioned cult of similarity. The true signs of its hegemony do not become obvious where he suddenly and startlingly uncovers similarities in actions, physiognomies, or speech mannerisms. The similarity of one thing to another which we are used to, which occupies us in a wakeful state, reflects only vaguely the deeper resemblance of the dream world in which everything that happens appears not in identical but in similar guise, opaquely similar one to another. Children know a symbol of this world: the stocking which has the structure of this dream world when, rolled up in the laundry hamper, it is a "bag" and a "present" at the same time. And just as children do not tire of quickly changing the bag and its contents into a third thing—namely, a stocking—Proust could not get his fill of emptying the dummy, his self, at one stroke in order to keep garnering that third thing, the image which satisfied his curiosity—indeed, assuaged his homesickness. He lay on his bed racked with homesickness, homesick for the world distorted in the state of resemblance, a world in which the true surrealist face of existence breaks through. To this world belongs what happens in Proust, and the deliberate and fastidious way in which it appears. It is never isolated, rhetorical, or visionary; carefully heralded and securely supported, it bears a fragile, precious reality: the image. It detaches itself from the structure of Proust's sentences as that summer day at Balbec—old, immemorial, mummified—emerged from the lace curtains under Françoise's hands.

II

We do not always proclaim loudly the most important thing we have to say. Nor do we always privately share it with those closest to us, our intimate friends, those who have been most devotedly ready to receive our confession. If it is true that not only people but also ages have such a chaste—that is, such a devious and frivolous—way of communicating what is most their own to a passing acquaintance, then the nineteenth century did not reveal itself to Zola or Anatole France, but to the young Proust, the insignificant snob, the playboy and socialite who snatched in passing the most astounding confidences from a declining age as from another, bone-weary Swann. It took Proust to make the nineteenth century ripe for memoirs. What before him had been a period devoid of tension now became a field of force in which later writers aroused multifarious currents. Nor is it accidental that the two most significant works of this kind were written by authors who were personally close to Proust as admirers and friends: the memoirs of Princess Clermont-Tonnerre and the

autobiographical work of Léon Daudet; the first volumes of both
works were published recently. An eminently Proustian inspiration led Léon Daudet, whose political folly is too gross and too
obtuse to do much harm to his admirable talent, to turn his life
into a city. *Paris vécu*, the projection of a biography onto the
city map, in more than one place is touched by the shadows of
Proustian characters. And the very title of Princess Clermont-
Tonnerre's book, *Au Temps des équipages*, would have been un-
thinkable prior to Proust. This book is the echo which softly
answers Proust's ambiguous, loving, challenging call from the
Faubourg Saint-Germain. In addition, this melodious performance is shot through with direct and indirect references to Proust
in its tenor and its characters, which include him and some of his
favorite objects of study from the Ritz. There is no denying, of
course, that this puts us in a very aristocratic milieu, and, with
figures like Robert de Montesquiou, whom Princess Clermont-
Tonnerre depicts masterfully, in a very special one at that. But
this is true of Proust as well, and in his writings Montesquiou has
a counterpart. All this would not be worth discussing, especially
since the question of models would be secondary and unimportant for Germany, if German criticism were not so fond of taking the easy way out. Above all, it could not resist the opportunity to descend to the level of the lending-library crowd. Hack
critics were tempted to draw conclusions about the author from
the snobbish milieu of his writings, to characterize Proust's works
as an internal affair of the French, a literary supplement to the
Almanach de Gotha. It is obvious that the problems of Proust's
characters are those of a satiated society. But there is not one
which would be identical with those of the author, which are
subversive. To reduce this to a formula, it was to be Proust's aim
to design the entire inner structure of society as a physiology of
chatter. In the treasury of its prejudices and maxims there is not
one that is not annihilated by a dangerous comic element. Pierre-
Quint was the first to draw attention to it. "When humorous
works are mentioned," he wrote, "one usually thinks of short,
amusing books in illustrated jackets. One forgets about *Don
Quixote, Pantagruel,* and *Gil Blas*—fat, ungainly tomes in small

print." These comparisons, of course, do not do full justice to the explosive power of Proust's critique of society. His style is comedy, not humor; his laughter does not toss the world up but flings it down—at the risk that it will be smashed to pieces, which will then make him burst into tears. And unity of family and personality, of sexual morality and professional honor, are indeed smashed to bits. The pretensions of the bourgeoisie are shattered by laughter. Their return and reassimilation by the aristocracy is the sociological theme of the work.

Proust did not tire of the training which moving in aristocratic circles required. Assiduously and without much constraint, he conditioned his personality, making it as impenetrable and resourceful, as submissive and difficult, as it had to be for the sake of his mission. Later on this mystification and ceremoniousness became so much part of him that his letters sometimes constitute whole systems of parentheses, and not just in the grammatical sense—letters which despite their infinitely ingenious, flexible composition occasionally call to mind the specimen of a letter writer's handbook: "My dear Madam, I just noticed that I forgot my cane at your house yesterday; please be good enough to give it to the bearer of this letter. P.S. Kindly pardon me for disturbing you; I just found my cane." Proust was most resourceful in creating complications. Once, late at night, he dropped in on Princess Clermont-Tonnerre and made his staying dependent on someone bringing him his medicine from his house. He sent a valet for it, giving him a lengthy description of the neighborhood and of the house. Finally he said: "You cannot miss it. It is the only window on the Boulevard Haussmann in which there still is a light burning!" Everything but the house number! Anyone who has tried to get the address of a brothel in a strange city and has received the most long-winded directions, everything but the name of the street and the house number, will understand what is meant here and what the connection is with Proust's love of ceremony, his admiration of the Duc de Saint-Simon, and, last but not least, his intransigent French spirit. Is it not the quintessence of experience to find out how very difficult it is to learn many things which apparently could be told in very few words? It is simply that such words are part of a language established along lines of caste and class and unintelligible to outsiders. No wonder that the secret language of the salons excited Proust. When he later embarked on his merciless depiction of the *petit clan*, the Courvoisiers, the "esprit d'Oriane," he had through his association with the Bibescos become conversant with the improvisations of a code language to which we too have recently been introduced.

In his years of life in the salons Proust developed not only the vice of flattery to an eminent—one is tempted to say, to a theological—degree, but the vice of curiosity as well. We detect in him the reflection of the laughter which like a flash fire curls the lips of the Foolish Virgins represented on the intrados of many of the cathedrals which Proust loved. It is the smile of curiosity. Was it curiosity that made him such a great parodist? If so, we would know how to evaluate the term "parodist" in this context. Not very highly. For though it does justice to his abysmal malice, it skirts the bitterness, savagery, and grimness of the magnificent pieces which he wrote in the style of Balzac, Flaubert, Sainte-Beuve, Henri de Régnier, the Goncourts, Michelet, Renan, and his favorite Saint-Simon, and which are collected in the volume *Pastiches et mélanges*. The mimicry of a man of curiosity is the brilliant device of this series, as it is also a feature of his entire creativity in which his passion for vegetative life cannot be taken seriously enough. Ortega y Gasset was the first to draw attention to the vegetative existence of Proust's characters, which are planted so firmly in their social habitat, influenced by the position of the sun of aristocratic favor, stirred by the wind that blows from Guermantes or Méséglise, and inextricably intertwined in the thicket of their fate. This is the environment that gave rise to the poet's mimicry. Proust's most accurate, most convincing insights fasten on their objects as insects fasten on leaves, blossoms, branches, betraying nothing of their existence until a leap, a beating of wings, a vault, show the startled observer that some incalculable individual life has imperceptibly crept into an alien world. The true reader of Proust is constantly jarred by small shocks. In the parodies he finds again, in the guise of a play with "styles," what affected him in an altogether different way as this spirit's struggle for survival under the leafy canopy of society. At this point we must say something about the close and fructifying interpenetration of these two vices, curiosity and flattery. There is a revealing passage in the writings of Princess Clermont-Tonnerre. "And finally we cannot suppress the fact that Proust became enraptured with the study of domestic servants—whether it be that an element which he encountered nowhere else intrigued his investigative faculties or that he envied servants their greater opportunities for observing the intimate details of things that aroused his interest. In any case, domestic servants in their various embodiments and types were his passion." In the exotic shadings of a Jupien, a Monsieur Aimé, a Célestine Albalat, their ranks extend from Françoise, a figure with the coarse, angular features of St. Martha that seems to be straight out of a Book of Hours, to those grooms and *chasseurs* who are paid for loafing rather than working. And perhaps the greatest concentration of this connoisseur of ceremonies was reserved for the depiction of these lower ranks. Who can tell how much servant curiosity became part of Proust's flattery, how much servant flattery became mixed with his curiosity, and where this artful copy of the role of the servant on the heights of the social scale had its limits? Proust presented such a copy, and he could not help doing so, for, as he once admitted, "*voir*" and "*désirer imiter*" were one and the same thing to him. This attitude, which was both sovereign and obsequious, has been preserved by Maurice Barrès in the most apposite words that have ever been written about Proust: "*Un poète persan dans une loge de portière.*" *

There was something of the detective in Proust's curiosity. The upper ten thousand were to him a clan of criminals, a band of conspirators beyond compare: the Camorra of consumers. It excludes from its world everything that has a part in production, or at least demands that this part be gracefully and bashfully concealed behind the kind of manner that is sported by the polished professionals of consumption. Proust's analysis of snobbery,

* "A Persian poet in a porter's lodge."

which is far more important than his apotheosis of art, constitutes the apogee of his criticism of society. For the attitude of the snob is nothing but the consistent, organized, steely view of life from the chemically pure standpoint of the consumer. And because even the remotest as well as the most primitive memory of nature's productive forces was to be banished from this satanic magic world, Proust found a perverted relationship more serviceable than a normal one even in love. But the pure consumer is the pure exploiter—logically and theoretically—and in Proust he is that in the full concreteness of his actual historical existence. He is concrete because he is impenetrable and elusive. Proust describes a class which is everywhere pledged to camouflage its material basis and for this very reason is attached to a feudalism which has no intrinsic economic significance but is all the more serviceable as a mask of the upper middle class. This disillusioned, merciless deglamorizer of the ego, of love, of morals—for this is how Proust liked to view himself—turns his whole limitless art into a veil for this one most vital mystery of his class: the economic aspect. He did not mean to do it a service. Here speaks Marcel Proust, the hardness of his work, the intransigence of a man who is ahead of his class. What he accomplishes he accomplishes as its master. And much of the greatness of this work will remain inaccessible or undiscovered until this class has revealed its most pronounced features in the final struggle.

III

In the last century there was an inn by the name of "Au Temps Perdu" at Grenoble; I do not know whether it still exists. In Proust, too, we are guests who enter through a door underneath a suspended sign that sways in the breeze, a door behind which eternity and rapture await us. Fernandez rightly distinguished between a *thème de l'éternité* and a *thème du temps* in Proust. But his eternity is by no means a platonic or a utopian one; it is rapturous. Therefore, if "time reveals a new and hitherto unknown kind of eternity to anyone who becomes engrossed in its passing," this certainly does not enable an individual to approach "the higher regions which a Plato or Spinoza reached with one beat of the wings." It is true that in Proust we find rudiments of an enduring idealism, but it would be a mistake to make these the basis of an interpretation, as Benoist-Méchin has done most glaringly. The eternity which Proust opens to view is convoluted time, not boundless time. His true interest is in the passage of time in its most real—that is, space-bound—form, and this passage nowhere holds sway more openly than in remembrance within and aging without. To observe the interaction of aging and remembering means to penetrate to the heart of Proust's world, to the universe of convolution. It is the world in a state of resemblances, the domain of the *correspondances;* the Romanticists were the first to comprehend them and Baudelaire embraced them most fervently, but Proust was the only one who managed to reveal them in our lived life. This is the work of the *mémoire involontaire*, the rejuvenating force which is a match for the inexorable process of aging. When the past is reflected in the dewy fresh "instant," a painful shock of rejuvenation pulls it together once more as irresistibly as the Guermantes way and Swann's way become intertwined for Proust when, in the thirteenth volume, he roams about the Combray area for the last time and discovers the intertwining of the roads. In a trice the landscape jumps about like a child. *"Ah! que le monde est grand à la clarté des lampes! Aux yeux du souvenir que le monde est petit!"* * Proust has brought off the tremendous feat of letting the whole world age by a lifetime in an instant. But this very concentration in which things that normally just fade and slumber consume themselves in a flash is called rejuvenation. *À la Recherche du temps perdu* is the constant attempt to charge an entire lifetime with the utmost awareness. Proust's method is actualization, not reflection. He is filled with the insight that none of us has time to live the true dramas of the life that we are destined for. This is what ages us—this and nothing else. The wrinkles and creases on our faces are the registration of the great

* "Oh, how large the world is in the brightness of the lamps. How small the world is in the eyes of recollection."

passions, vices, insights that called on us; but we, the masters, were not home.

Since the spiritual exercises of Loyola there has hardly been a more radical attempt at self-absorption. Proust's, too, has as its center a loneliness which pulls the world down into its vortex with the force of a maelstrom. And the overloud and inconceivably hollow chatter which comes roaring out of Proust's novels is the sound of society plunging down into the abyss of this loneliness. This is the location of Proust's invectives against friendship. It was a matter of perceiving the silence at the bottom of this crater, whose eyes are the quietest and most absorbing. Something that is manifested irritatingly and capriciously in so many anecdotes is the combination of an unparalleled intensity of conversation with an unsurpassable aloofness from his partner. There has never been anyone else with Proust's ability to show us things; Proust's pointing finger is unequaled. But there is another gesture in amicable togetherness, in conversation: physical contact. To no one is this gesture more alien than to Proust. He cannot touch his reader either; he could not do so for anything in the world. If one wanted to group literature around these poles, dividing it into the directive and the touching kind, the core of the former would be the work of Proust, the core of the latter, the work of Péguy. This is basically what Fernandez has formulated so well: "Depth, or, rather, intensity, is always on his side, never on that of his partner." This is demonstrated brilliantly and with a touch of cynicism in Proust's literary criticism, the most significant document of which is an essay that came into being on the high level of his fame and the low level of his deathbed: "À Propos de Baudelaire." The essay is Jesuitic in its acquiescence in his own maladies, immoderate in the garrulousness of a man who is resting, frightening in the indifference of a man marked by death who wants to speak out once more, no matter on what subject. What inspired Proust here in the face of death also shaped him in his intercourse with his contemporaries: so spasmodic and harsh an alternation of sarcasm and tenderness that its recipients threatened to break down in exhaustion.

The provocative, unsteady quality of the man affects even

the reader of his works. Suffice it to recall the endless succession of *"soit que . . . ,"* by means of which an action is shown in an exhaustive, depressing way in the light of the countless motives upon which it may have been based. And yet these paratactic sequences reveal the point at which weakness and genius coincide in Proust: the intellectual renunciation, the tested skepticism with which he approached things. After the self-satisfied inwardness of Romanticism Proust came along, determined, as Jacques Rivière puts it, not to give the least credence to the *"Sirènes intérieures."* "Proust approaches experience without the slighest metaphysical interest, without the slightest penchant for construction, without the slightest tendency to console." Nothing is truer than that. And thus the basic feature of this work, too, which Proust kept proclaiming as being planned, is anything but the result of construction. But it is as planned as the lines on the palm of our hand or the arrangement of the stamen in a calyx. Completely worn out, Proust, that aged child, fell back on the bosom of nature—not to drink from it, but to dream to its heartbeat. One must picture him in this state of weakness to understand how felicitously Jacques Rivière interpreted the weakness when he wrote: "Marcel Proust died of the same inexperience which permitted him to write his works. He died of ignorance of the world and because he did not know how to change the conditions of his life which had begun to crush him. He died because he did not know how to make a fire or open a window." And, to be sure, of his psychogenic asthma.

The doctors were powerless in the face of this malady; not so the writer, who very systematically placed it in his service. To begin with the most external aspect, he was a perfect stage director of his sickness. For months he connected, with devastating irony, the image of an admirer who had sent him flowers with their odor, which he found unbearable. Depending on the ups and downs of his malady he alarmed his friends, who dreaded and longed for the moment when the writer would suddenly appear in their drawing rooms long after midnight—*brisé de fatigue* and for just five minutes, as he said—only to stay till the gray of dawn, too tired to get out of his chair or interrupt his conversation. Even as a writer of letters he extracted the most singular effects from his malady. "The wheezing of my breath is drowning out the sounds of my pen and of a bath which is being drawn on the floor below." But that is not all, nor is it the fact that his sickness removed him from fashionable living. This asthma became part of his art—if indeed his art did not create it. Proust's syntax rhythmically and step by step reproduces his fear of suffocating. And his ironic, philosophical, didactic reflections invariably are the deep breath with which he shakes off the weight of memories. On a larger scale, however, the threatening, suffocating crisis was death, which he was constantly aware of, most of all while he was writing. This is how death confronted Proust, and long before his malady assumed critical dimensions— not as a hypochondriacal whim, but as a *"réalité nouvelle,"* that new reality whose reflections on things and people are the marks of aging. A physiology of style would take us into the innermost core of this creativeness. No one who knows with what great tenacity memories are preserved by the sense of smell, and smells not at all in the memory, will be able to call Proust's sensitivity to smells accidental. To be sure, most memories that we search for come to us as visual images. Even the free-floating forms of the *mémoire involontaire* are still in large part isolated, though enigmatically present, visual images. For this very reason, anyone who wishes to surrender knowingly to the innermost overtones in this work must place himself in a special stratum—the bottommost—of this involuntary memory, one in which the materials of memory no longer appear singly, as images, but tell us about a whole, amorphously and formlessly, indefinitely and weightily, in the same way as the weight of his net tells a fisherman about his catch. Smell—that is the sense of weight of someone who casts his nets into the sea of the *temps perdu*. And his sentences are the entire muscular activity of the intelligible body; they contain the whole enormous effort to raise this catch.

For the rest, the closeness of the symbiosis between this particular creativity and this particular malady is demonstrated most clearly by the fact that in Proust there never was a breakthrough of that heroic defiance with which other creative people have risen up against their infirmities. And therefore one can say, from another point of view, that so close a complicity with life and the course of the world as Proust's would inevitably have led to ordinary, indolent contentment on any basis but that of such great and constant suffering. As it was, however, this malady was destined to have its place in the great work process assigned to it by a furor devoid of desires or regrets. For the second time there rose a scaffold like Michelangelo's on which the artist, his head thrown back, painted the Creation on the ceiling of the Sistine Chapel: the sickbed on which Marcel Proust consecrates the countless pages which he covered with his handwriting, holding them up in the air, to the creation of his microcosm.

✤

The Work of Art
in the Age of Mechanical Reproduction

"Our fine arts were developed, their types and uses were established, in times very different from the present, by men whose power of action upon things was insignificant in comparison with ours. But the amazing growth of our techniques, the adaptability and precision they have attained, the ideas and habits they are creating, make it a certainty that profound changes are impending in the ancient craft of the Beautiful. In all the arts there is a physical component which can no longer be considered or treated as it used to be, which cannot remain unaffected by our modern knowledge and power. For the last twenty years neither matter nor space nor time has been what it was from time immemorial. We must expect great innovations to transform the entire technique of the arts, thereby affecting artistic invention itself and perhaps even bringing about an amazing change in our very notion of art." *

—Paul Valéry, PIÈCES SUR L'ART,
"La Conquète de l'ubiquité," Paris.

PREFACE

When Marx undertook his critique of the capitalistic mode of production, this mode was in its infancy. Marx directed his efforts in such a way as to give them prognostic value. He went back to the basic conditions underlying capitalistic production and through his presentation showed what could be expected of capitalism in the future. The result was that one could expect it not only to exploit the proletariat with increasing intensity, but ultimately to create conditions which would make it possible to abolish capitalism itself.

The transformation of the superstructure, which takes place

* Quoted from Paul Valéry, *Aesthetics*, "The Conquest of Ubiquity," translated by Ralph Manheim, p. 225. Pantheon Books, Bollingen Series, New York, 1964.

217

far more slowly than that of the substructure, has taken more than half a century to manifest in all areas of culture the change in the conditions of production. Only today can it be indicated what form this has taken. Certain prognostic requirements should be met by these statements. However, theses about the art of the proletariat after its assumption of power or about the art of a classless society would have less bearing on these demands than theses about the developmental tendencies of art under present conditions of production. Their dialectic is no less noticeable in the superstructure than in the economy. It would therefore be wrong to underestimate the value of such theses as a weapon. They brush aside a number of outmoded concepts, such as creativity and genius, eternal value and mystery—concepts whose uncontrolled (and at present almost uncontrollable) application would lead to a processing of data in the Fascist sense. The concepts which are introduced into the theory of art in what follows differ from the more familiar terms in that they are completely useless for the purposes of Fascism. They are, on the other hand, useful for the formulation of revolutionary demands in the politics of art.

I

In principle a work of art has always been reproducible. Man-made artifacts could always be imitated by men. Replicas were made by pupils in practice of their craft, by masters for diffusing their works, and, finally, by third parties in the pursuit of gain. Mechanical reproduction of a work of art, however, represents something new. Historically, it advanced intermittently and in leaps at long intervals, but with accelerated intensity. The Greeks knew only two procedures of technically reproducing works of art: founding and stamping. Bronzes, terra cottas, and coins were the only art works which they could produce in quantity. All others were unique and could not be mechanically reproduced. With the woodcut graphic art became mechanically reproducible for the first time, long before script became reproducible by print. The enormous changes which printing, the mechanical reproduction of writing, has brought about in literature are a familiar story. However, within the phenomenon which we are here examining from the perspective of world history, print is merely a special, though particularly important, case. During the Middle Ages engraving and etching were added to the woodcut; at the beginning of the nineteenth century lithography made its appearance.

With lithography the technique of reproduction reached an essentially new stage. This much more direct process was distinguished by the tracing of the design on a stone rather than its incision on a block of wood or its etching on a copperplate and permitted graphic art for the first time to put its products on the market, not only in large numbers as hitherto, but also in daily changing forms. Lithography enabled graphic art to illustrate everyday life, and it began to keep pace with printing. But only a few decades after its invention, lithography was surpassed by photography. For the first time in the process of pictorial reproduction, photography freed the hand of the most important artistic functions which henceforth devolved only upon the eye looking into a lens. Since the eye perceives more swiftly than the hand can draw, the process of pictorial reproduction was accelerated so enormously that it could keep pace with speech. A film operator shooting a scene in the studio captures the images at the speed of an actor's speech. Just as lithography virtually implied the illustrated newspaper, so did photography foreshadow the sound film. The technical reproduction of sound was tackled at the end of the last century. These convergent endeavors made predictable a situation which Paul Valéry pointed up in this sentence: "Just as water, gas, and electricity are brought into our houses from far off to satisfy our needs in response to a minimal effort, so we shall be supplied with visual or auditory images, which will appear and disappear at a simple movement of the hand, hardly more than a sign" (*op. cit.*, p. 226). Around 1900 technical reproduction had reached a standard that not only permitted it to reproduce all transmitted works of art and thus to cause the most profound change in their impact upon the public; it also had captured a place of its own among the artistic processes. For the study of this standard nothing is more revealing than the nature of the repercussions that these two different manifestations—the reproduction of works of art and the art of the film—have had on art in its traditional form.

II

Even the most perfect reproduction of a work of art is lacking in one element: its presence in time and space, its unique existence at the place where it happens to be. This unique existence of the work of art determined the history to which it was subject throughout the time of its existence. This includes the changes which it may have suffered in physical condition over the years as well as the various changes in its ownership.[1] The traces of the first can be revealed only by chemical or physical analyses which it is impossible to perform on a reproduction; changes of ownership are subject to a tradition which must be traced from the situation of the original.

The presence of the original is the prerequisite to the concept of authenticity. Chemical analyses of the patina of a bronze can help to establish this, as does the proof that a given manuscript of the Middle Ages stems from an archive of the fifteenth century. The whole sphere of authenticity is outside technical—and, of course, not only technical—reproducibility.[2] Confronted with its manual reproduction, which was usually branded as a forgery, the original preserved all its authority; not so *vis à vis* technical reproduction. The reason is twofold. First, process reproduction is more independent of the original than manual reproduction. For example, in photography, process reproduction can bring out those aspects of the original that are unattainable to the naked eye yet accessible to the lens, which is adjustable and chooses its angle at will. And photographic reproduction, with the aid of certain processes, such as enlargement or slow motion, can capture images which escape natural vision. Secondly, technical reproduction can put the copy of the original into situations which would be out of reach for the original itself. Above all, it enables the original to meet the beholder halfway, be it in the form of a photograph or a phonograph record. The cathedral leaves its locale to be received in the studio of a lover of art; the choral production, performed in an auditorium or in the open air, resounds in the drawing room.

The situations into which the product of mechanical reproduction can be brought may not touch the actual work of art, yet the quality of its presence is always depreciated. This holds not only for the art work but also, for instance, for a landscape which passes in review before the spectator in a movie. In the case of the art object, a most sensitive nucleus—namely, its authenticity—is interfered with whereas no natural object is vulnerable on that score. The authenticity of a thing is the essence of all that is transmissible from its beginning, ranging from its substantive duration to its testimony to the history which it has experienced. Since the historical testimony rests on the authenticity, the former, too, is jeopardized by reproduction when substantive duration ceases to matter. And what is really jeopardized when the historical testimony is affected is the authority of the object.[3]

One might subsume the eliminated element in the term "aura" and go on to say: that which withers in the age of mechanical reproduction is the aura of the work of art. This is a symptomatic process whose significance points beyond the realm of art. One might generalize by saying: the technique of reproduction detaches the reproduced object from the domain of tradition. By making many reproductions it substitutes a plurality of copies for a unique existence. And in permitting the reproduction to meet the beholder or listener in his own particular situation, it reactivates the object reproduced. These two processes lead to a tremendous shattering of tradition which is the obverse of the contemporary crisis and renewal of mankind. Both processes are intimately connected with the contemporary mass movements. Their most powerful agent is the film. Its social significance, particularly in its most positive form, is inconceivable without its destructive, cathartic aspect, that is, the liquidation of the traditional value of the cultural heritage. This phenomenon is most palpable in the great historical films. It extends to ever new positions. In 1927 Abel Gance exclaimed enthusiastically: "Shakespeare, Rembrandt, Beethoven will make films . . . all legends, all mythologies and all myths, all founders of religion, and the very religions . . . await their exposed resurrection, and the heroes crowd each other at the gate." * Presumably without intending it, he issued an invitation to a far-reaching liquidation.

III

During long periods of history, the mode of human sense perception changes with humanity's entire mode of existence. The manner in which human sense perception is organized, the medium in which it is accomplished, is determined not only by nature but by historical circumstances as well. The fifth century, with its great shifts of population, saw the birth of the late Roman art industry and the Vienna Genesis, and there developed not only an art different from that of antiquity but also a new kind of perception. The scholars of the Viennese school, Riegl and Wickhoff, who resisted the weight of classical tradition under which these later art forms had been buried, were the first to draw conclusions from them concerning the organization of perception at the time. However far-reaching their insight, these scholars limited themselves to showing the significant, formal hallmark which characterized perception in late Roman times. They did not attempt—and, perhaps, saw no way—to show the social transformations expressed by these changes of perception. The conditions for an analogous insight are more favorable in the present. And if changes in the medium of contemporary perception can be comprehended as decay of the aura, it is possible to show its social causes.

The concept of aura which was proposed above with reference to historical objects may usefully be illustrated with reference to the aura of natural ones. We define the aura of the latter as the unique phenomenon of a distance, however close it may be. If, while resting on a summer afternoon, you follow with

* Abel Gance, "Le Temps de l'image est venu," *L'Art cinématographique*, Vol. 2, pp. 94 f, Paris, 1927.

your eyes a mountain range on the horizon or a branch which casts its shadow over you, you experience the aura of those mountains, of that branch. This image makes it easy to comprehend the social bases of the contemporary decay of the aura. It rests on two circumstances, both of which are related to the increasing significance of the masses in contemporary life. Namely, the desire of contemporary masses to bring things "closer" spatially and humanly, which is just as ardent as their bent toward overcoming the uniqueness of every reality by accepting its reproduction.[4] Every day the urge grows stronger to get hold of an object at very close range by way of its likeness, its reproduction. Unmistakably, reproduction as offered by picture magazines and newsreels differs from the image seen by the unarmed eye. Uniqueness and permanence are as closely linked in the latter as are transitoriness and reproducibility in the former. To pry an object from its shell, to destroy its aura, is the mark of a perception whose "sense of the universal equality of things" has increased to such a degree that it extracts it even from a unique object by means of reproduction. Thus is manifested in the field of perception what in the theoretical sphere is noticeable in the increasing importance of statistics. The adjustment of reality to the masses and of the masses to reality is a process of unlimited scope, as much for thinking as for perception.

I V

The uniqueness of a work of art is inseparable from its being imbedded in the fabric of tradition. This tradition itself is thoroughly alive and extremely changeable. An ancient statue of Venus, for example, stood in a different traditional context with the Greeks, who made it an object of veneration, than with the clerics of the Middle Ages, who viewed it as an ominous idol. Both of them, however, were equally confronted with its uniqueness, that is, its aura. Originally the contextual integration of art in tradition found its expression in the cult. We know that the earliest art works originated in the service of a ritual—first the magical, then the religious kind. It is significant that the existence of the work of art with reference to its aura is never entirely separated from its ritual function.[5] In other words, the unique value of the "authentic" work of art has its basis in ritual, the location of its original use value. This ritualistic basis, however remote, is still recognizable as secularized ritual even in the most profane forms of the cult of beauty.[6] The secular cult of beauty, developed during the Renaissance and prevailing for three centuries, clearly showed that ritualistic basis in its decline and the first deep crisis which befell it. With the advent of the first truly revolutionary means of reproduction, photography, simultaneously with the rise of socialism, art sensed the approaching crisis which has become evident a century later. At the time, art reacted with the doctrine of *l'art pour l'art*, that is, with a theology of art. This gave rise to what might be called a negative theology in the form of the idea of "pure" art, which not only denied any social function of art but also any categorizing by subject matter. (In poetry, Mallarmé was the first to take this position.)

An analysis of art in the age of mechanical reproduction must do justice to these relationships, for they lead us to an all-important insight: for the first time in world history, mechanical reproduction emancipates the work of art from its parasitical dependence on ritual. To an ever greater degree the work of art reproduced becomes the work of art designed for reproducibility.[7] From a photographic negative, for example, one can make any number of prints; to ask for the "authentic" print makes no sense. But the instant the criterion of authenticity ceases to be applicable to artistic production, the total function of art is reversed. Instead of being based on ritual, it begins to be based on another practice—politics.

V

Works of art are received and valued on different planes. Two polar types stand out: with one, the accent is on the cult value; with the other, on the exhibition value of the work.[8] Artistic production begins with ceremonial objects destined to serve in a cult. One may assume that what mattered was their existence, not their being on view. The elk portrayed by the man of the Stone Age on the walls of his cave was an instrument of magic. He did expose it to his fellow men, but in the main it was meant for the spirits. Today the cult value would seem to demand that the work of art remain hidden. Certain statues of gods are accessible only to the priest in the cella; certain Madonnas remain covered nearly all year round; certain sculptures on medieval cathedrals are invisible to the spectator on ground level. With the emancipation of the various art practices from ritual go increasing opportunities for the exhibition of their products. It is easier to exhibit a portrait bust that can be sent here and there than to exhibit the statue of a divinity that has its fixed place in the interior of a temple. The same holds for the painting as against the mosaic or fresco that preceded it. And even though the public presentability of a mass originally may have been just as great as that of a symphony, the latter originated at the moment when its public presentability promised to surpass that of the mass.

With the different methods of technical reproduction of a work of art, its fitness for exhibition increased to such an extent that the quantitative shift between its two poles turned into a qualitative transformation of its nature. This is comparable to the situation of the work of art in prehistoric times when, by the absolute emphasis on its cult value, it was, first and foremost, an instrument of magic. Only later did it come to be recognized as a work of art. In the same way today, by the absolute emphasis on its exhibition value the work of art becomes a creation with entirely new functions, among which the one we are conscious of, the artistic function, later may be recognized as incidental.[9] This much is certain: today photography and the film are the most serviceable exemplifications of this new function.

VI

In photography, exhibition value begins to displace cult value all along the line. But cult value does not give way without resistance. It retires into an ultimate retrenchment: the human countenance. It is no accident that the portrait was the focal point of early photography. The cult of remembrance of loved ones, absent or dead, offers a last refuge for the cult value of the picture. For the last time the aura emanates from the early photographs in the fleeting expression of a human face. This is what constitutes their melancholy, incomparable beauty. But as man withdraws from the photographic image, the exhibition value for the first time shows its superiority to the ritual value. To have pinpointed this new stage constitutes the incomparable significance of Atget, who, around 1900, took photographs of deserted Paris streets. It has quite justly been said of him that he photographed them like scenes of crime. The scene of a crime, too, is deserted; it is photographed for the purpose of establishing evidence. With Atget, photographs become standard evidence for historical occurrences, and acquire a hidden political significance. They demand a specific kind of approach; free-floating contemplation is not appropriate to them. They stir the viewer; he feels challenged by them in a new way. At the same time picture magazines begin to put up signposts for him, right ones or wrong ones, no matter. For the first time, captions have become obligatory. And it is clear that they have an altogether different character than the title of a painting. The directives which the captions give to those looking at pictures in illustrated magazines soon become even more explicit and more imperative in the film where the meaning of each single picture appears to be prescribed by the sequence of all preceding ones.

VII

The nineteenth-century dispute as to the artistic value of painting versus photography today seems devious and confused. This does not diminish its importance, however; if anything, it underlines it. The dispute was in fact the symptom of a historical transformation the universal impact of which was not realized by either of the rivals. When the age of mechanical reproduction separated art from its basis in cult, the semblance of its autonomy disappeared forever. The resulting change in the function of art transcended the perspective of the century; for a long time it even escaped that of the twentieth century, which experienced the development of the film.

Earlier much futile thought had been devoted to the question of whether photography is an art. The primary question—whether the very invention of photography had not transformed the entire nature of art—was not raised. Soon the film theoreticians asked the same ill-considered question with regard to the film. But the difficulties which photography caused traditional aesthetics were mere child's play as compared to those raised by the film. Whence the insensitive and forced character of early theories of the film. Abel Gance, for instance, compares the film with hieroglyphs: "Here, by a remarkable regression, we have come back to the level of expression of the Egyptians. . . . Pictorial language has not yet matured because our eyes have not yet adjusted to it. There is as yet insufficient respect for, insufficient cult of, what it expresses." * Or, in the words of Séverin-Mars: "What art has been granted a dream more poetical and more real at the same time! Approached in this fashion the film might represent an incomparable means of expression. Only the most high-minded persons, in the most perfect and mysterious moments of their lives, should be allowed to enter its ambience." † Alexandre Arnoux concludes his fantasy about the silent film with the question: "Do not all the bold descriptions we have given amount to the definition of prayer?" ‡ It is instructive to note how their desire to class the film among the "arts" forces these theoreticians to read ritual elements into it—with a striking lack of discretion. Yet when these speculations were published, films like *L'Opinion publique* and *The Gold Rush* had already appeared. This, however, did not keep Abel Gance from adducing hieroglyphs for purposes of comparison, nor Séverin-Mars from speaking of the film as one might speak of paintings by Fra Angelico. Characteristically, even today ultrareactionary authors give the film a similar contextual significance—if not an

* Abel Gance, *op. cit.*, pp. 100-1.
† Séverin-Mars, quoted by Abel Gance, *op. cit.*, p. 100.
‡ Alexandre Arnoux, *Cinéma pris*, 1929, p. 28.

outright sacred one, then at least a supernatural one. Commenting on Max Reinhardt's film version of *A Midsummer Night's Dream,* Werfel states that undoubtedly it was the sterile copying of the exterior world with its streets, interiors, railroad stations, restaurants, motorcars, and beaches which until now had obstructed the elevation of the film to the realm of art. "The film has not yet realized its true meaning, its real possibilities . . . these consist in its unique faculty to express by natural means and with incomparable persuasiveness all that is fairylike, marvelous, supernatural." *

VIII

The artistic performance of a stage actor is definitely presented to the public by the actor in person; that of the screen actor, however, is presented by a camera, with a twofold consequence. The camera that presents the performance of the film actor to the public need not respect the performance as an integral whole. Guided by the cameraman, the camera continually changes its position with respect to the performance. The sequence of positional views which the editor composes from the material supplied him constitutes the completed film. It comprises certain factors of movement which are in reality those of the camera, not to mention special camera angles, close-ups, etc. Hence, the performance of the actor is subjected to a series of optical tests. This is the first consequence of the fact that the actor's performance is presented by means of a camera. Also, the film actor lacks the opportunity of the stage actor to adjust to the audience during his performance, since he does not present his performance to the audience in person. This permits the audience to take the position of a critic, without experiencing any personal contact with the actor. The audience's identification with the actor is really an identification with the camera. Consequently the audience takes the position of the camera; its ap-

* Franz Werfel, "Ein Sommernachtstraum, Ein Film von Shakespeare und Reinhardt," *Neues Wiener Journal,* cited in *Lu* 15, November, 1935.

proach is that of testing.[10] This is not the approach to which cult
values may be exposed. INDUCES A CRITICAL STANCE

I X

For the film, what matters primarily is that the actor represents himself to the public before the camera, rather than representing someone else. One of the first to sense the actor's metamorphosis by this form of testing was Pirandello. Though his
remarks on the subject in his novel *Si Gira* were limited to the
negative aspects of the question and to the silent film only, this
hardly impairs their validity. For in this respect, the sound film
did not change anything essential. What matters is that the part
is acted not for an audience but for a mechanical contrivance—
in the case of the sound film, for two of them. "The film actor,"
wrote Pirandello, "feels as if in exile—exiled not only from the
stage but also from himself. With a vague sense of discomfort
he feels inexplicable emptiness: his body loses its corporeality,
it evaporates, it is deprived of reality, life, voice, and the noises
caused by his moving about, in order to be changed into a mute
image, flickering an instant on the screen, then vanishing into
silence. . . . The projector will play with his shadow before the
public, and he himself must be content to play before the camera." * This situation might also be characterized as follows: for
the first time—and this is the effect of the film—man has to operate with his whole living person, yet forgoing its aura. For
aura is tied to his presence; there can be no replica of it. The
aura which, on the stage, emanates from Macbeth, cannot be
separated for the spectators from that of the actor. However, the
singularity of the shot in the studio is that the camera is substituted for the public. Consequently, the aura that envelops the
actor vanishes, and with it the aura of the figure he portrays.

It is not surprising that it should be a dramatist such as Pirandello who, in characterizing the film, inadvertently touches on
the very crisis in which we see the theater. Any thorough study

* Luigi Pirandello, *Si Gira*, quoted by Léon Pierre-Quint, "Signification
du cinéma," *L'Art cinématographique, op. cit.*, pp. 14-15.

proves that there is indeed no greater contrast than that of the stage play to a work of art that is completely subject to or, like the film, founded in, mechanical reproduction. Experts have long recognized that in the film "the greatest effects are almost always obtained by 'acting' as little as possible. . . ." In 1932 Rudolf Arnheim saw "the latest trend . . . in treating the actor as a stage prop chosen for its characteristics and . . . inserted at the proper place." [11] With this idea something else is closely connected. The stage actor identifies himself with the character of his role. The film actor very often is denied this opportunity. His creation is by no means all of a piece; it is composed of many separate performances. Besides certain fortuitous considerations, such as cost of studio, availability of fellow players, décor, etc., there are elementary necessities of equipment that split the actor's work into a series of mountable episodes. In particular, lighting and its installation require the presentation of an event that, on the screen, unfolds as a rapid and unified scene, in a sequence of separate shootings which may take hours at the studio; not to mention more obvious montage. Thus a jump from the window can be shot in the studio as a jump from a scaffold, and the ensuing flight, if need be, can be shot weeks later when outdoor scenes are taken. Far more paradoxical cases can easily be construed. Let us assume that an actor is supposed to be startled by a knock at the door. If his reaction is not satisfactory, the director can resort to an expedient: when the actor happens to be at the studio again he has a shot fired behind him without his being forewarned of it. The frightened reaction can be shot now and be cut into the screen version. Nothing more strikingly shows that art has left the realm of the "beautiful semblance" which, so far, had been taken to be the only sphere where art could thrive.

X

The feeling of strangeness that overcomes the actor before the camera, as Pirandello describes it, is basically of the same kind as the estrangement felt before one's own image in the mirror.

SIGNS → SIGNIFIED

But now the reflected image has become separable, transportable. And where is it transported? Before the public.[12] Never for a moment does the screen actor cease to be conscious of this fact. While facing the camera he knows that ultimately he will face the public, the consumers who constitute the market. This market, where he offers not only his labor but also his whole self, his heart and soul, is beyond his reach. During the shooting he has as little contact with it as any article made in a factory. This may contribute to that oppression, that new anxiety which, according to Pirandello, grips the actor before the camera. The film responds to the shriveling of the aura with an artificial build-up of the "personality" outside the studio. The cult of the movie star, fostered by the money of the film industry, preserves not the unique aura of the person but the "spell of the personality," the phony spell of a commodity. So long as the movie-makers' capital sets the fashion, as a rule no other revolutionary merit can be accredited to today's film than the promotion of a revolutionary criticism of traditional concepts of art. We do not deny that in some cases today's films can also promote revolutionary criticism of social conditions, even of the distribution of property. However, our present study is no more specifically concerned with this than is the film production of Western Europe.

It is inherent in the technique of the film as well as that of sports that everybody who witnesses its accomplishments is somewhat of an expert. This is obvious to anyone listening to a group of newspaper boys leaning on their bicycles and discussing the outcome of a bicycle race. It is not for nothing that newspaper publishers arrange races for their delivery boys. These arouse great interest among the participants, for the victor has an opportunity to rise from delivery boy to professional racer. Similarly, the newsreel offers everyone the opportunity to rise from passer-by to movie extra. In this way any man might even find himself part of a work of art, as witness Vertoff's *Three Songs About Lenin* or Ivens' *Borinage*. Any man today can lay claim to being filmed. This claim can best be elucidated by a comparative look at the historical situation of contemporary literature.

For centuries a small number of writers were confronted by

many thousands of readers. This changed toward the end of the last century. With the increasing extension of the press, which kept placing new political, religious, scientific, professional, and local organs before the readers, an increasing number of readers became writers—at first, occasional ones. It began with the daily press opening to its readers space for "letters to the editor." And today there is hardly a gainfully employed European who could not, in principle, find an opportunity to publish somewhere or other comments on his work, grievances, documentary reports, or that sort of thing. Thus, the distinction between author and public is about to lose its basic character. The difference becomes merely functional; it may vary from case to case. At any moment the reader is ready to turn into a writer. As expert, which he had to become willy-nilly in an extremely specialized work process, even if only in some minor respect, the reader gains access to authorship. In the Soviet Union work itself is given a voice. To present it verbally is part of a man's ability to perform the work. Literary license is now founded on polytechnic rather than specialized training and thus becomes common property.[13]

All this can easily be applied to the film, where transitions that in literature took centuries have come about in a decade. In cinematic practice, particularly in Russia, this change-over has partially become established reality. Some of the players whom we meet in Russian films are not actors in our sense but people who portray *themselves*—and primarily in their own work process. In Western Europe the capitalistic exploitation of the film denies consideration to modern man's legitimate claim to being reproduced. Under these circumstances the film industry is trying hard to spur the interest of the masses through illusion-promoting spectacles and dubious speculations.

XI

The shooting of a film, especially of a sound film, affords a spectacle unimaginable anywhere at any time before this. It presents a process in which it is impossible to assign to a spectator a viewpoint which would exclude from the actual scene such

Does not object to Film's hyper
reality —coercive
vantage point
of the
lens

extraneous accessories as camera equipment, lighting machinery, staff assistants, etc.—unless his eye were on a line parallel with the lens. This circumstance, more than any other, renders superficial and insignificant any possible similarity between a scene in the studio and one on the stage. In the theater one is well aware of the place from which the play cannot immediately be detected as illusionary. There is no such place for the movie scene that is being shot. Its illusionary nature is that of the second degree, the result of cutting. That is to say, in the studio the mechanical equipment has penetrated so deeply into reality that its pure aspect freed from the foreign substance of equipment is the result of a special procedure, namely, the shooting by the specially adjusted camera and the mounting of the shot together with other similar ones. The equipment-free aspect of reality here has become the height of artifice; the sight of immediate reality has become an orchid in the land of technology.

Even more revealing is the comparison of these circumstances, which differ so much from those of the theater, with the situation in painting. Here the question is: How does the cameraman compare with the painter? To answer this we take recourse to an analogy with a surgical operation. The surgeon represents the polar opposite of the magician. The magician heals a sick person by the laying on of hands; the surgeon cuts into the patient's body. The magician maintains the natural distance between the patient and himself; though he reduces it very slightly by the laying on of hands, he greatly increases it by virtue of his authority. The surgeon does exactly the reverse; he greatly diminishes the distance between himself and the patient by penetrating into the patient's body, and increases it but little by the caution with which his hand moves among the organs. In short, in contrast to the magician—who is still hidden in the medical practitioner—the surgeon at the decisive moment abstains from facing the patient man to man; rather, it is through the operation that he penetrates into him.

Magician and surgeon compare to painter and cameraman. The painter maintains in his work a natural distance from reality, the cameraman penetrates deeply into its web.[14] There is a tremendous difference between the pictures they obtain. That of the painter is a total one, that of the cameraman consists of multiple fragments which are assembled under a new law. Thus, for contemporary man the representation of reality by the film is incomparably more significant than that of the painter, since it offers, precisely because of the thoroughgoing permeation of reality with mechanical equipment, an aspect of reality which is free of all equipment. And that is what one is entitled to ask from a work of art.

OBSCURES ITS OWN ARTIFICE / NECESSARILY
CXT. TO THE SHOT / THESE DISTINCTIONS

XII   *— Between painting AND FILM Don't HOLD STRICTLY*
SPEAKING

Mechanical reproduction of art changes the reaction of the masses toward art. The reactionary attitude toward a Picasso painting changes into the progressive reaction toward a Chaplin movie. The progressive reaction is characterized by the direct, intimate fusion of visual and emotional enjoyment with the orientation of the expert. Such fusion is of great social significance. The greater the decrease in the social significance of an art form, the sharper the distinction between criticism and enjoyment by the public. The conventional is uncritically enjoyed, and the truly new is criticized with aversion. With regard to the screen, the critical and the receptive attitudes of the public coincide. The decisive reason for this is that individual reactions are predetermined by the mass audience response they are about to produce, and this is nowhere more pronounced than in the film. The moment these responses become manifest they control each other. Again, the comparison with painting is fruitful. A painting has always had an excellent chance to be viewed by one person or by a few. The simultaneous contemplation of paintings by a large public, such as developed in the nineteenth century, is an early symptom of the crisis of painting, a crisis which was by no means occasioned exclusively by photography but rather in a relatively independent manner by the appeal of art works to the masses.

Painting simply is in no position to present an object for simultaneous collective experience, as it was possible for architecture at all times, for the epic poem in the past, and for the movie today. Although this circumstance in itself should not lead one to conclusions about the social role of painting, it does constitute a serious threat as soon as painting, under special conditions and, as it were, against its nature, is confronted directly by the masses. In the churches and monasteries of the Middle Ages and at the princely courts up to the end of the eighteenth century, a collective reception of paintings did not occur simultaneously, but by graduated and hierarchized mediation. The change that has come about is an expression of the particular conflict in which painting was implicated by the mechanical reproducibility of paintings. Although paintings began to be publicly exhibited in galleries and salons, there was no way for the masses to organize and control themselves in their reception.[15] Thus the same public which responds in a progressive manner toward a grotesque film is bound to respond in a reactionary manner to surrealism.

XIII

The characteristics of the film lie not only in the manner in which man presents himself to mechanical equipment but also in the manner in which, by means of this apparatus, man can represent his environment. A glance at occupational psychology illustrates the testing capacity of the equipment. Psychoanalysis illustrates it in a different perspective. The film has enriched our field of perception with methods which can be illustrated by those of Freudian theory. Fifty years ago, a slip of the tongue passed more or less unnoticed. Only exceptionally may such a slip have revealed dimensions of depth in a conversation which had seemed to be taking its course on the surface. Since the *Psychopathology of Everyday Life* things have changed. This book isolated and made analyzable things which had heretofore floated along unnoticed in the broad stream of perception. For the entire spectrum of optical, and now also acoustical, perception the film has brought about a similar deepening of apperception. It is only an obverse of this fact that behavior items shown in a movie can be analyzed much more precisely and from more points of view than those presented on paintings or on the stage. As compared with painting, filmed behavior lends itself more readily to analysis because of its incomparably more precise statements of the situation. In comparison with the stage scene, the filmed behavior item lends itself more readily to analysis because it can be isolated more easily. This circumstance derives its chief importance from its tendency to promote the mutual penetration of art and science. Actually, of a screened behavior item which is neatly brought out in a certain situation, like a muscle of a body, it is difficult to say which is more fascinating, its artistic value or its value for science. To demonstrate the identity of the artistic and scientific uses of photography which heretofore usually were separated will be one of the revolutionary functions of the film.[16]

By close-ups of the things around us, by focusing on hidden details of familiar objects, by exploring commonplace milieus under the ingenious guidance of the camera, the film, on the one hand, extends our comprehension of the necessities which rule our lives; on the other hand, it manages to assure us of an immense and unexpected field of action. Our taverns and our metropolitan streets, our offices and furnished rooms, our railroad stations and our factories appeared to have us locked up hopelessly. Then came the film and burst this prison-world asunder by the dynamite of the tenth of a second, so that now, in the midst of its far-flung ruins and debris, we calmly and adventurously go traveling. With the close-up, space expands; with slow motion, movement is extended. The enlargement of a snapshot does not simply render more precise what in any case was visible, though unclear: it reveals entirely new structural formations of the subject. So, too, slow motion not only presents familiar qualities of movement but reveals in them entirely unknown ones "which, far from looking like retarded rapid movements, give the effect of singularly gliding, floating, supernatural motions." * Evidently a different nature opens itself to the camera than opens to the naked eye—if only because an unconsciously penetrated space is substituted for a space consciously explored

* Rudolf Arnheim, *loc. cit.*, p. 138.

by man. Even if one has a general knowledge of the way people walk, one knows nothing of a person's posture during the fractional second of a stride. The act of reaching for a lighter or a spoon is familiar routine, yet we hardly know what really goes on between hand and metal, not to mention how this fluctuates with our moods. Here the camera intervenes with the resources of its lowerings and liftings, its interruptions and isolations, its extensions and accelerations, its enlargements and reductions. The camera introduces us to unconscious optics as does psychoanalysis to unconscious impulses.

XIV

One of the foremost tasks of art has always been the creation of a demand which could be fully satisfied only later.[17] The history of every art form shows critical epochs in which a certain art form aspires to effects which could be fully obtained only with a changed technical standard, that is to say, in a new art form. The extravagances and crudities of art which thus appear, particularly in the so-called decadent epochs, actually arise from the nucleus of its richest historical energies. In recent years, such barbarisms were abundant in Dadaism. It is only now that its impulse becomes discernible: Dadaism attempted to create by pictorial—and literary—means the effects which the public today seeks in the film.

Every fundamentally new, pioneering creation of demands will carry beyond its goal. Dadaism did so to the extent that it sacrificed the market values which are so characteristic of the film in favor of higher ambitions—though of course it was not conscious of such intentions as here described. The Dadaists attached much less importance to the sales value of their work than to its uselessness for contemplative immersion. The studied degradation of their material was not the least of their means to achieve this uselessness. Their poems are "word salad" containing obscenities and every imaginable waste product of language. The same is true of their paintings, on which they mounted buttons and tickets. What they intended and achieved was a relentless destruction of the aura of their creations, which they branded as reproductions with the very means of production. Before a painting of Arp's or a poem by August Stramm it is impossible to take time for contemplation and evaluation as one would before a canvas of Derain's or a poem by Rilke. In the decline of middle-class society, contemplation became a school for asocial behavior; it was countered by distraction as a variant of social conduct.[18] Dadaistic activities actually assured a rather vehement distraction by making works of art the center of scandal. One requirement was foremost: to outrage the public.

From an alluring appearance or persuasive structure of sound the work of art of the Dadaists became an instrument of ballistics. It hit the spectator like a bullet, it happened to him, thus acquiring a tactile quality. It promoted a demand for the film, the distracting element of which is also primarily tactile, being based on changes of place and focus which periodically assail the spectator. Let us compare the screen on which a film unfolds with the canvas of a painting. The painting invites the spectator to contemplation; before it the spectator can abandon himself to his associations. Before the movie frame he cannot do so. No sooner has his eye grasped a scene than it is already changed. It cannot be arrested. Duhamel, who detests the film and knows nothing of its significance, though something of its structure, notes this circumstance as follows: "I can no longer think what I want to think. My thoughts have been replaced by moving images." * The spectator's process of association in view of these images is indeed interrupted by their constant, sudden change. This constitutes the shock effect of the film, which, like all shocks, should be cushioned by heightened presence of mind.[19] By means of its technical structure, the film has taken the physical shock effect out of the wrappers in which Dadaism had, as it were, kept it inside the moral shock effect.[20]

* Georges Duhamel, *Scènes de la vie future,* Paris, 1930, p. 52.

X V

The mass is a matrix from which all traditional behavior toward works of art issues today in a new form. Quantity has been transmuted into quality. The greatly increased mass of participants has produced a change in the mode of participation. The fact that the new mode of participation first appeared in a disreputable form must not confuse the spectator. Yet some people have launched spirited attacks against precisely this superficial aspect. Among these, Duhamel has expressed himself in the most radical manner. What he objects to most is the kind of participation which the movie elicits from the masses. Duhamel calls the movie "a pastime for helots, a diversion for uneducated, wretched, worn-out creatures who are consumed by their worries . . . , a spectacle which requires no concentration and presupposes no intelligence . . . , which kindles no light in the heart and awakens no hope other than the ridiculous one of someday becoming a 'star' in Los Angeles." * Clearly, this is at bottom the same ancient lament that the masses seek distraction whereas art demands concentration from the spectator. That is a commonplace. The question remains whether it provides a platform for the analysis of the film. A closer look is needed here. Distraction and concentration form polar opposites which may be stated as follows: A man who concentrates before a work of art is absorbed by it. He enters into this work of art the way legend tells of the Chinese painter when he viewed his finished painting. In contrast, the distracted mass absorbs the work of art. This is most obvious with regard to buildings. Architecture has always represented the prototype of a work of art the reception of which is consummated by a collectivity in a state of distraction. The laws of its reception are most instructive.

Buildings have been man's companions since primeval times. Many art forms have developed and perished. Tragedy begins with the Greeks, is extinguished with them, and after centuries its "rules" only are revived. The epic poem, which had its origin

* Duhamel, *op. cit.*, p. 58.

in the youth of nations, expires in Europe at the end of the Renaissance. Panel painting is a creation of the Middle Ages, and nothing guarantees its uninterrupted existence. But the human need for shelter is lasting. Architecture has never been idle. Its history is more ancient than that of any other art, and its claim to being a living force has significance in every attempt to comprehend the relationship of the masses to art. Buildings are appropriated in a twofold manner: by use and by perception—or rather, by touch and sight. Such appropriation cannot be understood in terms of the attentive concentration of a tourist before a famous building. On the tactile side there is no counterpart to contemplation on the optical side. Tactile appropriation is accomplished not so much by attention as by habit. As regards architecture, habit determines to a large extent even optical reception. The latter, too, occurs much less through rapt attention than by noticing the object in incidental fashion. This mode of appropriation, developed with reference to architecture, in certain circumstances acquires canonical value. For the tasks which face the human apparatus of perception at the turning points of history cannot be solved by optical means, that is, by contemplation, alone. They are mastered gradually by habit, under the guidance of tactile appropriation.

The distracted person, too, can form habits. More, the ability to master certain tasks in a state of distraction proves that their solution has become a matter of habit. Distraction as provided by art presents a covert control of the extent to which new tasks have become soluble by apperception. Since, moreover, individuals are tempted to avoid such tasks, art will tackle the most difficult and most important ones where it is able to mobilize the masses. Today it does so in the film. Reception in a state of distraction, which is increasing noticeably in all fields of art and is symptomatic of profound changes in apperception, finds in the film its true means of exercise. The film with its shock effect meets this mode of reception halfway. The film makes the cult value recede into the background not only by putting the public in the position of the critic, but also by the fact that at the movies this position requires no attention. The public is an examiner, but an absent-minded one.

[handwritten marginal note: Think of the auditor in the storstelle / sounds of spinning Bergdem / Distraction listener absorbs is not absorbed]

EPILOGUE

The growing proletarianization of modern man and the increasing formation of masses are two aspects of the same process. Fascism attempts to organize the newly created proletarian masses without affecting the property structure which the masses strive to eliminate. Fascism sees its salvation in giving these masses not their right, but instead a chance to express themselves.[21] The masses have a right to change property relations; Fascism seeks to give them an expression while preserving property. The logical result of Fascism is the introduction of aesthetics into political life. The violation of the masses, whom Fascism, with its *Führer* cult, forces to their knees, has its counterpart in the violation of an apparatus which is pressed into the production of ritual values.

[handwritten marginal note: Heg. concess]

All efforts to render politics aesthetic culminate in one thing: war. War and war only can set a goal for mass movements on the largest scale while respecting the traditional property system. This is the political formula for the situation. The technological formula may be stated as follows: Only war makes it possible to mobilize all of today's technical resources while maintaining the property system. It goes without saying that the Fascist apotheosis of war does not employ such arguments. Still, Marinetti says in his manifesto on the Ethiopian colonial war: "For twenty-seven years we Futurists have rebelled against the branding of war as antiaesthetic. . . . Accordingly we state: . . . War is beautiful because it establishes man's dominion over the subjugated machinery by means of gas masks, terrifying megaphones, flame throwers, and small tanks. War is beautiful because it initiates the dreamt-of metalization of the human body. War is beautiful because it enriches a flowering meadow with the fiery orchids of machine guns. War is beautiful because it combines the gunfire, the cannonades, the cease-fire, the scents, and the stench of putrefaction into a symphony. War is beautiful because it creates new architecture, like that of the big tanks, the geometrical formation flights, the smoke spirals from burning villages, and many others. . . . Poets and artists of Futurism! . . . remember these principles of an aesthetics of war so that your struggle for a new literature and a new graphic art . . . may be illumined by them!'"

This manifesto has the virtue of clarity. Its formulations deserve to be accepted by dialecticians. To the latter, the aesthetics of today's war appears as follows: If the natural utilization of productive forces is impeded by the property system, the increase in technical devices, in speed, and in the sources of energy will press for an unnatural utilization, and this is found in war. The destructiveness of war furnishes proof that society has not been mature enough to incorporate technology as its organ, that technology has not been sufficiently developed to cope with the elemental forces of society. The horrible features of imperialistic warfare are attributable to the discrepancy between the tremendous means of production and their inadequate utilization in the process of production—in other words, to unemployment and the lack of markets. Imperialistic war is a rebellion of technology which collects, in the form of "human material," the claims to which society has denied its natural material. Instead of draining rivers, society directs a human stream into a bed of trenches; instead of dropping seeds from airplanes, it drops incendiary bombs over cities; and through gas warfare the aura is abolished in a new way.

"*Fiat ars—pereat mundus,*" says Fascism, and, as Marinetti admits, expects war to supply the artistic gratification of a sense perception that has been changed by technology. This is evidently the consummation of "*l'art pour l'art.*" Mankind, which in Homer's time was an object of contemplation for the Olympian gods, now is one for itself. Its self-alienation has reached such a degree that it can experience its own destruction as an aesthetic pleasure of the first order. This is the situation of politics which Fascism is rendering aesthetic. Communism responds by politicizing art.

Notes

1. Of course, the history of a work of art encompasses more than this. The history of the "Mona Lisa," for instance, encompasses the kind and number of its copies made in the 17th, 18th, and 19th centuries.

2. Precisely because authenticity is not reproducible, the intensive penetration of certain (mechanical) processes of reproduction was instrumental in differentiating and grading authenticity. To develop such differentiations was an important function of the trade in works of art. The invention of the woodcut may be said to have struck at the root of the quality of authenticity even before its late flowering. To be sure, at the time of its origin a medieval picture of the Madonna could not yet be said to be "authentic." It became "authentic" only during the succeeding centuries and perhaps most strikingly so during the last one.

3. The poorest provincial staging of *Faust* is superior to a Faust film in that, ideally, it competes with the first performance at Weimar. Before the screen it is unprofitable to remember traditional contents which might come to mind before the stage—for instance, that Goethe's friend Johann Heinrich Merck is hidden in Mephisto, and the like.

4. To satisfy the human interest of the masses may mean to have one's social function removed from the field of vision. Nothing guarantees that a portraitist of today, when painting a famous surgeon at the breakfast table in the midst of his family, depicts his social function more precisely than a painter of the 17th century who portrayed his medical doctors as representing this profession, like Rembrandt in his "Anatomy Lesson."

5. The definition of the aura as a "unique phenomenon of a distance however close it may be" represents nothing but the formulation of the cult value of the work of art in categories of space and time perception. Distance is the opposite of closeness. The essentially distant object is the unapproachable one. Unapproachability is indeed a major quality of the cult image. True to its nature, it remains "distant, however close it may be." The closeness which one may gain from its subject matter does not impair the distance which it retains in its appearance.

6. To the extent to which the cult value of the painting is secularized the ideas of its fundamental uniqueness lose distinctness. In
the imagination of the beholder the uniqueness of the phenomena
which hold sway in the cult image is more and more displaced by
the empirical uniqueness of the creator or of his creative achievement.
To be sure, never completely so; the concept of authenticity always
transcends mere genuineness. (This is particularly apparent in the
collector who always retains some traces of the fetishist and who,
by owning the work of art, shares in its ritual power.) Nevertheless,
the function of the concept of authenticity remains determinate in
the evaluation of art; with the secularization of art, authenticity dis-
places the cult value of the work.

7. In the case of films, mechanical reproduction is not, as with
literature and painting, an external condition for mass distribution.
Mechanical reproduction is inherent in the very technique of film
production. This technique not only permits in the most direct way
but virtually causes mass distribution. It enforces distribution because
the production of a film is so expensive that an individual who, for
instance, might afford to buy a painting no longer can afford to buy
a film. In 1927 it was calculated that a major film, in order to pay
its way, had to reach an audience of nine million. With the sound
film, to be sure, a setback in its international distribution occurred
at first: audiences became limited by language barriers. This coincided with the Fascist emphasis on national interests. It is more
important to focus on this connection with Fascism than on this setback, which was soon minimized by synchronization. The simulta-
neity of both phenomena is attributable to the depression. The same
disturbances which, on a larger scale, led to an attempt to maintain
the existing property structure by sheer force led the endangered
film capital to speed up the development of the sound film. The introduction of the sound film brought about a temporary relief, not
only because it again brought the masses into the theaters but also
because it merged new capital from the electrical industry with that
of the film industry. Thus, viewed from the outside, the sound film
promoted national interests, but seen from the inside it helped to
internationalize film production even more than previously.

8. This polarity cannot come into its own in the aesthetics of
Idealism. Its idea of beauty comprises these polar opposites without
differentiating between them and consequently excludes their polarity. Yet in Hegel this polarity announces itself as clearly as possible

within the limits of Idealism. We quote from his *Philosophy of History:*

> "Images were known of old. Piety at an early time required them for worship, but it could do without *beautiful* images. These might even be disturbing. In every beautiful painting there is also something nonspiritual, merely external, but its spirit speaks to man through its beauty. Worshipping, conversely, is concerned with the work as an object, for it is but a spiritless stupor of the soul. . . . Fine art has arisen . . . in the church . . . , although it has already gone beyond its principle as art."

Likewise, the following passage from *The Philosophy of Fine Art* indicates that Hegel sensed a problem here.

> "We are beyond the stage of reverence for works of art as divine and objects deserving our worship. The impression they produce is one of a more reflective kind, and the emotions they arouse require a higher test. . . ."—G. W. F. Hegel, *The Philosophy of Fine Art*, trans., with notes, by F. P. B. Osmaston, Vol. i, p. 12, London, 1920.

The transition from the first kind of artistic reception to the second characterizes the history of artistic reception in general. Apart from that, a certain oscillation between these two polar modes of reception can be demonstrated for each work of art. Take the Sistine Madonna. Since Hubert Grimme's research it has been known that the Madonna originally was painted for the purpose of exhibition. Grimme's research was inspired by the question: What is the purpose of the molding in the foreground of the painting which the two cupids lean upon? How, Grimme asked further, did Raphael come to furnish the sky with two draperies? Research proved that the Madonna had been commissioned for the public lying-in-state of Pope Sixtus. The Popes lay in state in a certain side chapel of St. Peter's. On that occasion Raphael's picture had been fastened in a nichelike background of the chapel, supported by the coffin. In this picture Raphael portrays the Madonna approaching the papal coffin in clouds from the background of the niche, which was demarcated by green drapes. At the obsequies of Sixtus a pre-eminent exhibition value of Raphael's picture was taken advantage of. Some time later it was placed on the high altar in the church of the Black Friars at Piacenza. The reason for this exile is to be found in the Roman rites which forbid the use of paintings exhibited at obsequies as cult objects on the high altar. This regulation devalued Raphael's picture to some degree. In order to obtain an adequate price nevertheless, the Papal See resolved to add to the bargain the tacit toleration of the picture above the high altar. To avoid attention the picture was given to the monks of the far-off provincial town.

9. Bertolt Brecht, on a different level, engaged in analogous reflections: "If the concept of 'work of art' can no longer be applied to the thing that emerges once the work is transformed into a commodity, we have to eliminate this concept with cautious care but without fear, lest we liquidate the function of the very thing as well. For it has to go through this phase without mental reservation, and not as noncommittal deviation from the straight path; rather, what happens here with the work of art will change it fundamentally and erase its past to such an extent that should the old concept be taken up again—and it will, why not?—it will no longer stir any memory of the thing it once designated."

10. "The film . . . provides—or could provide—useful insight into the details of human actions. . . . Character is never used as a source of motivation; the inner life of the persons never supplies the principal cause of the plot and seldom is its main result." (Bertolt Brecht, *Versuche*, "Der Dreigroschenprozess," p. 268.) The expansion of the field of the testable which mechanical equipment brings about for the actor corresponds to the extraordinary expansion of the field of the testable brought about for the individual through economic conditions. Thus, vocational aptitude tests become constantly more important. What matters in these tests are segmental performances of the individual. The film shot and the vocational aptitude test are taken before a committee of experts. The camera director in the studio occupies a place identical with that of the examiner during aptitude tests.

11. Rudolf Arnheim, *Film als Kunst*, Berlin, 1932, pp. 176 f. In this context certain seemingly unimportant details in which the film director deviates from stage practices gain in interest. Such is the attempt to let the actor play without make-up, as made among others by Dreyer in his *Jeanne d'Arc*. Dreyer spent months seeking the forty actors who constitute the Inquisitors' tribunal. The search for these actors resembled that for stage properties that are hard to come by. Dreyer made every effort to avoid resemblances of age, build, and physiognomy. If the actor thus becomes a stage property, this latter, on the other hand, frequently functions as actor. At least it is not unusual for the film to assign a role to the stage property.

Instead of choosing at random from a great wealth of examples, let us concentrate on a particularly convincing one. A clock that is working will always be a disturbance on the stage. There it cannot be permitted its function of measuring time. Even in a naturalistic play, astronomical time would clash with theatrical time. Under these circumstances it is highly revealing that the film can, whenever appropriate, use time as measured by a clock. From this more than from many other touches it may clearly be recognized that under certain circumstances each and every prop in a film may assume important functions. From here it is but one step to Pudovkin's statement that "the playing of an actor which is connected with an object and is built around it . . . is always one of the strongest methods of cinematic construction." (W. Pudovkin, *Filmregie und Filmmanuskript*, Berlin, 1928, p. 126.) The film is the first art form capable of demonstrating how matter plays tricks on man. Hence, films can be an excellent means of materialistic representation.

12. The change noted here in the method of exhibition caused by mechanical reproduction applies to politics as well. The present crisis of the bourgeois democracies comprises a crisis of the conditions which determine the public presentation of the rulers. Democracies exhibit a member of government directly and personally before the nation's representatives. Parliament is his public. Since the innovations of camera and recording equipment make it possible for the orator to become audible and visible to an unlimited number of persons, the presentation of the man of politics before camera and recording equipment becomes paramount. Parliaments, as much as theaters, are deserted. Radio and film not only affect the function of the professional actor but likewise the function of those who also exhibit themselves before this mechanical equipment, those who govern. Though their tasks may be different, the change affects equally the actor and the ruler. The trend is toward establishing controllable and transferrable skills under certain social conditions. This results in a new selection, a selection before the equipment from which the star and the dictator emerge victorious.

13. The privileged character of the respective techniques is lost. Aldous Huxley writes:

"Advances in technology have led . . . to vulgarity. . . . Process reproduction and the rotary press have made possible the indefinite multiplication of writing and pictures. Universal education and relatively high wages have created an enormous public who know how to read and can afford to buy reading and pictorial matter. A great industry has been called into existence in order to supply these commodities. Now, artistic talent is a very rare phenomenon; whence it follows . . . that, at every epoch and in all countries, most art has been bad. But the proportion of trash in the total artistic output is greater now than at any other period. That it must be so is a matter of simple arithmetic. The population of Western Europe has a little more than doubled during the last century. But the amount of reading—and seeing—matter has increased, I should imagine, at least twenty and possibly fifty or even a hundred times. If there were n men of talent in a population of x millions, there will presumably be 2n men of talent among 2x millions. The situation may be summed up thus. For every page of print and pictures published a century ago, twenty or perhaps even a hundred pages are published today. But for every man of talent then living, there are now only two men of talent. It may be of course that, thanks to universal education, many potential talents which in the past would have been stillborn are now enabled to realize themselves. Let us assume, then, that there are now three or even four men of talent to every one of earlier times. It still remains true to say that the consumption of reading—and seeing—matter has far outstripped the natural production of gifted writers and draughtsmen. It is the same with hearing-matter. Prosperity, the gramophone and the radio have created an audience of hearers who consume an amount of hearing-matter that has increased out of all proportion to the increase of population and the consequent natural increase of talented musicians. It follows from all this that in all the arts the output of trash is both absolutely and relatively greater than it was in the past; and that it must remain greater for just so long as the world continues to consume the present inordinate quantities of reading-matter, seeing-matter, and hearing-matter."—Aldous Huxley, *Beyond the Mexique Bay. A Traveller's Journal,* London, 1949, pp. 274 ff. First published in 1934.

This mode of observation is obviously not progressive.

14. The boldness of the cameraman is indeed comparable to that of the surgeon. Luc Durtain lists among specific technical sleights of hand those "which are required in surgery in the case of certain difficult operations. I choose as an example a case from oto-rhino-laryngology; . . . the so-called endonasal perspective procedure; or

I refer to the acrobatic tricks of larynx surgery which have to be performed following the reversed picture in the laryngoscope. I might also speak of ear surgery which suggests the precision work of watchmakers. What range of the most subtle muscular acrobatics is required from the man who wants to repair or save the human body! We have only to think of the couching of a cataract where there is virtually a debate of steel with nearly fluid tissue, or of the major abdominal operations (laparotomy)."—Luc Durtain, *op. cit.*

15. This mode of observation may seem crude, but as the great theoretician Leonardo has shown, crude modes of observation may at times be usefully adduced. Leonardo compares painting and music as follows: "Painting is superior to music because, unlike unfortunate music, it does not have to die as soon as it is born. . . . Music which is consumed in the very act of its birth is inferior to painting which the use of varnish has rendered eternal." (Trattato I, 29.)

16. Renaissance painting offers a revealing analogy to this situation. The incomparable development of this art and its significance rested not least on the integration of a number of new sciences, or at least of new scientific data. Renaissance painting made use of anatomy and perspective, of mathematics, meteorology, and chromatology. Valéry writes: "What could be further from us than the strange claim of a Leonardo to whom painting was a supreme goal and the ultimate demonstration of knowledge? Leonardo was convinced that painting demanded universal knowledge, and he did not even shrink from a theoretical analysis which to us is stunning because of its very depth and precision. . . ."—Paul Valéry, *Pièces sur l'art,* "Autour de Corot," Paris, p. 191.

17. "The work of art," says André Breton, "is valuable only in so far as it is vibrated by the reflexes of the future." Indeed, every developed art form intersects three lines of development. Technology works toward a certain form of art. Before the advent of the film there were photo booklets with pictures which flitted by the onlooker upon pressure of the thumb, thus portraying a boxing bout or a tennis match. Then there were the slot machines in bazaars; their picture sequences were produced by the turning of a crank.

Secondly, the traditional art forms in certain phases of their development strenuously work toward effects which later are effortlessly attained by the new ones. Before the rise of the movie the

Dadaists' performances tried to create an audience reaction which Chaplin later evoked in a more natural way.

Thirdly, unspectacular social changes often promote a change in receptivity which will benefit the new art form. Before the movie had begun to create its public, pictures that were no longer immobile captivated an assembled audience in the so-called *Kaiserpanorama*. Here the public assembled before a screen into which stereoscopes were mounted, one to each beholder. By a mechanical process individual pictures appeared briefly before the stereoscopes, then made way for others. Edison still had to use similar devices in presenting the first movie strip before the film screen and projection were known. This strip was presented to a small public which stared into the apparatus in which the succession of pictures was reeling off. Incidentally, the institution of the *Kaiserpanorama* shows very clearly a dialectic of the development. Shortly before the movie turned the reception of pictures into a collective one, the individual viewing of pictures in these swiftly outmoded establishments came into play once more with an intensity comparable to that of the ancient priest beholding the statue of a divinity in the cella.

18. The theological archetype of this contemplation is the awareness of being alone with one's God. Such awareness, in the heyday of the bourgeoisie, went to strengthen the freedom to shake off clerical tutelage. During the decline of the bourgeoisie this awareness had to take into account the hidden tendency to withdraw from public affairs those forces which the individual draws upon in his communion with God.

19. The film is the art form that is in keeping with the increased threat to his life which modern man has to face. Man's need to expose himself to shock effects is his adjustment to the dangers threatening him. The film corresponds to profound changes in the apperceptive apparatus—changes that are experienced on an individual scale by the man in the street in big-city traffic, on a historical scale by every present-day citizen.

20. As for Dadaism, insights important for Cubism and Futurism are to be gained from the movie. Both appear as deficient attempts of art to accommodate the pervasion of reality by the apparatus. In contrast to the film, these schools did not try to use the apparatus as such for the artistic presentation of reality, but aimed at some sort of alloy in the joint presentation of reality and apparatus. In Cubism,

the premonition that this apparatus will be structurally based on optics plays a dominant part; in Futurism, it is the premonition of the effects of this apparatus which are brought out by the rapid sequence of the film strip.

21. One technical feature is significant here, especially with regard to newsreels, the propagandist importance of which can hardly be overestimated. Mass reproduction is aided especially by the reproduction of masses. In big parades and monster rallies, in sports events, and in war, all of which nowadays are captured by camera and sound recording, the masses are brought face to face with themselves. This process, whose significance need not be stressed, is intimately connected with the development of the techniques of reproduction and photography. Mass movements are usually discerned more clearly by a camera than by the naked eye. A bird's-eye view best captures gatherings of hundreds of thousands. And even though such a view may be as accessible to the human eye as it is to the camera, the image received by the eye cannot be enlarged the way a negative is enlarged. This means that mass movements, including war, constitute a form of human behavior which particularly favors mechanical equipment.

Theses on the Philosophy of History

I

The story is told of an automaton constructed in such a way that it could play a winning game of chess, answering each move of an opponent with a countermove. A puppet in Turkish attire and with a hookah in its mouth sat before a chessboard placed on a large table. A system of mirrors created the illusion that this table was transparent from all sides. Actually, a little hunchback who was an expert chess player sat inside and guided the puppet's hand by means of strings. One can imagine a philosophical counterpart to this device. The puppet called "historical materialism" is to win all the time. It can easily be a match for anyone if it enlists the services of theology, which today, as we know, is wizened and has to keep out of sight.

METAPHYSICCI
UNDERPINNING

II

"One of the most remarkable characteristics of human nature," writes Lotze, "is, alongside so much selfishness in specific instances, the freedom from envy which the present displays toward the future." Reflection shows us that our image of happiness is thoroughly colored by the time to which the course of our own existence has assigned us. The kind of happiness that could arouse envy in us exists only in the air we have breathed, among people we could have talked to, women who could have given themselves to us. In other words, our image of happiness is indissolubly bound up with the image of redemption. The same applies to our view of the past, which is the concern of history. The past carries with it a temporal index by which it is referred to redemption. There is a secret agreement between past generations and the present one. Our coming was expected on earth. Like every generation that preceded us, we have been endowed with a *weak* Messianic power, a power to which the past has a claim. That claim cannot be settled cheaply. Historical materialists are aware of that.

III

A chronicler who recites events without distinguishing between major and minor ones acts in accordance with the following truth: nothing that has ever happened should be regarded as lost for history. To be sure, only a redeemed mankind receives the fullness of its past—which is to say, only for a redeemed mankind has its past become citable in all its moments. Each moment it has lived becomes a *citation à l'ordre du jour*—and that day is Judgment Day.

IV

> *Seek for food and clothing first, then*
> *the Kingdom of God shall be added unto you.*
> —Hegel, 1807

The class struggle, which is always present to a historian influenced by Marx, is a fight for the crude and material things without which no refined and spiritual things could exist. Nevertheless, it is not in the form of the spoils which fall to the victor that the latter make their presence felt in the class struggle. They manifest themselves in this struggle as courage, humor, cunning, and fortitude. They have retroactive force and will constantly call in question every victory, past and present, of the rulers. As flowers turn toward the sun, by dint of a secret heliotropism the past strives to turn toward that sun which is rising in the sky of history. A historical materialist must be aware of this most inconspicuous of all transformations. WILLIAMS' MODEL

V

The true picture of the past flits by. The past can be seized only as an image which flashes up at the instant when it can be recognized and is never seen again. "The truth will not run away from us": in the historical outlook of historicism these words of Gottfried Keller mark the exact point where historical materialism cuts through historicism. For every image of the past that is not recognized by the present as one of its own concerns threatens to disappear irretrievably. (The good tidings which the historian of the past brings with throbbing heart may be lost in a void the very moment he opens his mouth.)

VI

To articulate the past historically does not mean to recognize it "the way it really was" (Ranke). It means to seize hold of a memory as it flashes up at a moment of danger. Historical materialism wishes to retain that image of the past which unexpectedly appears to man singled out by history at a moment of danger. The danger affects both the content of the tradition and its receivers. The same threat hangs over both: that of becoming a tool of the ruling classes. In every era the attempt must be made anew to wrest tradition away from a conformism that is about to overpower it. The Messiah comes not only as the redeemer, he comes as the subduer of Antichrist. Only that historian will have the gift of fanning the spark of hope in the past who is firmly convinced that *even the dead* will not be safe from the enemy if he wins. And this enemy has not ceased to be victorious.

NARRATIVE w/ GOOD
GUYS AND BAD

VII

Consider the darkness and the great cold
In this vale which resounds with mysery.
    —Brecht, THE THREEPENNY OPERA

To historians who wish to relive an era, Fustel de Coulanges recommends that they blot out everything they know about the later course of history. There is no better way of characterizing the method with which historical materialism has broken. It is a process of empathy whose origin is the indolence of the heart, *acedia*, which despairs of grasping and holding the genuine historical image as it flares up briefly. Among medieval theologians it was regarded as the root cause of sadness. Flaubert, who was familiar with it, wrote: "*Peu de gens devineront combien il a fallu être triste pour ressusciter Carthage.*" * The nature of this sadness stands out more clearly if one asks with whom the adherents of historicism actually empathize. The answer is inevitable: with the victor. And all rulers are the heirs of those who conquered before them. Hence, empathy with the victor invariably benefits the rulers. Historical materialists know what that means. Whoever has emerged victorious participates to this day in the triumphal procession in which the present rulers step over those who are lying prostrate. According to traditional practice, the spoils are carried along in the procession. They are called cultural treasures, and a historical materialist views them with cautious detachment. For without exception the cultural treasures he surveys have an origin which he cannot contemplate without horror. They owe their existence not only to the efforts of the great minds and talents who have created them, but also to the anonymous toil of their contemporaries. There is no document of civilization which is not at the same time a document of barbarism. And just as such a document is not free of barbarism, barbarism taints also the manner in which it was transmitted from one owner to another. A historical materialist therefore dissoci-

* "Few will be able to guess how sad one had to be in order to resuscitate Carthage."

ates himself from it as far as possible. He regards it as his task to
brush history against the grain.

— echoes of the grain (handwritten)

VIII

The tradition of the oppressed teaches us that the "state of
emergency" in which we live is not the exception but the rule.
We must attain to a conception of history that is in keeping with
this insight. Then we shall clearly realize that it is our task to
bring about a real state of emergency, and this will improve
our position in the struggle against Fascism. One reason why
Fascism has a chance is that in the name of progress its opponents
treat it as a historical norm. The current amazement that the
things we are experiencing are "still" possible in the twentieth
century is *not* philosophical. This amazement is not the beginning of knowledge—unless it is the knowledge that the view of
history which gives rise to it is untenable.

IX

Mein Flügel ist zum Schwung bereit,
ich kehrte gern zurück,
denn blieb ich auch lebendige Zeit,
ich hätte wenig Glück.
　　—Gerhard Scholem, "Gruss vom Angelus" *

A Klee painting named "Angelus Novus" shows an angel looking as though he is about to move away from something he is
fixedly contemplating. His eyes are staring, his mouth is open,
his wings are spread. This is how one pictures the angel of history. His face is turned toward the past. Where we perceive a
chain of events, he sees one single catastrophe which keeps piling
wreckage upon wreckage and hurls it in front of his feet. The
angel would like to stay, awaken the dead, and make whole what
has been smashed. But a storm is blowing from Paradise; it has

---

* *My wing is ready for flight,*
I would like to turn back.
If I stayed timeless time,
I would have little luck.

got caught in his wings with such violence that the angel can no longer close them. This storm irresistibly propels him into the future to which his back is turned, while the pile of debris before him grows skyward. This storm is what we call progress.

X

The themes which monastic discipline assigned to friars for meditation were designed to turn them away from the world and its affairs. The thoughts which we are developing here originate from similar considerations. At a moment when the politicians in whom the opponents of Fascism had placed their hopes are prostrate and confirm their defeat by betraying their own cause, these observations are intended to disentangle the political world-lings from the snares in which the traitors have entrapped them. Our consideration proceeds from the insight that the politicians' stubborn faith in progress, their confidence in their "mass basis," and, finally, their servile integration in an uncontrollable ap-paratus have been three aspects of the same thing. It seeks to convey an idea of the high price our accustomed thinking will have to pay for a conception of history that avoids any com-plicity with the thinking to which these politicians continue to adhere.

X I

The conformism which has been part and parcel of Social Democracy from the beginning attaches not only to its political tactics but to its economic views as well. It is one reason for its later breakdown. Nothing has corrupted the German working class so much as the notion that it was moving with the current. It regarded technological developments as the fall of the stream with which it thought it was moving. From there it was but a step to the illusion that the factory work which was supposed to tend toward technological progress constituted a political achieve-ment. The old Protestant ethics of work was resurrected among

German workers in secularized form. The Gotha Program * already bears traces of this confusion, defining labor as "the source of all wealth and all culture." Smelling a rat, Marx countered that ". . . the man who possesses no other property than his labor power" must of necessity become "the slave of other men who have made themselves the owners. . . ." However, the confusion spread, and soon thereafter Josef Dietzgen proclaimed: "The savior of modern times is called work. The . . . improvement . . . of labor constitutes the wealth which is now able to accomplish what no redeemer has ever been able to do." This vulgar-Marxist conception of the nature of labor bypasses the question of how its products might benefit the workers while still not being at their disposal. It recognizes only the progress in the mastery of nature, not the retrogression of society; it already displays the technocratic features later encountered in Fascism. Among these is a conception of nature which differs ominously from the one in the Socialist utopias before the 1848 revolution. The new conception of labor amounts to the exploitation of nature, which with naïve complacency is contrasted with the exploitation of the proletariat. Compared with this positivistic conception, Fourier's fantasies, which have so often been ridiculed, prove to be surprisingly sound. According to Fourier, as a result of efficient co-operative labor, four moons would illuminate the earthly night, the ice would recede from the poles, sea water would no longer taste salty, and beasts of prey would do man's bidding. All this illustrates a kind of labor which, far from exploiting nature, is capable of delivering her of the creations which lie dormant in her womb as potentials. Nature, which, as Dietzgen puts it, "exists gratis," is a complement to the corrupted conception of labor.

---

* The Gotha Congress of 1875 united the two German Socialist parties, one led by Ferdinand Lassalle, the other by Karl Marx and Wilhelm Liebknecht. The program, drafted by Liebknecht and Lassalle, was severely attacked by Marx in London. See his "Critique of the Gotha Program."

XII

We need history, but not the way a spoiled loafer
in the garden of knowledge needs it.
—Nietzsche, OF THE USE AND ABUSE OF HISTORY

√   Not man or men but the struggling, oppressed class itself is
the depository of historical knowledge. In Marx it appears as the
last enslaved class, as the avenger that completes the task of lib-
eration in the name of generations of the downtrodden. This
conviction, which had a brief resurgence in the Spartacist group,*
has always been objectionable to Social Democrats. Within three
decades they managed virtually to erase the name of Blanqui,
though it had been the rallying sound that had reverberated
through the preceding century. Social Democracy thought fit to
assign to the working class the role of the redeemer of future
generations, in this way cutting the sinews of its greatest strength.
This training made the working class forget both its hatred and
its spirit of sacrifice, for both are nourished by the image of enslaved ancestors rather than that of liberated grandchildren.

XIII

Every day our cause becomes clearer and people get smarter.
—Wilhelm Dietzgen, DIE RELIGION DER SOZIALDEMOKRATIE

Social Democratic theory, and even more its practice, have
been formed by a conception of progress which did not adhere
to reality but made dogmatic claims. Progress as pictured in the
minds of Social Democrats was, first of all, the progress of mankind itself (and not just advances in men's ability and knowledge). Secondly, it was something boundless, in keeping with the
infinite perfectibility of mankind. Thirdly, progress was regarded
as irresistible, something that automatically pursued a straight or
spiral course. Each of these predicates is controversial and open

---

* Leftist group, founded by Karl Liebknecht and Rosa Luxemburg at
the beginning of World War I in opposition to the pro-war policies of the
German Socialist party, later absorbed by the Communist party.

to criticism. However, when the chips are down, criticism must penetrate beyond these predicates and focus on something that they have in common. The concept of the historical progress of mankind cannot be sundered from the concept of its progression through a homogeneous, empty time. A critique of the concept of such a progression must be the basis of any criticism of the concept of progress itself.

X I V

Origin is the goal.
—Karl Kraus, WORTE IN VERSEN, Vol. I

History is the subject of a structure whose site is not homogeneous, empty time, but time filled by the presence of the now [*Jetztzeit*].* Thus, to Robespierre ancient Rome was a past charged with the time of the now which he <u>blasted</u> out of the continuum of history. The French Revolution viewed itself as Rome reincarnate. It evoked ancient Rome the way fashion evokes costumes of the past. Fashion has a flair for the topical, no matter where it stirs in the thickets of long ago; it is a tiger's leap into the past. This jump, however, takes place in an arena where the ruling class gives the commands. The same leap in the open air of history is the dialectical one, which is how Marx understood the revolution.

X V

The awareness that they are about to make the continuum of history explode is characteristic of the revolutionary classes at the moment of their action. The great revolution introduced a new calendar. The initial day of a calendar serves as a historical time-lapse camera. And, basically, it is the same day that keeps recurring in the guise of holidays, which are days of remembrance. Thus the calendars do not measure time as clocks do; they are

---

* Benjamin says "*Jetztzeit*" and indicates by the quotation marks that he does not simply mean an equivalent to *Gegenwart*, that is, present. He clearly is thinking of the mystical *nunc stans.*

monuments of a historical consciousness of which not the slightest trace has been apparent in Europe in the past hundred years. In the July revolution an incident occurred which showed this consciousness still alive. On the first evening of fighting it turned out that the clocks in towers were being fired on simultaneously and independently from several places in Paris. An eye-witness, who may have owed his insight to the rhyme, wrote as follows:

> Qui le croirait! on dit, qu'irrités contre l'heure
> De nouveaux Josués au pied de chaque tour,
> Tiraient sur les cadrans pour arrêter le jour.*

XVI

A historical materialist cannot do without the notion of a present which is not a transition, but in which time stands still and has come to a stop. For this notion defines the present in which he himself is writing history. Historicism gives the "eternal" image of the past; historical materialism supplies a unique experience with the past. The historical materialist leaves it to others to be drained by the whore called "Once upon a time" in historicism's bordello. He remains in control of his powers, man enough to blast open the continuum of history.

XVII

Historicism rightly culminates in universal history. Materialistic historiography differs from it as to method more clearly than from any other kind. Universal history has no theoretical armature. Its method is additive; it musters a mass of data to fill the homogeneous, empty time. Materialistic historiography, on the other hand, is based on a constructive principle. Thinking involves not only the flow of thoughts, but their arrest as well. Where thinking suddenly stops in a configuration pregnant with tensions, it gives that configuration a shock, by which it crystal-

---

* Who would have believed it! we are told that new Joshuas
  at the foot of every tower, as though irritated with
  time itself, fired at the dials in order to stop the day.

lizes into a monad. A historical materialist approaches a historical subject only where he encounters it as a monad. In this structure he recognizes the sign of a Messianic cessation of happening, or, put differently, a revolutionary chance in the fight for the oppressed past. He takes cognizance of it in order to blast a specific era out of the homogeneous course of history—blasting a specific life out of the era or a specific work out of the lifework. As a result of this method the lifework is preserved in this work and at the same time canceled*; in the lifework, the era; and in the era, the entire course of history. The nourishing fruit of the historically understood contains time as a precious but tasteless seed.

XVIII

"In relation to the history of organic life on earth," writes a modern biologist, "the paltry fifty millennia of *homo sapiens* constitute something like two seconds at the close of a twenty-four-hour day. On this scale, the history of civilized mankind would fill one-fifth of the last second of the last hour." The present, which, as a model of Messianic time, comprises the entire history of mankind in an enormous abridgment, coincides exactly with the stature which the history of mankind has in the universe.

A

Historicism contents itself with establishing a causal connection between various moments in history. But no fact that is a cause is for that very reason historical. It became historical posthumously, as it were, through events that may be separated from it by thousands of years. A historian who takes this as his point of departure stops telling the sequence of events like the beads of a rosary. Instead, he grasps the constellation which his own era has formed with a definite earlier one. Thus he establishes a conception of the present as the "time of the now" which is shot through with chips of Messianic time.

* The Hegelian term *aufheben* in its threefold meaning: to preserve, to elevate, to cancel.

B

The soothsayers who found out from time what it had in store certainly did not experience time as either homogeneous or empty. Anyone who keeps this in mind will perhaps get an idea of how past times were experienced in remembrance—namely, in just the same way. We know that the Jews were prohibited from investigating the future. The Torah and the prayers instruct them in remembrance, however. This stripped the future of its magic, to which all those succumb who turn to the soothsayers for enlightenment. This does not imply, however, that for the Jews the future turned into homogeneous, empty time. For every second of time was the strait gate through which the Messiah might enter.

Editor's Note

Benjamin's work consists of two books on German literature—his dissertation on "The Concept of Art Criticism in German Romanticism" (*Der Begriff der Kunstkritik in der deutschen Romantik*, Bern, 1920) and "The Origin of German Tragedy" (*Der Ursprung des deutschen Trauerspiels*, Berlin, 1928)—of two books of general reflections in the form of short essays or aphorisms—"One-Way Street" (*Einbahnstrasse*, Berlin, 1928) and "A Berlin Childhood around 1900" (*Berliner Kindheit um Neunzehnhundert*, written during the late thirties and published posthumously, Frankfurt, 1950)—and of a great number of literary and critical essays, book reviews, and commentaries.

The chief purpose of this collection is to convey the importance of Benjamin as a literary critic. It contains the full-length essays with two very regrettable exceptions—the study of "Goethe's *Elective Affinities*" (published in Hugo von Hofmannsthal's *Neue Deutsche Beiträge* in two instalments, 1924 and 1925) and the article on "Karl Kraus" (in the *Frankfurter Zeitung*, 1931). Since Karl Kraus is still practically unknown in English-speaking countries and since the Goethe essay consists to a large extent of a polemic against Friedrich Gundolf's *Goethe*, equally unknown, these two essays would have needed so many explanatory notes that the thrust of the text itself would have been ruined.

The translation of the text follows the two-volume German edition of Benjamin's writings which, under the title *Schriften*, was edited and introduced by Theodor W. Adorno and published by the Suhrkamp Verlag in 1955. The title of the present collection, but not its content, is identical with the title of a selection from the *Schriften*, published by Suhrkamp in 1961; Benjamin himself had approved this title for an earlier selection of some of his works. The German text is chiefly drawn from the published texts in various magazines and newspapers. Professor Adorno points out in his Introduction that it is not definitive: in the few instances where the original manuscripts could be consulted, it turned out that Benjamin's handwriting was difficult to read, and as for the typescripts and printed newspaper or magazine copies, they "unquestionably contain numerous errors." In the only case in which I was able to compare the original manuscript with the printed text, "Theses on the Philosophy of History," which Benjamin gave me shortly before his death, I found many important variants.

As I mentioned in the Introduction (Note 7), manuscripts, typescripts, and reprints of Benjamin's work are scattered. Most manuscripts are in the possession of Professor Theodor W. Adorno in Frankfurt; a number of letters and manuscripts are in the East German Zentralarchiv in Potsdam. Professor Gershom Scholem in Jerusalem possesses a collection of reprints and carbon copies of typescripts.

The two-volume *Schriften* does not contain the collected works. Large portions of what Benjamin considered his main oeuvre, "Paris, the Capital of the Nineteenth Century," seem to have been finished in manuscript, and a number of his essays and reviews, published during his lifetime, have not been reprinted. Two volumes of letters, edited by T. W. Adorno and G. Scholem, were published in 1966; a collection of essays on Brecht, which includes several previously unpublished articles and notes on "Conversations with Brecht," also appeared in 1966 under the editorship of Rolf Tiedemann. Finally, a collection of German letters, written between 1783 and 1833, with commentaries and first published under the pseudonym Detlev Holz with the title *Deutsche Menschen* in Switzerland in 1936, has been reissued in Germany.

The original sources of the essays published in this collection are as follows:

"Unpacking My Library": *Literarische Welt*, 1931.

"The Task of the Translator": his introduction to his translation of Baudelaire's *Tableaux parisiens*, Heidelberg, 1923.

"The Storyteller": *Orient und Okzident*, 1936.

"Franz Kafka": *Jüdische Rundschau*, 1934.

"Some Reflections on Kafka": the text is based upon a letter to Scholem, dated Paris, June 12, 1938; now published in *Briefe*, II, 756–64.

"What Is Epic Theater?": *Mass und Wert*, 1939.

"On Some Motifs in Baudelaire": *Zeitschrift für Sozialforschung*, VIII, 1-2, 1939.

"The Image of Proust": *Literarische Welt*, 1929.

Editor's Note

"The Work of Art in the Age of Mechanical Reproduction":
Zeitschrift für Sozialforschung, V, 1, 1936.

"Theses on the Philosophy of History": completed in spring
1940, first published in *Neue Rundschau,* 61, 3, 1950.

Index of Names

Adorno, Theodor Wiesengrund, 1903– , German professor of philosophy and sociology, 2, 10–13, 15, 17, 52, 53, 265 f.

Anselm of Canterbury, St., 1033–1109, Scholastic philosopher, 128

Arnheim, Rudolf, 1904– , German-born American educator, psychologist, and art historian, 230, 236 n., 246

Arnobius, ca. A.D. 300, early Christian apologist, 131

Arnoux, Alexandre, 1884– , French novelist, essayist, playwright, 227

Arp, Hans, 1887–1966, Alsatian sculptor, painter, poet, 238

Atget, Eugène, 1856–1927, French photographer, 226

Aurevilly, Jules Barbey d', 1808–1889, French man of letters, 184

Bachofen, Johann Jakob, 1815–1887, Swiss philosopher and archaeologist, famous author of *Mutterrecht und Urreligion*, 62, 130 f.

Balzac, Honoré de, 1799–1850, 64, 208

Barbier, Henri Auguste, 1805–1882, French poet and satirist, 168, 171, 195

Barrès, Maurice, 1862–1923, French writer and publicist, 209

Baudelaire, Charles, 1821–1867, 4, 11, 52, 54, 155–200, 212

Beethoven, Ludwig van, 1770–1827, 222

Benoist-Méchin, Jacques, 1901– , French historian, diplomat, and man of letters, 211